Youth policy, civil society and the modern Irish state

MANCHESTER
1824

Manchester University Press

IRISH SOCIETY

SERIES EDITOR
Rob Kitchin

ALREADY PUBLISHED
Rory Hearne *Public Private Partnerships in Ireland*

YOUTH POLICY, CIVIL SOCIETY AND THE MODERN IRISH STATE

Fred Powell, Martin Geoghegan, Margaret Scanlon and Katharina Swirak

MANCHESTER UNIVERSITY PRESS
Manchester and New York
*distributed in the United States exclusively
by Palgrave Macmillan*

Published by Manchester University Press
Oxford Road, Manchester M13 9NR, UK
and Room 400, 175 Fifth Avenue, New York, NY 10010, USA
www.manchesteruniversitypress.co.uk

Distributed in the United States exclusively by
Palgrave Macmillan, 175 Fifth Avenue,
New York, NY 10010, USA

Distributed in Canada exclusively by
UBC Press, University of British Columbia, 2029 West Mall,
Vancouver, BC, Canada V6T 1Z2

British Library Cataloguing-in-Publication Data is available

Library of Congress Cataloging-in-Publication Data is available

ISBN 978 0 7190 9542 9 paperback

First published by Manchester University Press in hardback 2012

This paperback edition first published 2014

Printed by Lightning Source

Contents

Series editor's foreword

Over the past twenty years Ireland has undergone enormous social, cultural and economic change. From a poor, peripheral country on the edge of Europe with a conservative culture dominated by tradition and Church, Ireland transformed into a global, cosmopolitan country with a dynamic economy. At the heart of the processes of change was a new kind of political economic model of development that ushered in the so-called Celtic Tiger years, accompanied by renewed optimism in the wake of the ceasefires in Northern Ireland and the peace dividend of the Good Friday Agreement. As Ireland emerged from decades of economic stagnation and The Troubles came to a peaceful end, the island became the focus of attention for countries seeking to emulate its economic and political miracles. Every other country, it seemed, wanted to be the next Tiger, modelled on Ireland's successes. And then came the financial collapse of 2008, the bursting of the property bubble, bank bailouts, austerity plans, rising unemployment and a return to emigration. From being the paradigm case of successful economic transformation, Ireland has become an internationally important case study of what happens when an economic model goes disastrously wrong.

The Irish Society series provides a critical, interdisciplinary and in-depth analysis of Ireland that reveals the processes and forces shaping social, economic, cultural and political life, and their outcomes for communities and social groups. The books seek to understand the evolution of social, economic and spatial relations from a broad range of perspectives, and explore the challenges facing Irish society in the future given present conditions and policy instruments. The series examines all aspects of Irish society including, but not limited to: social exclusion, identity, health, welfare, life cycle, family life and structures, labour and work cultures, spatial and sectoral economy, local and regional development, politics and the political system, government and governance, environment, migration and spatial planning. The series is supported by the Irish Social Sciences Platform (ISSP), an all-island platform of integrated social science research and graduate education focusing on the social, cultural and economic transformations shaping Ireland in the 21st century. Funded by the Programme for Research in Third Level Institutions, the ISSP brings together leading social science academics from all of Ireland's universities and other third level institutions.

Given the marked changes in Ireland's fortunes over the past two decades it is important that rigorous scholarship is applied to understand the forces at work, how they have affected different people and places in uneven and unequal ways, and what needs to happen to create a fairer and prosperous society. The Irish Society series provides such scholarship.

Rob Kitchin

List of tables

Acknowledgements

The research reported in this book was conducted as part of a project entitled Civil Society, Youth and Youth Policy in Modern Ireland, which was funded by the Irish Research Council for the Humanities and Social Sciences (IRCHSS). The project was located within the Institute of Social Science in the 21st Century (ISS21), established at UCC from funding provided through the Programme for Research in Third Level Institutions (PRTLI), cycle 4. We are particularly grateful to the ISS21 Director, Linda Connolly, and to the Research Manager, Caitríona Ní Laoire for their support during the project. We are also grateful to the Irish Social Science Platform (ISSP) for creating the series, in particular Rob Kitchin.

We would like to thank the following members of our research advisory panel for their guidance and support: Eamonn Lynch (Scouting Ireland), Diarmuid Kearney and Tom Dunne (Youth Work Ireland), Denis O'Brien (Foróige), Conor Rowley (Office of the Minister for Children and Youth Affairs), Pat O'Brien (Irish Girl Guides), Mark Dunwoody and David Brown (Church of Ireland Youth Department), Pat Forde (North Connaught Youth and Community Services) and Gertrude Cotter (NASC, Irish Immigrant Support Centre).

The project team would like to sincerely thank the Youth Officers at the Vocational Education Committees who helped in the administration of the survey. Special thanks are also due to the youth workers and volunteers who contributed to the research, either by completing questionnaires or participating in interviews. The CEOs and regional directors of several youth work organisations also participated in interviews and put us in contact with other personnel within their organisations. Their help is gratefully acknowledged.

In conducting research on the history of youth movements we are particularly indebted to Brian Meyer and David Stern (Scouting Ireland) and Daniel Scott-Davies (The Scout Association, London) who introduced us to the Scouting archives, and who shared with us their considerable knowledge of Scouting history. Thanks also to Philip Daley for providing access to historical sources for The Boys' Brigade. Elaine Graham and Winnie Wilmot (YWCA), Joan Nicoll (The Girls' Brigade Ireland) and Margaret Dunne (the Irish Girl Guides) advised us on locating historical sources for their respective organisations and their help is gratefully acknowledged.

We would also like to thank the archivists and other staff at the following institutions for their help: Representative Church Body Library, Dublin; The National Library of Ireland; The National Archives, Ireland; The National Archives, UK; University College Dublin Archives; Dublin Diocesan Archives; Cork City Library Archive; Cork City and County Archives.

Finally, we would like to thank all our colleagues within the School of Applied Social Studies for their interest and support for the project.

Introduction

It's doubly galling that children were so much a part of the revolutionary rhetoric and yet everything we did flew in the face of the notion that children were meant to be prized.[1] (Diarmaid Ferriter, *Irish Times*, 28 May 2010)

What does 'youth' mean? At the outset of this study we were confronted by this seminal question. A senior government official on our research advisory committee suggested to us that we should use the chronological definition contained in the Irish Youth Work Act 2001. On the face of it, this was good advice. But an examination of the Youth Work Act 2001 reveals more than one chronological definition. At the outset, the Youth Work Act 2001 (Section 2) defines youth very broadly: 'young person means a person who has not attained the age of 25'. But subsequently the Youth Work Act 2001 (Section 8) refers to youth work as being provided for 'persons who have attained the age of 10 years but not 21 years'. Childhood refers to all citizens under the age of 18 years, who are not entitled to civil or political rights but do have a social right to care and protection. According to the legal principle, *parens patriae*, the State is the higher or ultimate parent of the child. The publication of the Ryan Report in 2009 showed how little had been done to vindicate that right.

Chronology is too simple a parameter to explain a social phenomenon as complex as youth, which is both ambiguous and uneven in its various meanings. The fundamental ambiguity in the Irish Youth Work Act 2001 exposes a problem in Ireland, Europe and beyond in defining what we mean when we talk about 'the youth population'. Who exactly are they? What are they? How are they socially constructed? These are not easy questions to answer, and are further complicated by historical differences between the divergent meanings of 'youth policy' and 'child care policy'. Barker (2008: 422) asserts 'youth is a cultural category differentially articulated with (constructed in relation to) class, gender and race. In addition, youth is understood as a spatial matter, that is, youth may be produced differently, in divergent spaces and places, youth is enacted in clubs, pubs, schools and parks'. Furthermore 'youth policy' may or may not have a coherent meaning, largely depending on the country in which the youth population (an equally elusive notion) reside. While some states have an overarching conception of youth policy, others respond in an *ad hoc* fashion, state department by state department, often in response to moral panics (e.g. child abuse) and pathological views of young people (e.g. delinquency).

Our study grew out of a European project involving ten member states funded by a Council of Europe-European Union partnership in 2007 (Bohn, 2007). One of the challenges faced in that research was the complexity involved in defining youth policy in a cross-national comparative study. An earlier Instituto di Ricerca (IARD) (2001: 2) research project, entitled *Study on the State of Young People and Youth Policy in Europe*, shed considerable light on these issues:

> The concept of youth in a policy context is the product of national and historical traditions. In European countries with a long historical tradition of youth work and youth policy, there is a marked tendency to define youth policy as policies directed towards 'young people' which includes some or all cohorts of children, and sometimes even expands into age groups beyond the age of 24. In other European countries, the generic term 'young people' is not used at all in policy contexts and in these countries there is a separation between child policy and youth policy. Because of the fundamentally different youth concepts – the narrow one, which excludes children, and the wide-ranging one – it is very difficult to compare youth policy across Europe. These differences in the definition of youth are of importance when examining the two main approaches to youth policy in Europe: youth as a human resource versus youth as a problem. In countries where youth is chiefly perceived as (social) minors, there is a tendency to consider young people as a potential problem, as being in danger, as people that must be protected against threats to their development. In countries in which youth policy is based on a narrower and more adult point of view, there seems to be a tendency to regard youth as a resource.

The IARD Final Reports (IARD, 2001: 57) concluded on the basis of a classification of European countries into four groups where Ireland (in common with the Netherlands and Luxembourg) were 'countries where youth policy covers the age range from the age of early primary school to 25 years'. This parameter complements the broad definition in the Irish Youth Work Act 2001. The National Youth Work Development Plan 2003–2007 (NYWDP) also states 'a young person means a person who has not attained the age of twenty-five' (Department of Education and Science, 2003: 2). On the other hand, the Child Care Act 1992 defines childhood as the state of any young person under the age of eighteen years.

Our national study was confronted with this European problem of definitional complexity, as well as several other seminal issues. First, in relation to chronology we addressed youth policy as an overarching concept that embraces age groups that range from pre-school years up to adulthood, in essence the entire population under the age of twenty-five years. Second, there was the issue of the governance of youth policy. The Office of the Minister for Children and Youth Affairs (OMCYA) coordinates Irish youth policy but does not deliver it. The model of youth policy in Ireland is based upon a long tradition of community-orientated youth work, in which the youth service is largely 'devolved' by the State to civil society in the form of voluntary and community organisations (IARD, 2001: 106). However, targeted youth projects are a major focus of state intervention. Child care policy until 1970 was also devolved by the State to the Church and voluntary sector. Since then it has become a state responsibility in the form of the Health Service Executive (HSE). Human rights violations dominate debates about services for children both historically and contemporaneously, evidenced by a series of reports. Third, youth policy is framed within a discourse of problematisation (i.e. child abuse, social exclusion, drug awareness, youth justice). As the IARD Final Report (2001: 106–107) puts it, 'the dominant image of youth [in Ireland] is youth as a problem'. Cultural images such as the so-called 'joy-riders' of the 1980s and 1990s, their assumed progeny ('boy racers' and their 'modded' cars), as well as the ubiquitous image of the alcopop-swilling teen (usually female) binge drinker reinforce this popular association of youth with crime, violence and delinquency (Barker, 2008: 408–409). These images compete with images of child abuse victims in the media. Fourth, there is the issue of the developmental trajectory of Irish youth policy. In some European countries youth policy is described as 'static'. The universalistic welfare state in 'static' countries (e.g. Scandinavia) has developed youth policy to a point where it has reached a high level of sophistication and is consequently in a steady state. In other jurisdictions, with less well-developed welfare regimes, such as Ireland, Britain and the Mediterranean countries, youth policy tends to be defined as 'dynamic' because it is still in a state of evolution. Irish youth policy has evolved over several centuries. But as the country modernised post-1958, the Irish state (under pressure from social reformers) began to take on a much more active role in the formulation and promotion of youth policy, particularly in response to evidence of institutional child abuse. There has been considerable tension between traditionalist policy actors (the Civil Service and the Catholic Church) and reformist policy actors (campaign groups, professional associations and voluntary organisations). Much of the thrust of the resulting debate has centred upon community-based forms of social intervention and support, as opposed to the traditional model of institutional care for disadvantaged youth, where human rights were systematically violated. Because of the definitional complexity and historic legacy of abuse, we have included both youth policy and child care policy in our study. The recent decision by the Irish government to establish an Office of the Minister for Children and Youth Affairs clearly defines

Irish youth policy in this broad way. However it is important to note that many policy-makers and practitioners in youth work have very real concerns about this policy development, which they fear may eclipse their identity and marginalise their contribution.

Finally, beyond these legal and policy issues there are deeper questions that inform and shape the definition and foundational meaning of youth, youth policy and childhood in a postmodern world where the social is decentred and identities destabilised. Philippe Aries (1962) advanced his thesis of 'the discovery of childhood' as the product of modernity. Norbert Elias (1994) viewed the emergence of childhood as part of a civilisation process, which he called 'civility'. Talcot Parsons (1942, 1963) conceptualised youth as a product of capitalism that had created a rupture in society, resulting in an extended transition to adulthood. In modern society, a cultural space was created outside the traditional family aimed at the socialisation of youth for more complex occupational roles and social responsibilities. Formal education became the chief mechanism by which the socialisation functions of the family were displaced by the State in urban industrial society. Youth work found a space in this new order to offer informal education and personal development through recreational and leisure pursuits in the community. This modernist process led to the deconstruction of pre-modern youth, as an invisible organic part of traditional extended family life within a rural agriculturally-based economy without age stages, into the structured urban industrial world of education and employment. Postmodernity has thrown up new socio-historical cultural configurations of fragmentation, individualisation and consumerism in risk society (Beck, 1992; Giddens, 1991). This is the social and cultural space that youth in Celtic Tiger/Post-Celtic Tiger Ireland finds itself as a social group, adrift in a world without clear coordinates or easily identifiable purpose (Crook et al., 1992; Putnam, 2000). A shrinking state and weakening civil society are challenged to address this social vacuum in the lives of postmodern youth. The revelations of the Ryan Report during 2009 have so far elicited a very weak policy response, consistent with the traditional disengagement of the Irish state with children's rights. While unborn children enjoy constitutional protection in Ireland, born children have no such rights, although a constitutional referendum on children's rights is promised.

The National Youth Work Development Plan 2003–2007 addresses the impact of postmodern change on Irish youth in terms of a series of socio-cultural factors: demography; diversity; blurring of boundaries; complex transitions; choices and pressures, as well as individualism and consumerism (Department of Education and Science, 2003: 2–4). In the wake of the 2008 crash, unemployment and poverty need to be added to this list. The NYWDP notes that youth is declining as a proportion of the population but 'the make up of the youth population is much more culturally diverse than heretofore, increasing the need for intercultural/multicultural aptitudes and awareness among young people and those who work with them' (Department of Education and Science, 2003: 2–3). It convincingly seeks to grapple with the foundational meaning of youth in the postmodern world, arguing that the boundaries between childhood and adulthood have become more fluid, leading to a blurring of previous distinctions. This has impacted on the transition from childhood to adulthood: 'The transition that has for so long been associated with youth is being significantly extended. In addition, the transition – in fact, the transitions – are becoming more complex' (Department of Education and Science, 2003: 3). The NYWDP discusses the critical issues of consumerism and individualism in terms of lifestyle choices and pressures that drive young people earlier in their lives to embrace sexuality and relationships in a world where the solidity of the traditional family and community is under strain (Department of Education and Science, 2003: 3–4). The tension between group consciousness and atomistic individualism and the interweaving of ethics and aesthetics define modern youth culture (Gilroy, 2010).

Are these profound changes in postmodern society undermining the foundations of youth as a social and cultural construct? Is there a loss of meaning in a decentred world? Can we any longer address 'youth' as a coherent whole? Does this present youth policy with a crisis of obsolescence? Or does it present us with an opportunity to reimagine its mission? The NYWDP 2003–2007 (Department of Education and Science, 2003: 4) concludes that young people are more alienated, sceptical and questioning of established meanings contained in traditional religious verities and the authenticity of social institutions. This might be interpreted as a Baudrillardian version of postmodernity in which youth culture can simply be dismissed as stylised and ritualised forms of activity in a world that has become lost in a black hole of meaninglessness (Barker, 2008: 428). The NYWDP (Department of Education and Science, 2003: 4) rejects this 'death of meaning' thesis, optimistically concluding 'there is nothing to suggest that young people are any less interested than before in the spiritual dimension of their lives, in developing a belief system which makes sense of their experience and informs their relationships with others and with society'. But it issues a warning that youth policy must adapt to 'the changing nature of youth' and see it as an 'opportunity' and a 'challenge' (*ibid.*: 11–12).

This national study of Irish youth policy seeks to address the historical narratives of youth policy and child care and survey the current realities that confront the youth service (a contested term). In addressing these issues, the study aims to provide a historical and social scientific analysis of youth policy in Ireland, which embraces a triarchy of civil society, State and Church. It has both institutional (child abuse) and community (disadvantaged youth) dimensions. This has three main purposes: first, to document, analyse and theorise the development of social policy enacted specifically with young people in mind ('youth policy') from the beginning of modernity to the present day, including abused children; secondly to analyse associational activity and active citizenship in civil society as it pertains to young people, and to develop an analysis of 'youth work' as an expression of that active citizenship; and thirdly to develop a survey-based analysis of the contemporary provision of youth services to young people. We view these developments as important aspects of Irish society's journey to and through modernity, and on the changing self-image of Irish society through that process: from colonial Ireland and the struggle for independence, to the assertion of cultural values in the fledgling state; from the political upheavals and social contestation of the late 1920s and early 1930s, to the integrative project of autarkist independence; and from the economic modernisation of the 1960s, through the crises of the late 1970s and early 1980s, to the emergence in the 1990s of a qualitatively 'new' Ireland through the processes of globalisation, ethnic diversification and economic development, often popularly, and now erstwhile, described as 'Celtic Tiger' Ireland.

In doing this, the study explores the role played by youth organisations in civil society and their impact on Irish society, including historical research on the role of pre-independence institutions and youth movements; on religious youth organisations (institutional and community-based) in post-independence Ireland; on the emergence of 'youth clubs' and the burgeoning notion of 'youth work' in the 1960s; and on the increasingly professionalised and policy-driven interventions in young people's lives through 'child care' and 'youth services' from the mid-1980s to the present day. Further, the study focuses on analysing the changing social, cultural and political constructions of youth policy, of notions of 'youth' and 'childhood', and of the relationship between the State and voluntary organisations in civil society in the mixed economy of welfare that have occurred since the formation of the State. Complementing the historical and rhetorical arguments presented, the study also utilises empirical data from a national survey of over 600 youth organisations.

The study analyses what youth policy reveals about modern Irish society and its historical development: how 'youth' was and is conceived of; what form of interventions in young people's lives are and have been socially sanctioned; what associational activities in civil society have arisen to support and contradict these interventions; how youth policy has been socially, culturally and ideologically constructed; how the normative nature of youth has been, and continues to be, contested; and how Irish social services now orient and organise themselves to the challenge of providing a relevant service to Irish young people. It is a complex task because youth policy, as already noted, embraces both services for young people (generically referred to as 'youth work') and child care services (generically referred to as 'social work' and 'social care'). Manifestly, there are sporting and cultural organisations (e.g. the Gaelic Athletic Association and Irish Youth Theatre), schools and colleges, as well as services for the unemployed that for reasons of scope and resources could not be fully developed in our study. However, we are satisfied that our analysis accords with European 'broad' conceptions of youth policy and hope it will make a significant contribution to Irish discourse on youth policy.

Notes

1 Ferriter is referring to the Democratic Programme (1919) that promised a social (as well as a political) revolution with rights for children and young people. Like the social revolution, Irish youth were abandoned once independence had been won.

PART I

YOUTH NARRATIVES AND YOUTH MOVEMENTS

1

The search for an Irish youth narrative: minor citizens or urban tribe?

> Youth is ... treated as a key indicator of the state of the nation itself ... Young people are assumed to hold the key to the nation's future, and the treatment and management of 'youth' is expected to provide the solution to a nation's problems. (Griffin, 1993: 9–10)

Christine Griffin's quote reminds us not only how 'youth' is a socially and culturally constructed category, but also how its alternating definitions and applications can tell us something about a society's condition. Equally, an understanding of the core social, economic and political circumstances which shape particular societies in unique ways, has to form a basis of analysis if we are to understand how the social category of 'youth' has been established, shaped and utilised in concrete social and historical contexts. It is now widely accepted in discussions of the history and sociology of youth, that youth is a socially and culturally constructed category and not a biological given (McRobbie, 1991; Willis, 1977). This was not always the case: the 'father of adolescence', the American psychologist G.S. Hall, termed this stage in the life course in largely biological-developmental terms. Social historians of childhood, such as Philippe Aries (*Centuries of Childhood*, 1962) and Lloyd de Mause (*The History of Childhood*, 1974) have interrupted this 'grand narrative'. Despite fundamental later revisions by medieval historians (O'Day, 1994; Pollock, 1983), Aries' and de Mause's theses transformed public understanding of the nature and meaning of childhood and youth. By opening up the study of childhood to social-historical inquiry, they established the social-constructionist perspective on childhood and youth. Aries argued that children in medieval times were absorbed into the adult world from the age of about seven, when they were 'considered capable of doing without mothers or nannies, not long after tardy weaning' (Aries, 1962: 395). Mass compulsory primary education, introduced in the nineteenth century, was to make childhood and youth a universal institution and transform public consciousness of young people's particular needs, their place in society, legal status and most of all their vulnerability.

Youth are regarded – and regard themselves – in very different ways in different historical contexts and in different cultures. The meaning of 'youth' is not a fixed parameter, but is in constant negotiation between different social actors and institutions, between generations as well as in young people's intimate relationships with families and friends. Public discourse, institutional policies, everyday practices and last but not least academic study of 'youth' is permanently re-defining what 'youth' means in different contexts. These interpretations and understandings are not always homogenous and quite often in stark contrast from each other, as this chapter will show. Many of the commonly accepted definitions of 'youth' have also developed out of 'adults' preoccupations and panics – at least over certain groups of young people, and by certain groups of adults (Griffin, 1993).

In this chapter we sketch the trajectory of a distinctive youth narrative in modern Ireland. To do this, we have chosen to adopt a broad socio-historical framework of analysis, aiming at highlighting some of the major social, political and cultural shifts, continuities and disruptions that have occurred in the construction of youth in Ireland. We will do this specifically by looking at how the Irish state, the Catholic Church and civil society, have shaped the youth narrative and young people's lives in direct and indirect ways. Each of these social actors have employed particular mechanisms to understand and shape youth: the State through a variety of social policies particularly in the areas of education, welfare and employment; the Church through a moral discourse as well as executor of many of the state's policies, in areas such as education and institutional care, but most importantly probably in the creation of powerful images of 'devils' and 'angels'; and civil society through the mobilisation of young people into different youth movements and organisations. As will become apparent, certain themes were treated with a relative level of consistency over time, while others disappeared at certain points or emerged as new considerations around the discourse on youth in Ireland. It is important to note that even within the institutions of Church, State and civil society, there were often contradictions and disputes in the way in which young people were imagined. By understanding how the term youth was employed as a social category to achieve broader social or organisational goals, the chapter will provide insight into the key parameters that shaped young people's lives over time in Ireland.

The chapter is organised into four broad time periods: pre-independence Ireland (pre-1922), the young Irish state and the period of cultural isolationism (1922–1958), the modernising Irish state (1958–1987) and 'Celtic and Post-Celtic Tiger' Ireland (1987 to date). Within the framework of significant broad socio-cultural trends in each of these time periods, we will analyse, how State, Church and civil society have played out their conceptions of young people. These broad socio-cultural trends as well as their conception by these actors have continuously shaped young people's lives along lines of gender, class and religion – demanding differing levels of independence, yet compliance to gener-ally accepted social, economic and political norms when necessary. Our analysis will demonstrate both a certain level of continuity as well as transformation and change both in conceptions as well as lived realities of young people.

Pre-independence Ireland: colonised youth

Jordan (1998: 49) observes: 'Disease as well as malnutrition contributed to the slaughter of Victorian Ireland's children'. Young people's lives in post-famine Ireland have to be conceptualised in the framework of extreme poverty and deprivation. While the capacity of the colonial state and the Church to develop interventions for youth was relatively limited, there was a growing appreciation of the needs of children and young people, which was progressively dealt with through child care policy. We will first explore the contexts and landmarks which influenced the lives of young people in pre-independence Ireland. Timothy Guinnane's analysis of census data of 1901 and 1911 provides important insights into how the transition from childhood to adulthood was structured for rural young people (where most of the population lived) at the turn of the twenti-eth century. Rural demographics shaped young people's experience of growing up: emigration rates abroad or to the cities were so high, that in counties like Clare and Mayo over half of a birth cohort would have emigrated by the age of thirty (Guinnane, 1990: 447). Indeed, Fitzpatrick (1984) argues that children in Ireland were brought up as potential emigrants, knowing that they would even-tually travel. Once they reached adulthood and as a 'result of the "stem-family" succession system, which saw the eldest son inherit the farm', emigration con-stituted a regular and 'normal' element in young people's lifecycle (Fitzpatrick, 1984: 46). The Congested District Board for Ireland, set up in 1891, attempted to address this situation by introducing some 'industrial' projects aimed par-ticularly at young people, such as lace-making classes for girls (Guinnane, 1990: 446). However, overall young people's autonomy was extremely limited, leaving them with the options of direct emigration, entering another Irish household (through servitude), marrying, or migrating to the city (*ibid.*: 449).

While we have only limited access to the lived experience of young people due to the dearth of recorded recollections from young people's perspectives, those available, such as Patrick MacGill's *Children of the Dead End* (1914), reveal a rather gloomy experience of growing up in Ireland in the late nineteenth cen-tury. Other recollections available from the period of mid-nineteenth century Ireland demonstrate how the famine and endemic poverty caused serious and permanent damage to children's lives (Jordan, 1998). Jordan remarks how the 'collapse of public, externally oriented, morality' had such an intense effect on children and young people's psychology that it disturbed their healthy mental development, resulting in what Erikson has termed 'role confusion' (Jordan,

1998: 48). For instance, it has been estimated that in 1856 only one-third of children up to the age of sixteen had two living parents (*ibid.*: 49).

In these contexts, the definition of youth as legal and social category developed rather slowly, and then only conferred a right to care and protection – as minor citizens who lacked adult rights. Only 'infancy' was recognised by the law in pre-modern society, which included newborn babies and young people up to twenty-one years of age. Boys could marry at fourteen years, but were not allowed to dispose of their property until they had achieved the age of majority, which was twenty-one years. Gradually, during the nineteenth century, the doctrine of *parens patriae* (i.e. that the State is the higher or ultimate parent) began to interpose itself between family rights (particularly those of fathers – up to this time considered unchallengeable) and children. However, the court's primary interest was to regulate adults' relationships (i.e. those between fathers and mothers) when they impacted on the welfare of the child. Apart from the regulation of child labour, young people as such had no social rights before the 1870s (Morris *et al.*, 1980: 1–2). The power of the family was so great that the protection of children from cruelty in the United Kingdom only followed sixty-five years after animal welfare legislation had been introduced to protect animals from cruelty.

Children's right to care and protection was finally secured during the 1870s. The dramatic Mary Ellen case in New York in 1875 alerted the world to the problem of cruelty to children. In the absence of appropriate child protection legislation, local community leaders prevailed upon the Society for the Prevention of Cruelty to Animals to take Mary Ellen's case to court as an abused 'animal'. It did so successfully. Mary Ellen was provided with care and protection by the State and her guardians imprisoned for her abuse and neglect. This case resulted in the establishment of child protection organisations and legislation. In 1884 the National Society for the Prevention of Cruelty to Children was established in Britain. There followed a committee of the society in Dublin, formed in 1889. This initiative coincided with the Prevention of Cruelty and Protection of Children Act 1889, which provided protection for children from abuse or neglect (Robins, 1980: 307–308). The Children Act 1908, known as the Children's Charter, acknowledged children's rights in law to care and protection by the State and established juvenile courts.

Besides welfare policy for children, schooling provided another opportunity for both the colonial state and the Catholic Church to join hands in shaping young minds. Attempts to make school attendance compulsory for children between the ages of six and fourteen were only moderately successful. Despite a dismal Irish average daily attendance of 63% in 1900, which had only marginally improved to 66% in 1919, and was well below European standards, reform in this area had to await the inception of the new State in 1922 (Coolahan, 1981: 35–38). No doubt the substantial contribution children were required to make to the family economy in a predominantly rural society explains the resistance to this measure in Ireland. It was left to the Irish Free State to address this problem through the School Attendance Act 1926, which made school attendance compulsory for children between the ages of six and fifteen.

The emergence of active citizenship engaged in the arena of philanthropy, needs to be set in the social context of the Victorian world. The urbanisation that characterised the emergence of capitalism in the modern world had created the perception of a social gulf between classes in the major cities. It was believed that the traditional hierarchies and social bonds of rural life had been fundamentally undermined, creating a social crisis. There was also a profound sense of political crisis, as the spectre of social revolution by the new urban tribes engulfed Europe between the 1840s and 1880s. Blom (2008: 330) asserts that 'these new urban tribes were a central fact of the emerging social order. A realignment of identities was taking place everywhere, leaving most people suspended between their traditional communities (religious faith, regional origin and customs) and new communities – half chosen; half imposed by life in the modern city'.

Youth as a new urban tribe needed to be rooted in this changed environment. The foundation of the Boy Scouts and the Girl Guides in the early twentieth century by Robert Baden-Powell, established an international youth movement that aimed to transcend class, politics, race and religious beliefs (see Chapter 3). The Scouts and Guides sought to promote character-building and a sense of public service amongst the youth population in a globalised world transformed by industrialisation and urbanisation. It was paralleled by the emergence of the German *Wandervogel* movement and other initiatives across the world. Blom (2008: 328–329) argues that during this *belle époque* period youth initially emerged as a distinct urban tribe – 'a first recognition of youth as a world in itself and not just a kind of deficient adulthood, a group demanding recognition, entertainment and identity; but they still lacked a distinctive youth culture that would define their world as different.'

In this uncertain landscape dystopian images of the modern city began to emerge. The division between the prosperous West End of London and the impoverished East End provided a metaphor for the way the city was depicted and theorised in Victorian social commentary (Mooney, 1998: 56). Dublin, like other European cities, was increasingly becoming home to rural migrants without providing them with adequate housing opportunities. Jacinta Prunty (1995) effectively illustrates the paranoia which developed amongst the Dublin bourgeoisie about the city's slums which were seen as a threat to health, social order and morality. In this imagery of the poor, deprived urban areas came to be configured in the Victorian mind as 'dark' and 'hostile' places (Engels, 1999). The poor became the 'other' of Victorian society (Mooney, 1998: 59). In Dublin, the concern about the city and particularly young boys, also established a discourse on 'city morals', and the declining morality of young people who were increasingly losing interest in the Church was frequently a focus of public concern. Eager philanthropists urged for the establishment of social clubs for boys, while being very aware of the distinctive and 'inferior' social class of the boys they ought to address.

On the basis of this historical context, it can be argued that young people's lives slowly started to be valued and protected after 1870 with the introduction of several and partial reforms concerning children's welfare. Young people emerged as an urban tribe with distinct tastes and manners – while they were not yet a commercial urban tribe, they were a distinctive social group that would later develop into a mass youth culture in the 1960s (Blom, 2008: 329). Previous to that, young people's lives were determined greatly by the circumstances of their family of origin. Childhood prepared a few young people for inheriting the family farm; however for most children, their transition into adulthood was marked by a period of servitude in another Irish household, emigration abroad, migration to the cities or marriage into another family. The lifespan of adolescence slowly started to take shape through modernisation and a nascent system of mass education. While it was only a small proportion of the youth population, and initially only the younger children who regularly attended national schools, this marked the beginning of continuing state intervention in young people's lives. This gradual shift away from the family and into the school, which was led by the State and the Church, contributed to creating the citizen who was morally upright and not questioning the social hierarchy. Increased migration to the urban centre of Dublin from rural areas, without adequate provision of housing, created city slums. Young boys particularly became the face of urban poverty, and philanthropists started to address the situation by setting up boys' social clubs and running or supporting mostly uniformed youth organisations. In rural Ireland the formation of the Gaelic Athletic Association (GAA) in 1884 provided Irish youth with a vibrant nationalist sporting organisation, which quickly organised across the country (see Chapter 4). The GAA was to prove one of the most successful and enduring expressions of civil society activism (O'Broin and Kirby, 2009: 19). These early beginnings of voluntary youth work provided associational spaces for young people to explore their roles in life as minor citizens awaiting adulthood before they could embrace full citizenship.

The nascent Irish state: angels and devils?

Once established, the newly founded state of Ireland soon found opportunities to focus upon the youth issue. As this section will outline, a new configuration between Church and State had profound implications for growing up in Ireland. The nascent Irish Free State, established in 1922, had limited resources to devise and implement new social policies, but those it had were inevitably used to boost its identity as an independent nation state. Young people soon found themselves the focus of this strategy. Peter Lennon describes in his once controversial 1967 film documentary *Rocky Road to Dublin* that the 'sons and daughters of revolutionary heroes were expected to show forth well behaved gratitude and heroic obedience'. The State and Catholic Church focused on young people through the schooling system; the former interested in instilling the revolutionary momentum and the rich Gaelic culture and tradition in its young people; the latter interested in the infusion of all subjects with instruction in the faith and social control over Ireland's youth. The education system imagined young people as the well-spring of the nation who would participate as agents or, maybe more appropriately, recipients of change in the cultural revolution to come (Coolahan, 1981: 7). The introduction of Irish language as an obligatory subject in 1922 served as an attempt to re-establish 'Irishness' in Ireland and ensuring that future generations incorporated the ideologies of the nation and national culture. Cultural isolationism, as it was termed retrospectively, was promoted through the history curriculum, which was to be exclusively concerned with Irish history and geography and 'develop the best traits of the national character and inculcate national pride and self-respect' (Coolahan, 1981: 40). As O'Donoghue (1999) shows, this partnership between State and Church resulted in an alliance that would not shift until the 1960s, resulting in a 'narrow curriculum delivered through stultifying, test-driven teaching methods that rewarded mimetic skills over more transformative, critical thinking', instilling in the process a rural and middle-class Catholic social ethos coupled with conservative nationalism on Ireland's youth. Educators were to the largest extent priests, religious brothers and sisters, educating a loyal middle-class generation of young people, who would carry on their understanding of social Catholic hierarchy. The partnership was to maintain stability, as it was underwritten by the consensus that the curriculum was fulfilling three central tasks: a decent religious education, the needs of the Gaelicisation process and the provision of 'general education' preparing young people for clerical occupations or entry into professional training (O'Donoghue, 1999: 89). It was only publicly admitted in the 1960s that this romanticisation of young people would not be sufficient to prepare young people for a 'modern Ireland'. The Department of Education realised that it could no longer take a back seat in education policy, particularly secondary education, if it was to contribute to building a well-educated and modern citizenry. This resulted in fundamental educational policy changes and the introduction of free secondary education in 1968, resulting in immense shifts in access to education for Ireland's young people. The OECD Report *Investment in Education* (1966) played a seminal role in modernising the Irish education system.

The first significant policy directed at young people by the Irish Free State, was the Vocational Education Committee (VEC) Act of 1930. It arose out of a concern about unemployment and vagrancy amongst young working-class men on Irish, particularly Dublin's, streets. It aimed to prepare young people for

employment in trades, manufactures, agriculture and commerce. It also authorised the VECs to collect information with respect to the employment of people
under eighteen years. In Dublin, the Society of St Vincent de Paul and the Legion
of Mary received training by the Dublin VEC youth training schemes under the
aegis of *Comhairle le Leas Óige*, to train young people, amongst other things, in
the crafts and marketable trades, such as boot repair and woodwork (Kiely and
Kennedy, 2005: 193). *Comhairle le Leas Óige* (Council for the Welfare of Youth)
was founded in 1942 by the City of Dublin VEC and quickly flourished.

In rural Ireland a vigorous youth movement addressed itself to the problems of rural decline and isolation. *Muintir na Tire* (People of the Countryside)
was initially founded in 1931 by Canon John Hayes, a charismatic priest. He
opened up *Muintir na Tire* to all religious denominations, incurring the wrath of
the Archbishop of Dublin, John Charles McQuaid, who objected to the inclusion
of Protestants (Cooney, 1999: 157–158). Hayes sought to promote rural regeneration through community development which included the development of a
rural youth movement. But it was the establishment of *Macra na Feirme* (Sons
of the Farms) in 1944, aimed at young people between seventeen and thirty-five
years, that was to prove the main catalyst in the development of a rural youth
movement. Founded by Stephen Cullinan, a Kildare-based rural science teacher,
Macra na Feirme set about up-skilling young farmers in agricultural methods
and providing a social life through *Macra* clubs, where young people could
meet. It played a seminal role in the foundation of the *Irish Farmers' Journal*,
the Irish Creamery Mill Suppliers Association (ICMSA), the National Farmers'
Association (now IFA) and the Farm Apprenticeship Scheme. In 1952 *Macra na
Feirme* founded *Macra na Tuaithe* (Sons of the Land), which changed its name
to *Foróige* in 1981. *Foróige* (meaning 'youth development') works with young
people between the age of twelve to eighteen years and is one of the largest youth
organisations in Ireland (see Chapter 6).

The youth unemployment issue also started to become a matter of great
concern to the State, and to the voluntary sector. The Catholic Youth Conference
of 1941 assembled five youth organisations (Catholic Young Men's Society,
Catholic Boy Scouts of Ireland, the Catholic Girl Guides of Ireland, St John Bosco
Boys and the Legion of Mary) to discuss the issue of youth unemployment. The
Archbishop of Dublin, John Charles McQuaid, became chairman of the National
Commission on Youth Unemployment in 1943, an acknowledgement of his secular power by the State. The difficulty with this appointment soon become clear in
a heated letter exchange between the Archbishop and Sean Lemass, Minister of
Supplies (and future Taoiseach), in which the Archbishop unsuccessfully but in-
sistently demanded that he could not accept submissions from any non-Catholic
organisations (Cooney, 1999: 169). The final report of the National Commission
on Youth Unemployment in 1951 reflected a progressive element, in so far as
it linked youth unemployment to the general unemployment situation and it

favoured community care over Industrial and Reformatory schools, which it recommended should be reorganised into smaller units. But it also reinforced traditional views about the girl's role in the home and a strong uneasiness with the continuing emigration, particularly of young women.

Archbishop McQuaid's views on youth policy were coloured by his religious loyalties. He sought to make religious segregation a fundamental tenet of Irish youth work, viewing contact between Catholic and Protestant youth as 'dangerous' (Cooney, 1999: 292). His work in promoting youth clubs was part of his mission to develop 'social study among working men, employers and youth in accordance with catholic doctrine' (ibid.: 68). For Archbishop McQuaid, young people's development was of the utmost concern. In a drive to expand youth clubs under his control, Archbishop McQuaid told the first youth leader training course, attended by 200 youths from parishes throughout the Archdiocese of Dublin, that they were 'only apprentices in the supernatural apostolate of youth who needed to follow the men and women in the counsel that was the fruit of grace and age and prayer' (ibid.: 202). He was also concerned about club work for young women. Encouraging the work of the Sodality of Mary, he stated that 'Social clubs, work-rooms, tea and dinner rooms, not to mention Hospital visitation and almoner work, are among the chief instruments used for the retention of power and spread of influence' (McQuaid in Cooney, 1999: 87). In 1944 Archbishop McQuaid established the Diocesan youth service in Dublin, which became Catholic Youth Care in 1977.

It is important to note that the climate in which Archbishop McQuaid's intervention with youth took place was in the overall context of strict monocultural Catholic puritanism. This was exemplified through legislation such as the Censorship of Films Act 1923, the Intoxicating Liquor Acts 1924 and 1927, outlawing of Divorce Bills 1925, Censorship of Publications Act 1929, Criminal Law Amendment Act 1935 (banning the sale and importation of contraceptives), the Dance Hall Act 1935 and the Conditions of Employment Act 1936 (allowing prohibition of the employment of married female workers) (Burke, 1999; Whyte, 1980). Young people were particularly affected by a repressive social atmosphere, in which moral panics, particularly fuelled by the Catholic Church about the negative influence of foreign music and dances on young people's morals, justified intervention by the State. The Public Dance Halls Act of 1935, which was introduced at the behest of 'some members of the hierarchy' (i.e. bishops' council), added a further layer of social repression (Whyte, 1980: 50). It could be said, after ensuring its control over education, the Church aimed to increase its control of young people through its attempts to colonise their leisure time. The dance hall, in the Church's view, represented everything that was a threat to the young Irish nation: the body and the soul of the nation represented by young people were at stake. Young people now also posed a threat through their relative geographical mobility, which allowed them to travel to dances outside their

local area. The rise in the use of motor cars and immoral behaviour became a related concern of the clergy. After successful government lobbying, the Criminal
Law Amendment Bill 1932 included a definition of motor cars as a public space
allowing the police to monitor behaviour within them (Smyth, 1993: 54).

Young people often found themselves enrolled in maintaining this moral
framework. A demonstration of approximately 3,000 young people in Mohill,
Country Leitrim, against jazz music, which was frequently referred to in explicitly racist terms by district judges as 'nigger music' (Smyth, 1993), was supported
with well-wishes by the Church and de Valera (Smyth, 1993:54). In an article on
the impact of the Public Dance Halls Act on rural communities in County Clare,
Gearaid O'hAdllmhnran describes how some priests accompanied the police to
raid private house dances (O'hAdllmhnran, 2005: 14). The intrusion of the State
into private homes to uphold the repressive moral values of the Catholic Church,
which abhorred the free association between the sexes, demonstrates how far
and how powerfully the Church could restrict and restrain the social lives of
young people. The Public Dance Hall Act 1935 demonstrated that in Irish society young people's leisure time was to be controlled, the private sphere was to
be regulated and young people's leisure was to be monitored in a certain kind of
Catholic public sphere, reflected through the rise of parochial halls in the 1930s.
The parochial halls increasingly served as commercial dance halls while strictly
monitored by the clergy (O'hAdllmhnran, 2005: 16). Worries about illegitimate
motherhood that would necessitate young women to 'retire to the refuge of the
institutions' (*Irish Independent*, 7 October 1925, cited in O'Connor 2003: 55),
led bishops to single out young women as being 'especially prone to the evils
of modern dancing' (*ibid.*). Analysing the discourse of Church documents and
statements relating to dance from the early 1920s to the early 1930s, O'Connor
(*ibid.*: 530) shows how they often reflected a combination of discourses around
nation, sexuality, social class/respectability and gender. As we know now, and
as will be further discussed in Chapters 9 and 10, a hidden discourse of abuse,
paedophilia and rape, particularly in the institutional care context, existed in
parallel.

The cinema provided another medium through which this moral panic
about young people in the context of the nation-building process could be expressed. The first cinema was opened in Ireland in 1908 and proved a favourite
pastime of many young people. However, for the conservative elite the cinema
posed a new set of threats to young people's minds, by allowing them to get an
insight into the 'frivolous' lifestyle and values of Hollywood. Even in publications which were setting out to address probably justifiable concerns about the
psychological impact of fast and loud images on children's health, the dominat-
ing discourse was the cultural threat of the foreign world.

In the light of these contexts, it seems that the reality confronting Irish
youth in the middle of the twentieth century was grim. Archbishop McQuaid's

concerns were a reflection of this reality as a failure of traditional society to resist the cultural influences of modern mass society, while offering a lifestyle that was socially barren. Sweeney and Dunne (2003: 5) have, in a description of the lives of Irish youth during the 1950s, captured this bleak reality:

> In the 1950s young people tended to be detained in childhood or rushed into adulthood. There was little conception that they should be allowed to occupy, much less enjoy, an intervening period in which freedoms could be tested and aspects of the adult world tasted. They were detained in childhood, for example, by the large reliance on repeat years in the National School System to ensure basic literacy; most 14 year olds were either 'big' boys or girls in a national school or had entered the workforce and finished with their education entirely. They were kept in childhood by family systems where the combination of elders, the wait to inherit property, and low marriage rates meant single men in their 30s could be stopped from socialising if their parents refused to give them the pocket money for going out. Alternatively, young people were rushed into adulthood. This occurred largely by their having to emigrate and discover, usually in the British Midlands or in London, a kind of autonomy and self-reliance which had been denied to them by their environment at home.

Paternalistic reference to 'comely maidens' did little to inspire confidence amongst Irish youth that they were either understood or respected in their quest for an identity upon which they could construct a narrative that would give shape and meaning to their lives. This was the traditionalist vision of Irish youth that informed An Taoiseach (Prime Minister) Eamon de Valera's St Patrick's Day 1943 radio broadcast to the nation. It was very much a vision *for* Irish youth rather than a vision *from* them (Sweeney and Dunne, 2003: 5). Disempowered by tradition, the historical experience of Irish youth has been highly problematic. This reality conditioned the Irish youth narrative in the nascent Irish state as minor citizens with very limited rights and prospects.

Modernisation, young people and the rise of an urban tribe

As elsewhere in Europe, the 1960s in Ireland were a period of social disruption and political change, noted for the declining grip that the Catholic Church held over young people's lives and the rise of new youth organisations within civil society. The mid-1960s formed a fundamental turning point in Irish social history. The economy began to grow and the psychology of the nation/Irish people seemed to be growing in confidence. There was a change in the political atmosphere: the mistrust in the State slowly withered away, giving rise to higher expectations from it and authority to it, by its citizenry. A number of key events and developments characterised this transition. Domestic television services were launched in 1962, proving to be a 'steady conduit for a predominantly

urban and cosmopolitan set of images, not as individually powerful as its detrac-
tors feared, but as insidious in their cumulative effect' (Tobin, 1984: 60). Slowly,
but steadily, the Church began to lose its grip over its population. Following
the Second Vatican Council of 1965 the Church began to modernise and came
under more intense scrutiny in the media. Increasingly open discussions were
conducted on controversial social issues such as family planning, censorship or
the Church's role in education. Bishops were now frequently being interviewed
on Gay Byrne's culturally influential *Late Late Show*, a circumstance that was
previously unheard of (Whyte, 1980: 358). While some of the Catholic Church's
'narrow-mindedness, philistinism and autocracy' (Fanning, 2008: 170) survived, they were now being challenged by a new cultural openness and by huge
advances in educational levels. J.H. Whyte (1979) remarks that at the beginning
of the 1950s, Irish Catholicism appeared monolithic and triumphalist, however,
by the end of the 1960s it was self-questioning, more open-minded and divided
between different opinions. He concludes: 'Ireland changed during those years
[from the beginning of the 1950s to the end of the 1960s] more quickly than in
any period of similar length since the Reformation' (*ibid.*: 82).

    Once again, the issue of dance, music and leisure time provides us with
insights into the changing contexts of the Irish youth experience. Hitherto the
Irish youth music scene had been dominated by orchestras, dancing in commercial ballrooms, club halls or parish halls – often under the gaze of 'overzealous
priests' (Power, 2000: 11). Economic prosperity and the communications revolution allowed a large part of the youth population to participate in the craze
in one form or the other: 'youngsters listened to Radio Luxembourg under the
bedcovers and tuned into Rock-and-Roll' (*ibid.*: 13). As much as their peers
abroad, Ireland's young people were captured by the international music scene
and youth culture. The Beatles visited Ireland in 1963, connecting Ireland's youth
to their peers abroad. But Ireland had produced its very own version of youth
music – the Showbands, which mushroomed throughout Ireland throughout
the 1960s and 1970s and performed in ballrooms and huge sheds, which were
purpose-built by private investors to hold up to 4000 people. Showbands were
specifically an Irish phenomenon – and although the most successful would tour
abroad – they did not happen anywhere else and also disappeared completely
from the Irish music scene after approximately a decade. However, they were an
important expression of youth culture in a particularly Irish setting: at the height
of the boom there were approximately 450 ballrooms countrywide, entertaining
tens of thousands of Irish young people every weekend. On St Stephen's Nights
(26 December), Ireland danced 'like a nation possessed' (*ibid.*: 20). It was estimated that a total dancing population of 731,700 aged from fifteen to thirty-four
was out dancing (*ibid.*).

    The ballrooms of the 1960s were more than a mere social outlet for young
people spending Ireland's newly found wealth. They were an indicator of a

changing social culture in Ireland with a significant impact on many young people's lives. One could meet potential spouses more anonymously miles away from home, away from the watchful eye of the community and the parish priest. The ballrooms thus created opportunities and spaces where young men and women could mix, independently of their social background. Power (2000) goes so far as to say that class boundaries, which were much more apparent in the parochial hall of the 1950s, were now more permeable, bringing together young people from all walks of life. He describes the period of the 1960s as 'a remarkable period in contemporary Irish history. There was a hint of affluence for the first time. Young people aspired to things that their parents could never have imagined' (*ibid.*: 17). Ireland was changing from a rural agriculturally-based tightly knit world into a global urban industrial society from the 1960s that was part of gradually reconstructing Irish youth as an urban tribe. As Blom (2008: 329) asserts 'new tribes needed, new rituals'. Music provided the metaphor for change.

In addition to the broad cultural changes relating to lifestyle and fashion, the State too started to take a more direct interest in shaping young people's lives, particularly through formal education, this time without any strident opposition from the Catholic Church. Hallmarks of the Catholic Church's intervention in education became diluted: the ban imposed in the 1940s by Archbishop Charles McQuaid forbidding Catholic students from attending Trinity College Dublin was lifted in 1970; objections to community and multi-denominational schools were removed and parents were allowed to become involved in management of schools. The education reforms, which led the way to free secondary schooling in 1968 were initiated by the OECD-sponsored *Investment in Education* report, published in 1966. O'Sullivan (1992: 445) observes that the sponsorship of the report by the OECD conferred authority and legitimacy upon the State to replace 'personal development with the human capital paradigm as the institutional rationale for education'. These developments must be seen in a wider context of secularisation of Irish society. In fact, the article, which previously recognised the Catholic Church's 'special' place in society, was removed from the Constitution in 1972. The bishops' role shifted to a large extent by taking on a role of publicly criticising social policy related to unemployment and allied social problems (O'Donoghue, 1999: 148). If the Church did also not completely give up its pre-eminent role in Irish education, it recognised that it had to make concessions to the State. However, O'Donoghue critically remarks that the State while investing significantly in the education system, did not alter the fundamental basis of particularly Irish secondary education, but had instead 'replaced the Church as the orchestrator of the reproduction of class inequities through the education system' (*ibid.*: 149).

Ireland also opened up politically by joining the European Economic Community (now European Union) in 1973, adapting to the broad frameworks in which social policy was defined. This improved Ireland's commitment to equality (at least on paper) and provided a richer comparative policy experience to draw upon. Secondly, in time through its third Anti-Poverty Programme (1989–1994), which focused on social exclusion and marginalisation and the European Social Fund, the Irish Government was able to mobilise a series of social policy instruments which could assist young people, through training and employment programmes such as Youthstart and Community Employment Schemes and schemes designed for early school leavers.

The 1960s opened up new opportunities and challenges for young people and youth gradually found a stronger voice within civil society during this period. Youth in Ireland emerged as an urban tribe, with a distinctive youth culture. A range of new voluntary youth organisations emerged with more diverse agendas, such as disability, minority groups, provision of alternative recreational spaces and many more. The National Youth Federation (now Youth Work Ireland) was founded in 1962 with the aim to provide services to young people and those working with them. Ogra Chorcai, the Cork Youth Association was established in 1966. The National Youth Council of Ireland (NYCI) was founded in 1967 with the aim to coordinate and promote common interests of voluntary youth organisations and eventually gaining a role in official partnership talks through the Youth Work Act 2001. From the 1960s onwards, the State became more involved in youth provision, focusing upon developing a policy framework for the delivery of youth services (Kiely and Kennedy, 2005: 195). In 1978, the then Minister of State for Youth and Sport, Jim Tunney, in cooperation with the National Youth Council of Ireland, launched a campaign to attract more leaders into youth work and create a better image for the youth service, known as 'Breakthrough'. At the time there were 14,000 volunteer adult leaders engaged with a quarter of a million young people through various youth organisations (Wayman, 1980). Several major policy documents and reports were published over a ten-year time span by different government departments and the National Youth Council of Ireland on the development of an Irish Youth Work Service and other related themes indicating the increasing importance that was given to 'youth' (see Chapter 5). This culminated in the *National Youth Policy Committee Report* (colloquially known as the Costello Report) of 1984, which suggested a more active involvement by the State in the provision of youth services, particularly with regards to reliable and transparent funding allocation for the voluntary youth work sector. Due to several changes in government at crucial moments, the fundamental suggestions of the Costello Report were only taken up again in the Youth Work Act of 2001 and the National Youth Work Development Plan 2003–2007 (Department of Education and Science, 2003). (A more detailed discussion on current youth policy follows in Chapters 5–7). In an analysis of the underlying ideology and orientations in Irish youth work policy until 1985, Devlin argues that the application of a consensualist ideology in combination with the influence of Catholic social teaching resulted in a discourse around youth which essentially reinforced earlier constructions around gender, class and sexuality, allowing youth work and policy to focus once again on specific kinds of young people: urban, unemployed, alienated, vulnerable, disaffected, etc. Despite significant social changes that Ireland underwent during this period, young people remained amongst those with least power. This also reflected broader trends in Irish social policy, which employed social change as a rhetorical device, but ultimately left responsibility with individuals, in this case young people (Devlin, 1989). If Irish youth had emerged as an urban tribe, it was very much on the periphery of society in terms of power and influence as minor citizens.

Postmodern Irish youth?

The most recent period in Irish history has been characterised by transformation at a pace and scale which has had profound implications on young people's lives in Ireland. Notable in this transformation have been apparently strong levels of social fragmentation, growing individualisation and a seemingly dislocated youth culture reliant on consumption and lifestyle, rather than on traditional institutions such as Church and State. Modernisation did not commence in Ireland until the 1960s. With modernisation came modernity which turned itself into hyper-modernity during the Celtic Tiger Years of the 1990s and early 2000s. Irish GDP growth increased steadily after 1993, reaching its peaks of 10.6% in 1996 and 1997. Overall, average income rose by 125% in real terms between 1987 and 2005. Internationally, Ireland's exceptional pathway won her much praise and newly developing countries were keen to emulate the Celtic Tiger model. In 2004, the Economist Intelligence Unit ranked Ireland as the country with the best quality of life, according to a survey of 111 states. However, this growth has been highly controversial. Income inequality has risen in the time period from 2000–2005 (Kirby, 2008: 19). And indeed, a comparison of Ireland's income distribution after the Celtic Tiger boom with EU and OECD countries shows that only the United States, Russia and Mexico have higher levels of inequality (Smeeding and Nolan cited in Kirby, 2008: 22). Economic growth was also not translated into increased social spending. Overall expenditure by the government on social services decreased during the main years of the boom from 11.1 % GDP in 1995 to 7.5% GDP in 2000. Despite an increase in the early 2000s, it never reached pre-boom levels (Kirby, 2008: 30), confirming observations of the Irish minimalist welfare state. Systems failures of the health and childcare services were never addressed wholeheartedly during the boom times, leading to increased privatisation of public goods and a lower level of public social services.

These economic changes, closely intertwined with the process of economic, social and cultural globalisation, have stimulated fundamental social changes in Irish society: increasing inward migration from the mid-1990s onwards led to the emergence of a sort of multi-cultural Irish state; changing family structures have led to a more mainstream European model of nuclear families and the emergence of patchwork families; changing consumption patterns; finally, satellite towns have emerged all over the country, creating new communities, often without sustainable access to public services. In addition, these rapid changes in all spheres of life have not happened without critical analysis and observation on social change from within Ireland. Keohane and Kuhling (2004) demonstrate how accelerated modernisation in Ireland has created a 'Collision Culture' between the old and the new, between accelerated modernisation and the persistence of traditional social forms, creating tensions which affect the lived realities and psychologies of individuals.

But how have these changes and shifts in economy, society and culture particularly affected young people in Ireland and related discourses about youth? Several trends seem to be emerging. Young people tend to stay in education longer – participation rates in higher education have increased from 20% in 1980 to 55% in 2004 (O' Connell et al., 2006) – and more young people than ever before aim for advanced university degrees, staying in education longer. Postgraduate enrolments have increased by 46% in the period from 1998/1999 to 2004/2005 compared to an increase of 19% for undergraduate enrolments (ibid.). Nevertheless independent living outside the family home remains postponed with the majority of university students in Ireland still living at home while at university, in contrast with the UK or the US (Flynn, 2007 cited in Kerrins, 2008). And even when working, some young people in their twenties continue to live with their parents, moving in and out of the family home (Kerrins, 2008).

Young people are also faced with a more diverse landscape of family structures, taking away some of the pressures of societal expectations. Since 1996, the number of cohabiting couples in Ireland increased fourfold (Census, 2006), there has been an 80% increase in the number of lone-parent families since 1986, and roughly 25% of children are being raised in non-marital families. Marriage is not an absolutely necessary option anymore: 40% of respondents of the Graduate Careers Survey 2008 expect to be married and 30% expect to have children by the age of 30 (Kerrins, 2008). Against the background of the general secularisation of Irish society- surveys show that weekly mass attendance has declined from 87% of Catholics to around 65% in the period 1981 to 1998, to a reported 44% in 2003 (Share et al., 2007: 421). Young people's church attendance is significantly lower than that of older age cohorts. In urban areas, only 13% of young people between eighteen to thirty years (from a manual background) attended church services on a weekly basis, compared to 45% between thirty-one to forty-five and 78% between forty-six to sixty. The picture is more differentiated in rural areas and for young people from non-manual backgrounds, however also reflecting the general trend (Fahey in Share et al., 2007: 421).

Some of the more problematic manifestations of Celtic Tiger Ireland can also be seen in the fact that young people are affected on an individual level. Suicide rates have doubled between 1977 and 1996 amongst young men under thirty-five and this group has the highest suicide rate among their peers in Europe (Swanwick, 1997). Several studies have also found that binge drinking has become a regular feature of young people's lives in Ireland (Lalor et al., 2007: 123).

Shifts in identity from stable reference points such as work and family to the more fragmented spheres of style and consumption have specific implications for young people (Furlong and Cartmel, 2007). At the same time local places and structural factors (gender, class, location) remain critical reference points for young people and shape their experiences and opportunities for growing up. Maffesoli (1996) suggests that in postmodernity social class has lost significance and has been replaced by new 'tribal' determinants based on consumer-oriented parameters. He argues that 'the sexual, political and professional identities associated with modernity are being replaced by processes of identification with groups, with sentiments and with fashions' (cited in Jones, 2009: 69). Miles (2000) argues that the 'meanings underlying young people's lives as consumers represent the fundamental building blocks of their identities' (cited in Jones, 2009: 74). While also acknowledging that consumption is still constrained by structure, Miles et al. (1998) suggest that consumption allows young people to feel that they 'fit in', at the same time allowing them a semblance of individuality, and this combination potentially gives them a sense of stability not otherwise available in the risk society. Youth as an urban tribe are challenged by the conditions of postmodernity.

Wallace and Kovatcheva (1998: 209) propose that postmodernisation is deconstructing youth, which modernisation had constructed earlier as a social category. One of the tenets of postmodernity in relation to youth is that young people now identify by their consumer tastes and interests, based on information and communication technology, rather than by their social class position. This view proposes that new media technology allows young people to transcend their ascribed class position and they define themselves via their consumer styles. 'Generation X' is defined by self-conscious and 'reflexive' choices with regards to style and consumption, constantly constructing and re-constructing their identities from a fluid mix of identities from different parts of the world and different time periods. They demonstrate how the postmodern condition in the Eastern European context had specific implications for its young people: youth organisations that have previously monitored and controlled young people have disappeared, greater possibilities have opened up for young people, but equally greater chaos exists in the transition from school to work and continuing education; increased social exclusion of young people due to the weak welfare state and weaker family ties and a shift in young people's political involvement from traditional politics to social movements (Wallace and Kovatecheva, 1998:

212–215). Indeed, it is argued that in our current 'risk societies' (Beck, 1992), responsibility for self-protection is shifted to the individual. Young people are being repositioned as consumers of social policy and their risk profiles are managed based on a number of universal indicators.

In the Irish context Sweeney and Dunne (2003: 3) comment on this postmodern dilemma for young people:

> Today's teenagers effectively live life at the interface of two sets of forces, the clash between which, for some, is like the grinding of opposing tectonic plates. On the one hand, there seems to be little that cannot be experienced and lived now, if only there was enough money to help implement their plans. On the other hand, the spectre of the failed adult life looms ever larger unless they sacrifice more of their youthful freedoms now in order to knuckle down and secure the right education. Given that tensions inevitably arise between the pull of the present and the imperatives of the future, it is hardly surprising that so many young people find relief in the social environments that carry a high risk of exposure to the perils of drink, drugs, violence, infection and accidents. This is the vanishing present that all youth confront. They must achieve to be in a successful trajectory forwards adulthood. Yet the world they inhabit lacks clear definition. Civil society and the market compete for youths' attention and values.

But are young people in Ireland really caught as sort of passive agents in between these 'two tectonic plates', so disillusioned and hopeless about their economic and social futures that they choose riskier lifestyles? Or is this yet another moral panic, allowing youth organisations and the State to direct and control young people's lives, imposing expectations such as 'active citizenship' on young people? Pat O'Connor carried out a study of over 4,000 essays written by young people aged between ten and twelve years and fourteen to seventeen years on the occasion of the millennium to 'tell their life stories' and 'describe themselves and the Ireland that they inhabit' (O'Connor, 2008: 23). Her findings present a mixed picture, pointing on the one hand towards significant changes of young people's views, feelings and expectation of their lives, compared to earlier generations; while on the other hand expressing 'traditionally modern' views. In their discourses on time for example, O'Connor observed that the older girls from fourteen to seventeen years expressed considerable stress about future life plans, relating to choices of education and career. Also, all young people referred to relatively linear life models in terms of their future and did not suggest individualised life-models that one might expect in the postmodern condition. Similarly, in discourses about space, global elements related to consumer culture, global technology and entertainment, entered into young people's narratives. However the importance of their local area was strongly expressed and does not allow for a simple conclusion that would suggest that local place 'becomes thoroughly penetrated by disembedding mechanisms' (Giddens, 1991: 146). With regards to consumption, O'Connor's (2008) study presents a complex picture: 'although there was evidence from the qualitative study as regards the importance of money in the lives of the 14–17 year olds, only a tiny minority of the young people referred to shopping, designer labels or fast food'. Similarly MacKeogh's (2002) participant study on young people and television in Ireland has shown that young people use both 'criticism' and 'sarcasm' in their everyday experience of television, demonstrating that they are active recipients of media content, rather than passive and undiscriminatory recipients. It therefore seems rather too simplistic to talk about the emergence of a postmodern youth paradigm in the Irish context.

One element of the politics of youth that has seemingly not been affected by the postmodern conditions of Ireland is how general societal concerns around issues such as public order in communities or excessive consumption, particularly of alcohol, are once again dealt with through the image of youth. Connecting issues of morality, irresponsibility and young people are still publicly voiced. Cardinal Sean Brady in a public comment demonstrates this age-old concern once again: 'we may be witnessing another lost generation of young people, who instead of emigrating abroad, are leaving the shores of moderation, responsibility and spirituality' (Brady, 2003). It is interesting to note that in a society where excessive drinking characterises a phenomenon that is culturally accepted amongst all age groups, this bio-political concern is only expressed towards young people, thus neglecting the wider social context in which this occurs. Similarly, the introduction of the Anti-Social Behaviour Orders (ASBOs) in 2006, targeting young people from the age of twelve to seventeen years reveal a contradiction in how young people in Ireland are viewed and appreciated. While they are encouraged by the government and youth organisations to be involved in their communities as 'active citizens', the discourse around the creation of the ASBOs demonstrates how young people continue to be defined as a disorderly urban tribe, particularly by policy-makers (Hamilton and Seymour, 2006). And once again, young people's lives are being understood outside the general context, such as the lack of appropriate services and facilities and lack of opportunities for positive engagement of young people in communities. Against the background of increased child and youth friendly policies, initiated since the Children Act 2001, it appears that the contradictory construction of young people seems to continue in contemporary Ireland.

Conclusion

Just like the nation of Ireland herself, 'youth' and young people in Ireland have undergone enormous changes over the past 150 years. The symbolic and material treatment of youth by society in general and the institutions of Church, State and civil society more specifically, reflect broad social and cultural shifts and probably tell us as much about young people's lives and the construction of youth as about these three institutions themselves. In a broad historical context, it may seem that young people's autonomy and freedom to choose has increased significantly as the Irish welfare state developed, the Church's grip on society loosened and Ireland opened up to the world. However, it is important to remember that increasing choices available to young people in terms of biographical choices, lifestyles and consumption do not necessarily imply more freedom. A highly individualised and competitive liberal market economy today puts more diverse and often contradicting pressures on young people. Their ability to negotiate their way through them depends on multiple factors, such as economic, social and cultural capital, which remain unequally distributed. Similarly, certain anxieties about young people remain as valid in public and policy discourse today as ever before, perpetuating deficit constructions of young people. It can be said that several of the postmodern conditions, such as complex, extended and 'boomerang' transitions into adulthood, may well exist for some young people. But while social conditions have certainly changed and present a unique set of conditions and challenges to young Irish people, their identity is still very much rooted in the local and with their families. Identities may, however, be more malleable, constructed both in reality and virtual realities, and expressed through consumption and style. Nonetheless, socio-economic backgrounds of young people, gender, race/ethnicity and sexuality still define young people's experience of growing up in Ireland. It is therefore important not to neglect young people as a social category per se, but to consider their age in combination with these previous parameters as signifiers relevant to their exclusion and inclusion.

2

Remoralising working-class youth: women, religion and morality in nineteenth and early twentieth-century Ireland

> Forming these clubs and associations was often a formidable task, not only because so many boys and girls of the new Machine Age had drifted from ancient family, neighbourhood, or village moorings, but because society itself placidly accepted the fact that for many there was no fate worse than childhood. (Woodroofe, 1960: 313)

> There were no 'fallen men' in Ireland. (Ferriter, 2009: 17)

The mid-eighteenth to the early twentieth century was in many respects a golden age of voluntary activity. The proliferation of clubs, societies and associations during this time was a response to a rapidly changing world in which civil society flourished. As society became more complex, Morris (1990: 395) notes, 'those with power, those with no power and above all those with slender fragments of power which they sought to defend and extend began to organise themselves in a variety of specific ways'. Voluntary associations were a means by which the upper-working class and lower-middle class sought to protect, 'improve' and empower themselves. Many of these organisations, such as the Friendly Societies, offered saving schemes and sickness and death insurance; they ran evening classes or lectures series; they provided libraries and reading rooms, and so on. Moreover clubs and societies offered companionship in a geographically mobile world. This function is poignantly expressed in the stipulation of many of the friendly societies that members should always follow the coffin at the funeral of a fellow member – thus avoiding the ignominy of a lonely death with no friends (*ibid.*: 417). The churches (and their laity) were to play a vital role in the development of voluntary associations, becoming 'leisure centres with endless clusters of societies based upon sex, age, denomination and even occupation' (*ibid.*: 420). While these societies provided social and recreational activities, their aim was essentially religious: to disseminate Christian values and keep members within the church.

An important section of the organisations which emerged in the late nineteenth and early twentieth century catered specifically for young people. These included the uniformed church-based brigades, which combined physical activity (particularly drill) and Bible study, and which had distinctly military overtones (see Chapter 3). Organisations were also developed to provide supports for a slightly older age group who had left home to seek work, for example the Girls' Friendly Society (GFS), the Young Men's Christian Association (YMCA) and the Young Women's Christian Association (YWCA). These organisation provided a range of services including accommodation, employment agencies, travel arrangements, evening classes and leisure activities. Their objectives were in many respects similar to those of voluntary associations more generally. The GFS, for example, aimed to provide companionship for girls in much the same way as other societies of the time. However young people also represented particular challenges and possibilities. Several of the girls' organisations, for example, were concerned for the welfare of those leaving home for the first time, fearing that through their youth and naivety, girls might 'be led astray', particularly in the city. Notions about what it meant to be a 'man' or a 'woman', clearly informed the work of the different youth groups. While boys were taught to be manly (see Chapter 3), girls were encouraged to be modest, chaste and adept at the 'home arts'. Moreover the class hierarchies of the time were reflected in the structure and leadership of societies such as the GFS, with middle- and upper-class women appearing to be on a mission to remoralise the 'deserving poor', by making them virtuous and self-reliant.

In the course of this chapter we will explore the complex mix of philanthropy, morality and social class which characterised a number of women's organisations which emerged during the nineteenth century, focusing in particular on the Girls' Friendly Society (GFS). The history of the GFS in Ireland is explored in the first part of this chapter, including its religious and moral mission and its hierarchical class structure. It will be argued that while the society provided many practical benefits for its working-class members, the GFS was also a deeply conservative organisation in both moral and social terms. Of course conservative organisations can, as Pedersen (1981) argues, sometimes give rise to unexpected outcomes. It is one of the contradictions of the GFS, and other societies of the time, that while they emphasised women's domestic role they were also one of the few routes through which women (mainly of the middle and upper class) could enter public life. Comparisons will be made with the Young Women's Christian Association, an organisation with broadly similar aims, objectives and membership profile. In the second part of the chapter we will consider some of the Irish Catholic clubs and hostels which, although considerably smaller than the GFS and YWCA, offered much the same services (accommodation, employment agencies, meeting-places) and shared their preoccupation with 'protecting' young women, both physically and morally. The final section charts the development of the 'rescue' movement in Ireland and the emergence of the Magdalen asylums.

Our focus in this chapter is primarily on the control and regulation of young working-class women in an increasingly urban and industrial society, through the promotion of 'traditional' values (particularly in relation to sexual morality) and class deference. The moral climate of the Victorian era was central to the emergence of the various organisations referred to above. We will begin therefore by considering the changing attitudes to sexual morality during the nineteenth century, and how this impacted on the lives of women.

It should be noted that the organisations discussed in this chapter represent only one part of associational activity amongst girls and young women at this time. There were also uniformed groups such as the Girl Guides and the Girls' Brigade (outlined in Chapter 3) as well as organisations which worked for political change (discussed in Chapter 4).

Women, morality and religion

McLoughlin (2001) argues that in the nineteenth century Ireland was widely believed to be a country with low marriage rates, high marital fertility, minimal illegitimacy, and celibacy. The testaments of nineteenth-century travellers such as Dickens and Kohl would add weight to the view of Ireland as 'a country filled with virtuous virgins' and widespread abstinence. The reality, McLoughlin suggests, was somewhat different. There was not a single norm of sexual alliance in Ireland in this period, but rather a whole series of relationships both casual and permanent. At one end of the socio-economic scale, for instance, there were 'gentleman's misses' who often enjoyed a comfortable lifestyle outside of marriage. A far more common alliance was that between men and women of the very poorest ranks of society who entered into 'irregular unions' which were not recognised by Church or State. In addition there was a thriving trade in prostitution, particularly in the cities and garrison towns (Luddy, 1997; McLoughlin, 2001). By the late nineteenth century, however, there was less and less tolerance of sexual diversity and an increased emphasis on 'respectability'. Changing patterns of behaviour could in part be explained by the growing influence of the Church and (in the case of prostitution) the passing of the Contagious Diseases Acts of the 1860s. A more important consideration, Luddy (1997: 499) argues, was the economics of property owners and prosperous farmers whose 'ideology of sexual abstinence' for the sake of land inheritance eventually became the accepted basis for sexual morality of the entire society. The issue of pre-marital sexual relations was not, therefore, simply a moral issue but an economic one.

Victorian England was, of course, equally concerned with respectability, particularly relating to sexual morality. Prochaska (1990: 376) notes that by the

1870s and 1880s the social purity movement was at its peak, with 'interfering ladies' scolding 'suspicious-looking couples on park benches or on public transport'. The social purity philosophy regarded sex and sexuality as 'deeply problematic drives' (Hunt, 1990: 25) which, unless tightly controlled, would lead to ruination in this life and damnation in the next. Moreover 'uncontrolled sex' was seen as socially harmful, leading to overpopulation and social unrest among the poor; contributing to the breaking down of class or racial barriers; and threatening the integrity of the institution of marriage (*ibid.*: 26). Sexual victimisation arguments played a prominent role in social purity rhetoric. While some regarded men as the victims of sexually assertive women and homosexuals, others believed that it was women who needed to be protected from men. Both the Protestant and Catholic churches – as well as the lay philanthropic organisations closely linked with them – would become the standard-bearers in policing sexuality, particularly female sexuality. One of the means by which this would be achieved was through 'rescue' work with prostitutes and other 'fallen' women. In the nineteenth century at least thirty-three Magdalen asylums or refuges were established in Ireland, the majority of which were based in Dublin and Belfast (Luddy 1995a). Records from some of the lay asylums indicate that those admitted were often not prostitutes at all but women who had been 'seduced' and abandoned by their seducers and families (*ibid.*: 112). Luddy notes that by the end of the century there were homes and institutions which catered for all groups of 'outcast' women: 'whether prostitutes, unmarried mothers, female ex-prisoners or drunks, few could escape the "rescue" net' (*ibid.*: 148).

While some philanthropists worked to reform 'fallen' women, others directed their energies towards ensuring that 'respectable' young women remained so. Certain groups of girls and young women – often working-class – were seen to be in particular need of protection. Those who moved out of their own locality (and the watchful eye of family and clergy) to seek employment in towns and cities faced not only loneliness but the possibility of being 'led astray'. Thus the Bishop of Durham, in a sermon commemorating the anniversary of the Girls' Friendly Society, asserted that 'The Governess, the shop girl, the domestic servant, has no longer a fixed home, she is a wanderer on the earth. Here the catholicity of the Church should step in to counteract the evil …' (*GFS Annual Report* 1884: 7). The leisure time of young people became a site of surveillance, given the dangers which the music hall, the public house and dances were seen to represent. Voluntary societies and associations were formed, in both Britain and Ireland, to provide young people with more acceptable forms of recreation, often segregating the sexes and promoting habits of temperance, abstinence and thrift.

It is within this context that we can understand the emergence of the religiously inspired women's organisations in the latter part of the nineteenth century. The Girls' Friendly Society, in particular, epitomised many of the themes outlined above. While the society was concerned with the welfare of young women leaving home, its work was also part of a mission to propagate certain moral standards.

The moral mission of the Girls' Friendly Society

The GFS was founded in England by M.E. Townsend in 1875 as a social purity organisation to preserve chastity among young working-class women moving from rural homes to urban employment (Richmond, 2007). It was an immediate success and by 1885 had 821 branches in England and Wales (Harrison, 1973). Membership reached its peak in 1913 when there were 39,926 associates and 197,493 members (*ibid.*: 109). The Girls' Friendly Society for Ireland was established in 1877. Its objectives and target membership were set out as follows:

> It is just at the time when girls are leaving the National School, and going out into life that they most want help. The object of the Society is that the Associates should search them out, make friends with them, bring them into relation with the Clergyman of the Parish, and take a general interest in their welfare; and in the next place, that they should be able to commend such girls, when leaving home for service or other employment to the notice of an Associate in the Parish to which they are going; while, in like manner, girls would be commended to them by Associates at a distance. (M.E. Townsend cited in *GFS Annual Report*, 1880: 3)

In the same report Townsend constructs a worrying picture of the fate which might befall young women who move away from home, friends and family: 'from time to time there comes news of those that are gone, sometimes glad tidings, but alas! Too often tales of shame and misery; of wasted lives spent in the service of sin or vanity, instead of the service of Christ' (*ibid.*: 4). To counter this possibility the GFS set in place a system that supported young women in various stages of their adolescence and early adulthood. Central and regional registries were set up through which young women, particularly those going into service, could look for work. Lodges were opened in towns and cities to provide 'respectable' accommodation on both a short- and long-term basis. By 1901 there were ten lodges based mainly in Ulster, with two in Dublin and one in Cork (*GFS Annual Report* 1901). Arrangements were even made to meet young women at sea ports or train stations where, as one associate noted, they might otherwise be 'overcome' by the change of scenery and 'engage themselves without thought or advice' (*GFS Annual Report* 1883: 7). By the close of the century unemployment at home was forcing thousands of women to emigrate each year (Preston, 2004). The GFS duly set up an emigration department which looked after those young women travelling to situations abroad. The 1888 annual report urges associates to impress upon their members the advantages of arranging travel through this department, including travel in 'select parties, under the care of a Matron', receiving letters of introduction, and being met at various ports (*GFS Annual Report* 1888: 2). Arranged emigration would also have advantages for employers in the British colonies, where there was often a severe shortage of domestic servants (Gothard, 1992).

Classes (both religious and secular), social gatherings and 'healthful recreation' were provided through the local GFS branches. Friendships between members and associates were encouraged in order to counter the loneliness which young women might experience when separated from family and friends: 'One object of the society is to provide *for every working girl* a friend, and to prevent that feeling of *isolation* which they would otherwise experience when leaving home for a distant place' (*GFS Annual Report* 1883: 5–6).

The YWCA provided a similar range of services and facilities for its members, including employment agencies, 'homes' where young women could stay while awaiting employment, and a Traveller's Aid Department which arranged for members to be met and looked after while travelling. The association, which was formed in London in 1855, spread to Ireland during the 1860s and by 1900 operated homes in eight Irish towns and cities (Luddy, 1995a). Like the Girls' Friendly Society, the YWCA offered its members companionship and recreation, which was felt to be especially important for girls leaving home for the first time. Clubs were opened in a number of towns and cities, while 'holiday homes' in Kilkee, Greystones and Portrush provided cheap holiday accommodation during the summer months (Graham 2004: 7). In addition, courses were provided in the 'home arts and sciences' including cooking, dressmaking and nursing (Association of Charities, 1902: 197; *YWCA Report for Ireland*, 1887). In 1887 it was reported that the association had over 240 branches in Ireland and more than 9,000 members (*YWCA Report for Ireland*, 1887).

Through their programme of leisure activities, accommodation and employment agencies, the GFS and the YWCA hoped to not only provide practical assistance to young working women, but also to keep them safe from the life of 'sin', to which Townsend refers above. The GFS amenities, Richmond (2007: 308) notes, 'were designed to facilitate the preservation of purity by placing members under the constant surveillance and protection of the Society'. In addition, young women of dubious character were to be excluded, in case they might corrupt the others. One of the earliest GFS Annual Reports for Ireland (1880: 6) sets out three general rules, one of which stipulates that: 'No girl who has not borne a character for good conduct can be admitted as a member; if any member should lose her good character, her card will be forfeited'. Although the wording of Rule III is open to different interpretations, Richmond (2007) notes, it was generally understood to refer to sexual morality. Working Associates, whose duty it was to 'select and admit girls of good character', were warned to be vigilant: 'N.B. – Working Associates are to be particularly careful as to the character of girls whom they admit as Members. In doubtful cases, a short delay for probation is advised' (*GFS Annual Report* 1880: 7). The importance of 'purity' and 'virtue' is sometimes couched in evangelical rhetoric. In one report, for example, the GFS in Ireland is described as 'an army of upwards of 10,000 strong, enrolled under the banner of the King of Kings to do battle against sin and evil, and to raise the standard of womanhood' (*GFS Annual Report* 1889: 3). To this end they would also enlist the help of another organisation, the Mothers Union, which had been founded by Mrs Sumner in England in 1885 (Harrison, 1973). According to one GFS Annual Report for Ireland (1887: 4): 'In some places Mothers Unions have been established in connection with the Society, and these seem to furnish the 'missing link', getting the parents upon the side of all that is pure and holy to uphold our hands in training their children to serve God in pureness of living and truth'.

With their focus on character, purity and virtue, the GFS could be said to contribute to a wider discourse on womanhood at the time, reinforcing the perceived dichotomy between the respectable and the 'fallen'; the modest and the immodest. The Society, and others like it, played an important role in constructing an ideology of proper behaviour for women. The model GFS girl, as Harrison (1973: 116) has noted, was 'expected to be devout, kindly, serious-minded, uncomplaining and (by modern standards) relatively uninterested in the opposite sex'. Attempts to separate and classify women in moral terms were, of course, a far more pronounced element of rescue and reform work. Women who found their way into the Magdalen asylums, as Luddy (1997) notes, were immediately labelled. Even within workhouses attempts to classify and label women were evident: prostitutes mixing freely with other women came to be seen as a source of moral 'contamination' and steps were taken to keep them apart. From the middle of the nineteenth century Irish workhouses operated a 'classification' system which attempted to keep 'respectable' women and girls away from those considered to be 'unrespectable' (*ibid.*: 492). Although the GFS was clearly distinct from the rescue and reform groups, they too defined their members in terms of moral character. The threatened expulsion of those who lost their good name may be seen not only as a deterrent but also as an echo of that fear of moral contamination which troubled workhouse guardians and the rescue and reform philanthropists.

The expulsion of members (on the grounds of moral conduct) was not universally supported within the society, however. In Britain in 1879–1880, Mrs Papillon claimed that chastity could not be guaranteed in urban members, and with the aid of some urban associates provoked the Society's most serious internal dispute by campaigning to modify the GFS's third central rule and abandon chastity as a prerequisite for membership (Richmond, 2007). One of her main objections to Rule III was the fact that a sexual transgression led to expulsion, which would 'brand the girl publicly' (cited in Richmond 2007: 313).[1] Papillon's campaign was ultimately unsuccessful and she seceded to form the Young

Women's Help Society. Nonetheless disagreements over Rule III continued to haunt the GFS. The Society claimed to have close connections with the Anglican Church and while some members of the clergy strongly supported Rule III, others objected that it contravened the Christian principle of forgiveness for the penitent (Richmond, 2007).

Religion and youth movements

The GFS, while run by lay women, had close connections with the Church of Ireland. Associates had to be members of the Church of Ireland (though no restrictions were made as to members) and the society set out to follow, as much as possible, diocesan and parochial divisions (*GFS Annual Report*, 1880: 6). In addition the clergy appear to have formed a significant element in the network of contacts which the GFS constructed. Associates were instructed to 'take care that the Members are brought under the notice of the Clergyman of the parish; to keep him informed of the names and addresses of the Members on her list, to let him know when Members come into the parish or go from it' (*ibid.*: 8). In theory, if perhaps not always in practice, the GFS had set up a system for tracking its members and keeping them within the influence of the Church. Clergymen could also provide references for young women seeking employment. Ladies who wished to become working associates had themselves to provide a letter of introduction from the clergyman of their parish.

Given its connections with the Church of Ireland, it is not surprising that the GFS was strongest in those areas with a large Protestant population. The 1891 annual report, for example, notes that 'Down and Connor and Dromore, containing such a large Protestant population, still heads the list as to numbers' (*GFS Annual Report* 1891: 5). The Society appears to have struggled in remoter areas, particularly if there were few Protestants. Thus one associate, in explaining the difficulties of setting up a branch in Dingle, describes it as 'a very remote and backward place, and but a few Protestant girls' (*GFS Annual Report* 1883: 9). Similarly another associate in rural Donegal complains of 'a scattered population' and the absence of 'a gentleman's family' (*ibid.*: 8). In one Galway parish, competition from the Young Women's Christian Association for a small Protestant population forced the GFS to withdraw (*GFS Annual Report* 1890). Nonetheless the reports from the 1880s to 1905 show a steady increase in membership. In 1884 there were 800 honorary associates, 463 working associates and 3,243 members. By the end of the decade (1890) these figures had more than doubled to 8,396 members, 1,562 candidates, 954 working associates and 776 honorary associates. Growth over the next fifteen years was more gradual: in 1905 there were 9,650 members, 3151 candidates, 604 friendly helpers, 1437 working associates and 811 honorary associates. The GFS at this time had 196 branches in Ireland, the society operated in 504 parishes (GFS annual reports for 1884, 1890 and 1905).

The YWCA also had close connections with the Church of Ireland and regarded spiritual development as central to its role – indeed the origins of the association can be traced to a Prayer Union set up by Emma Roberts in London in 1855.[2] The Christian basis of the association's work was reflected in its various divisions which, in 1887, included an 'evangelization and extension department', a missionary working party and a total abstinence department (*YWCA Report for Ireland*, 1887). Moreover Bible classes and prayer meetings were regular features of its work with members. However tensions appear to have occasionally arisen (both within the YWCA and the GFS) from the need to conduct a spiritual and moral mission while at the same time catering for the recreational needs of young people. Thus in 1907 the Irish Council for the YWCA felt it necessary to pass a resolution restricting the types of 'amusements' which could be held under the auspices of the YWCA: 'social evenings that include dancing, theatricals, or such like secular amusements, must, for the spiritual welfare of the whole Association, not only be discouraged but not permitted to be held under the name of the Irish YWCA' (cited in Graham 2004: 12). The passing of this resolution is indicative of the tensions which can arise within an organisation which provides for the leisure-time of young people, but within a strict moral code. The YWCA had to provide some enticement for women to join and attend social gatherings; at the same time the organisers were expected to uphold (what would appear to be) a rather puritanical code of behaviour. The Council of the YWCA clearly felt that they were moving too far in the direction of that which they most feared – dancing and other 'secular' amusements. Tensions also appear to have surfaced within the GFS as it tried to balance the society's spiritual mission with its 'secular advantages'. The 1883 report notes that 'it is now better understood that the object of the GFS is not merely to advance the temporal interests of the Members … but to do them good by leading them to Christ' – a comment which seems to suggest that the society's appeal, at least initially, had been temporal rather than spiritual (*GFS Annual Report* 1883: 6).

Class composition and class interests

If evangelical zeal was one feature of philanthropy and voluntary work in the nineteenth century, then class divisions was another. In its early years the GFS appears to have been drawn up along class lines, with 'ladies as associates' and working girls (usually servants) as members (GFS, 1880: 3).[3] The Society had been formed, according to one of its first reports, 'for the benefit of girls of the working classes, whether at home or in domestic service, or in other employment' (*ibid.*: 3). Initially there were three levels of membership: honorary associates (who provided financial support and 'prayers'); working associates 'by whom the work of the society is done'; and members who made up the bulk of the numbers. The society would later reject the perception (which they concede was widespread at the time) that general membership was only for working-class girls (*GFS Annual Report* 1885). In the 1890s they claimed that the number from the 'upper classes', who joined as members, was growing, a welcome development not least because 'we hope for still more help from them in the future, as Associates, who thoroughly understand the working of the Society' (*GFS Annual Report* 1888: 3). The latter statement suggests that the society looked not to its working-class members to provide future leaders, but to the educated daughters of the upper classes. The extent to which the society in Ireland succeeded in attracting more middle-class girls as members (rather than associates) is unclear. However an examination of the various departments within the GFS in 1900 – including a department for girls in service, an emigration department and an Industrial Department – indicates that catering for the needs of working-class women featured prominently in their provision.[4] In addition, candidates for future membership included orphans and workhouse children, suggesting that the society worked with some of the poorest girls in Irish society at the time (*GFS Annual Reports* 1902 and 1903).

Richmond (2007) notes that from the outset domestic servants formed the largest single occupational group among members. But domestic service was a low-status occupation and despite efforts to recruit more girls from other occupations, the GFS 'was known, and stigmatised, as a Society for domestic servants' (*ibid.*: 306). The YWCA appears to have had a similar profile catering for servants and, to a lesser extent, governesses (Graham, 2004: 10); while the association's leaders were drawn from the middle and upper classes (Luddy, 1995a). Its internal organisation was based on four tiers of membership including honorary associates, working associates, prayer union members and general circle members (*YWCA Report for Ireland*, 1887).

The type of class distinctions evident in the GFS and YWCA would have been quite common in the philanthropic institutions of the nineteenth century. Upper and middle-class women were seen as having the time, resources, social networks, education and organisational skills necessary to manage these institutions. Many of these women would also have seen themselves as *morally* superior to their working-class sisters: dispensing moral guidance was part of their mission (Preston, 2004). Moreover voluntary work was one of the few means by which women could enter public life in the nineteenth century. As Luddy (1995b: 10) points out, philanthropic work brought middle-class women 'very clearly into the public realm where they controlled finances, raised funds, ran institutions and catered for the needs of the poor and destitute'. It is perhaps ironic that while many prominent figures within the GFS opposed suffrage, they themselves held positions of influence, helping to push women increasingly into public life.

Like most religiously-inspired voluntary organisations of the time, both the GFS and the YWCA were socially conservative. While the GFS was formed for

the 'benefit of girls of the working classes', this did not include intervening between employers and employees, as the following extract from their GFS Annual
Report (1880: 3–4) illustrates:

> [Associates] would watch over and befriend [girls in service] as opportunity
> offered, taking special care not to interfere with the duty and privilege of their
> mistress to be their best friend, but on the contrary, endeavouring to promote a
> feeling of unity between employers and employed.

According to the GFS rules, girls living at home could not join the society
without the consent of their parents, nor servants contrary to the wish of their
employers. In the case of members going into service, the Associate sent a letter
to the mistress, asking that the member be allowed to go to pay her subscription
and to attend classes or meetings. Associates were expected to seek permission
before visiting the member at her mistress's house. In addition, associates were
to encourage servants to remain with their current employers, and not assume
that the society could find them alternative employment:

> The Council also anxiously urge the Working Associates to lose no opportunity of
> impressing upon girls going into service the importance of keeping their places,
> remembering that a character for good service is the best and surest guarantee
> of future employment; and to be on their guard against leaving Members under
> any impression that might encourage them to leave their places without sufficient
> reason, in the expectation of getting another situation through the agency of the
> Society. (GFS Annual Report 1880: 8)

The above stipulation acts as a reminder that while the GFS undoubtedly supported young working women, the society also provided benefits for employers.
The GFS register was a means by which servants could be recruited, and working-class members were encouraged to show due respect for formal authority
(be it that of a parent or employer). The emigration of young women, which was
facilitated by the GFS and other organisations, had advantages for employers in
the British colonies where there was often a severe shortage of domestic servants
(Bush, 2000; Bush 1993; Gothard, 1992).[5] In addition, the types of classes provided by the society (cooking, laundry work, dressmaking) prepared young women
for a life in service or the home. This desire to create industrious workers, who
could support themselves and who knew their place, was a feature of Victorian
philanthropy more generally (Preston, 2004: xii). The friendly societies, Preston
argues, can be seen as one route the poor took to empower themselves, but they
also bolstered an authoritarian society (ibid.: 42).

     The GFS in Ireland and Britain appear to have done little to promote social
reform. Harrison (1973: 130) notes that the society was 'timid in its support
for legislation on shop hours and the protection of factory girls, and much

concerned to avoid antagonizing the employer'. The society's policy on industrial relations, he points out, was merely to stimulate thoughtfulness and a sense
of responsibility in the employer, and a dutiful acquiescence in his employee.
Similarly Luddy (1995a) has argued that both the GFS and the YWCA were
inactive in areas which urged legislation regarding the working and social conditions of the poor. Neither organisation, though heavily involved in attempts to
find situations for their members, attempted to challenge the conditions under
which women worked.

The GFS was similarly reticent on major issues of the day, including wom-
en's suffrage and Home Rule. In 1893, however, one Irish branch caused an upset
by publicly expressing anti-Home Rule views (Harrison 1973; Luddy 1995a).
Unionist sympathies have also been noted by Jackson (1990: 860), who argues
that both the GFS and the YWCA in Armagh were 'effectively Unionist and
protestant bodies'. Nonetheless there is evidence to suggest that some members
of the YWCA wanted to broaden the organisation's membership base. In a paper
(*Proposal Concerning the YWCA in Ireland*, c.1910) written in the early part of
the twentieth century, one YWCA member accused the association of not sufficiently representing the needs of Irish women, who consequently 'keep apart
from it as an alien Association'. The author goes on to assert that the focus of the
Irish Divisional Council tended to be on British affairs and that the most responsible positions were held by English women:

> The National problems of England and Ireland are different, and require different
> treatment. It is therefore not easy to see the gain to either country in the present
> arrangement, which tends to focus the attention of the Irish Divisional Council
> on British, rather than on Irish affairs. The YWCA throughout the world, no
> longer restricts itself to purely religious teaching. It frankly takes up education-
> al, social and industrial problems as they affect women, working them out on
> National lines in each country. In Ireland, the Association does not seem as yet to
> have recognised this new development.
>
> At least two great Irish problems i.e. the high rate of emigration, by which the
> country annually sustains serious loss, and the relations between Protestants and
> R.C.s are left entirely on one side. For the most part, Branches are managed on
> English lines, there is a tendency to put English women in the most responsible
> positions and Members are not encouraged to study Irish questions or to work
> for Ireland ... its ideals and methods are not Irish.

She goes on to suggest that 'the simple expedient of a National instead of a
Divisional Council would ... leave the Association, in this Country free to devote
its energies to the pressing needs of Ireland'. Other members must have also felt
the need for greater independence (though not necessarily for the same reasons)
because in 1916 the Irish Council wrote to the YWCA for Great Britain expressing its wish to separate. From 1917 it operated under the new designation of 'the

YWCA for Ireland' (Graham, 2004: 20). A letter written by S.R. Barcroft (c.1917) provides a number of reasons for the separation including differences in aims and practices arising from the 'new ideas' which became prevalent in the British YWCA after the commencement of the war; and the 'nationalist tendencies' of some members of the Irish Council (from which the author distances herself). Issues of nationalism and religion would also prove to be stumbling blocks for the development of the uniformed groups (particularly the Boy Scouts) in Ireland, an issue which will be explored in detail in Chapter 3.

Catholic clubs, registries and hostels

Both the GFS and the YWCA were English in origin and (as noted earlier) had close connections with the Church of Ireland, a denomination which accounted for only 13.1% of the Irish population at the beginning of the twentieth century.[6] The vast majority of the population were Catholic and while some organisations were formed for the benefit of Catholic girls and young women, these appear to have been comparatively few in number and limited in their scale of operation. As Whyte (1980: 62) has argued, the Catholic social movement was relatively weak in Ireland up to the 1930s. In this it contrasted with many areas of the Continent, where Catholics had developed a network of organisations with a social purpose including friendly societies, youth movements and adult education movements. Similarly MacCurtain et al. (1992: 24) note that in the philanthropic sphere lay Catholic women were 'conspicuous by their absence from the vast army of philanthropists which existed in nineteenth-century Ireland'. Protestant women appear to have had more freedom than their Catholic counterparts to run organisations; much of Catholic charity was taken over by religious congregations (Luddy, 1995a; MacCurtain, et al., 1992). In addition Protestant women, who formed a minority in Ireland, may have developed a sense of community and camaraderie through their voluntary and philanthropic work.

These arguments are borne out by newspaper articles from the 1870s and 1880s which comment on the lack of organisations for young Catholic women, compared with their Protestant sisters. One article, for example, praises the work of the GFS, arguing that Catholics should 'do for the Catholic youth of this country, what is being so vigorously carried on for the benefit of the Protestant youth not only of England, but also, by means of its branches, of Scotland and Ireland, and even of foreign countries' (*The Irish Monthly* 1879: 471). Another article asserts that homes for young women have 'been long supplied amongst our Protestant fellow-citizens' and that it was time for Catholics to make similar provision. The emphasis placed on the need for a specifically *Catholic* organisation also gives an indication of the sectarian nature of youth movements in Ireland, a feature which is shared with nineteenth-century philanthropy more generally (see Preston, 2004).

In urging the formation of Catholic organisations, these newspaper articles provide an insight into the perceived isolation (and consequent dangers) which Catholic girls and young women faced in the city of Dublin:

> It is, in fact, the large masses of Catholic young girls in this city for whom it is the aim and object of these few words to appeal; those principally who are employed in shops and trades, and also those, if possible, who may be earning their liveli- hood in service. The friends and parents of many of both these classes do not live in Dublin at all, and it may be that their homes, if they have them in the city, are but cheerless and miserable ones. They are poorly paid, scantily fed, and lodg- ings are dear, solitary, and often dreary. Hundreds of these girls are without the means or opportunity of procuring from year's end to year's end any reasonable and innocent distraction or recreation, except a walk on Sundays, which they are perhaps too exhausted and tired from their week's work to be able to enjoy. Let us think of this for a moment. They are young, and would laugh and enjoy them- selves, if they got a chance. Some of them are so uneducated that they cannot write, and can scarcely read. They are vain poor things, like most young people, and fond of finery, cheap ribbons, and smart bonnets. Like their betters, they want amusement, distraction, some outlet for their youthful spirits, some break in the eternal round of work. (*The Irish Monthly* 1879: 470)

The danger, as expressed in this article, is that these girls may be tempted by the 'gaiety and life of the streets', the 'glare of the public house' and be 'led away through giddiness into vice and its most deplorable consequences' (*ibid.*). The article is an interesting mix of compassion and condescension, which sheds some light on how young working women were viewed at this time. On the one hand the author expresses sympathy for the perceived loneliness and hardships endured by these girls; there may even be an implied criticism of employers and landlords in her assertion that working girls are 'poorly paid' and 'lodgings are dear'. At the same time, the girls described in the article are subject to derision, both on the grounds of their youth ('vain poor things, like most young people') and their lower-class status, which the author contrasts with that of 'their bet- ters'. Moreover they are represented as being vulnerable, passive, easily swayed and, therefore, in need of protection. A Catholic movement for the protection of young women is therefore proposed by the author, to be modelled on the Girls' Friendly Society.

In the last decades of the nineteenth and beginning of the twentieth cen- tury a number of clubs, registries and residential homes were set up for young Catholics. In 1880, St Martha's Home was founded in Dublin, providing accom- modation for female workers, particularly shop assistants, seamstresses and daily governesses. An article published in *The Irish Monthly* (1882) suggests that the founders and managers of St Martha's Home shared the same concerns as the GFS and YWCA. Here again we see a concern with young women who are new to Dublin, who may have no family or friends in the city, and who consequently are in need of respectable (and affordable) accommodation and companionship. The author even suggests that without the protection given by homes like St Martha's, these women might end up in one of the city's reformatories:

> We all know, and have frequently thought and admired, the splendid work which is carried out at High Park, and other reformatories in the city. But, through the agency of St Martha's, it is hoped many an inexperienced young person will be spared temptation and trial, and that in the threshold of the unknown world she is about to enter the kindly Saint's sympathy and encouragement will guide her safely along the path of duty and happiness. (*The Irish Monthly,* 10, 1882: 159).

In 1914 the Catholic Girls Club and Hostel was opened in Dublin, providing 'respectable lodgings' and a registry for those seeking employment (Annual Report 1919–1920). The numbers of those staying in the hostel and registered for work appears to have grown steadily in subsequent years (see Table 2.1). The club, hostel and registry office were managed by two 'Lady Workers' who lived on the premises, and 'besides managing the Hostel ... interest themselves in the welfare of the girls, and do all in their power to help and advise them, especially the young girls coming from the county' (Eveleen Moore report, 1922).[7] By 1919 there was a Working Girls Hostel, based at Hansbury Lane in Dublin. The International Catholic Girls Protection Society was also concerned with the welfare of young women travelling abroad to seek employment.

Table 2.1 Catholic Girls Club and Hostel: figures for 1914–1921

Year	Number of hostel residents	Club membership numbers	Number of situations procured through Registry office
1914	150	235	400
1915	610	250	450
1916	715	300	515
1917	720	323	538
1918	817	348	573
1919	886	400	586
1920	990	420	650
1921	1020	380	740

Source: Report of the work of the Catholic Girls Club produced by Eveleen Moore, Hon. Secretary, 1922.

The rescue movement, youth sexuality and patriarchy

While the organisations discussed so far were designed to assist and protect 're-spectable' young women who had left home to find work in the cities, others set out to reform prostitutes and discourage young women from being drawn into a life of vice. Prostitution was widespread in nineteenth-century Ireland, particularly in the cities and garrison towns (Luddy, 1997; McLoughlin, 2001). The authorities initially did little to restrict this practice. However by the latter part of the century there were growing fears that prostitution was leading to the spread of venereal disease and was also a source of 'moral contagion'. During the 1860s, the Contagious Diseases Acts introduced a system of compulsory medical examination of suspected prostitutes and subsequent detention (in Lock hospitals) for those found to be infected. The acts met with immediate opposition on the grounds that they focused a disproportionate share of the blame for venereal disease on prostitutes while overlooking their male clients (Richmond, 2007: 489–490). Philanthropists would wage their own war against prostitution, setting up asylums where 'fallen' women could seek refuge and be reformed. The first such asylum was opened by Arbella Denny in Dublin in 1767. She became interested in rescue work while involved in the reform of the Dublin Foundling Hospital (Luddy, 1995a: 110). There she met unmarried mothers who had been abandoned by their families, and was moved by their plight to take action. The Magdalen asylum which she subsequently opened in Leeson Street was based on the example of an asylum which had been established in London some years previously.

Between 1765 and 1914 at least thirty-three refuges or asylums were formed in Ireland for the rescue of 'fallen' women.[8] While the majority of inmates appear to have been prostitutes, the asylums also admitted unmarried women who had been 'seduced' and abandoned. Indeed some of the lay asylums preferred to work with young and 'seduced' women as they were seen as easier to reclaim than 'hardened prostitutes' (Luddy, 1995a: 112). The one requirement common to all these institutions in allowing admittance was the woman's promise to reform (ibid.). In a symbolic gesture, many asylums were named after Mary Magdalen, the biblical sinner who repented and became a follower of Jesus.

Initially Magdalen asylums were provided by lay women (both Catholic and Protestant) and religious orders, but by the middle of the nineteenth century the majority were under the control of Catholic nuns (Luddy, 1997: 497). After 1830 no lay Catholic asylum was established to look after prostitutes and those begun earlier in the century were all taken over by religious orders, including the Good Shepherd Sisters, the Sisters of Mercy and the Sisters of Charity. The Catholic hierarchy, Luddy notes, clearly 'felt that the only worthwhile impact to be made on fallen women could come from nuns' (ibid.: 497). The role of the Catholic laity was largely confined to fundraising and other forms of patronage. The Church's appropriation of the Catholic rescue movement coincided with a more general expansion of its influence: after the mid-century the majority of reformatory and industrial schools were run by religious congregations. Protestant-run asylums for fallen women continued to operate, of course, though the majority of these had closed their doors or changed their mission by the first decades of the twentieth century (Smith, 2007: xiv). Ironically it was during the same period – and particularly in the post-independence decades – that the institutional power of the Catholic Church in Ireland was at its greatest (discussed later in this chapter and in Chapters 9–10).

Luddy (1995a) argues that there was a seemingly contradictory attitude to the women admitted to the nineteenth-century Magdalen asylums. In many reports and documents the belief is expressed that these women were not in themselves evil, but had been led astray by bad company and other harmful influences. In a few instances the role of men in seducing and 'ruining' women is acknowledged and even criticised (*ibid.*: 113). However once inside the institutions responsibility for their actions was laid firmly on the shoulders of the women themselves. Magdalen asylums were places of confinement and the 'penitents' (as inmates were called) were expected to spend at least enough time there to bring about their reformation. Life within these institutions was highly structured and restrictive. It was believed that by stripping the prostitute of any independence, she would be more easily reformed (Preston, 2004: 50). Penitents were urged to disown their past and were often not even called by their own name. Instead they were given the names of saints (in religious-run asylums) or numbers. Few allowances were made for maternal feeling and the children of penitents were usually sent for adoption. Daily life was based on a strict regime of work (generally needle and laundry work), prayer and reflection. By stifling individuality and imposing strict discipline rescue workers hoped to reform fallen women and create 'a docile, uniform population of workers' (*ibid.*). However, the extent to which they achieved this objective is debatable. Luddy (1997: 495) argues that many of the women who entered the asylums proved resistant to change, using these homes as a temporary refuge rather than a means to a new way of life. Moreover surviving records indicate that women entered and left these institutions of their own accord:

> The decision to stay was made by the women themselves and although the nuns certainly did not encourage women to leave, they had little choice in the matter if the woman was determined to go. It would seem, from the number of re-entries, that some women may have used the asylums as a temporary shelter and once they were able to return to the outside world they did so. For others, the stability of life within a refuge, the order and discipline imposed may have brought a sense of security, and made it an attractive option to remain. (Luddy, 1997: 497)

Although life within the asylums was difficult, Luddy (1995a: 121) argues, those who ran them 'did so with a genuine measure of humanitarianism' in the conviction that prostitutes were certainly better off in the homes than on the streets. Religious salvation was seen as even more important than temporal welfare: it was believed that the unrepentant prostitute not only suffered in this life but would lose her eternal soul. However by focusing on the individual 'sinner', the rescue movement largely overlooked the role of male clients in perpetuating prostitution and the social and economic conditions which led women to choose this way of life.

The function of the Magdalen asylums was to change in the twentieth century when they increasingly became homes for unmarried mothers rather than prostitutes. The lay population saw these asylums not only as institutions of repentance but as hiding places for their disgraced daughters in a society which valued sexual abstinence, particularly amongst women. A woman who became pregnant outside of marriage was in a vulnerable position. If the man refused to marry her then she became 'a humiliation upon the family as well as an economic burden' (McLoughlin, 2001: 85). There were few employment opportunities available to women in Ireland and the stigma of an illegitimate child would further reduce her prospects, both of employment and of marriage. It was commonly assumed, Preston (2004: 48) notes, that women were more moral in sexual matters and if a woman sinned, she 'sank much lower in depravity than a man because she had so much further to fall'. Thus an idealised picture of women could be used against them when they fell short of certain expectations. Ferriter's (2009: 17) comment that 'there were no fallen men in Ireland' underlines the sexual double-standards and patriarchal nature of twentieth-century Irish society.

Institutionalised women in Free State Ireland

From the formation of the Irish State in 1922, the influence of the Catholic Church over various aspects of life – education, health, welfare – grew rapidly, with the willing support of successive governments. Policy reports from the period indicate that the fledgling state shared the Church's concerns about a perceived decline in moral standards. Thus in 1931 the *Report of the Committee on the Criminal Law Amendment Acts (1880–85) and Juvenile Prostitution* (commonly known as the Carrigan Report) noted a 'degeneration in the standard of social conduct' and 'looseness of morals' amongst the Irish population (1931: 12). This was attributed largely 'to the introduction of new forms of popular amusements', including 'Dance Halls, Picture Houses of sorts, and the opportunities afforded by the misuse of motor cars for luring girls' (*ibid.*). Measures were subsequently taken to curtail these amusements, most notably the Public Dance Halls Act 1935 (see Chapter 1). Other official investigations conducted at this time included the Inquiry Regarding Venereal Disease (1926), the Committee on Evil Literature (1927), and the 1927 Commission on the Relief of the Sick and Destitute Poor (Smith, 2007: 2). These inquiries, Smith notes, typically generated lengthy reports that resulted in legislation addressing social and moral issues, for example the Censorship of Publications Act 1929 and the Illegitimate Children (Affiliation Orders) Act 1930.

The spectacle of the unmarried mother and illegitimate child, in particular, represented an affront to the moral standards expected of the Irish people. During the 1920s and 1930s the Irish Free State worked with the Catholic hierarchy to establish a two-tiered institutional response to this 'problem' (Smith, 2007: 48). State-funded mother and baby homes were set up for 'first offenders' who were seen as redeemable, while the Magdalen asylums provided for less hopeful cases, i.e. those who had had more than one pregnancy. It was believed that such women were a source of 'moral contagion' who might corrupt vulnerable first-time mothers should they come into contact. Unlike the mother and baby homes, the Magdalen asylums were never governed by state legislation, they never received state capitation grants and consequently resisted all forms of government regulation and inspection (*ibid.*: 46). These institutions were to become known as the Magdalen laundries because of the type of work (generally unpaid) which the inmates undertook.

The importance of segregating 'first offenders' from 'hopeless cases' is made clear in Church and State reports and policy documents from the 1920s and 1930s. A submission from the Church hierarchy to the government in 1922, for example, suggests that the county homes – where some destitute unmarried mothers sought refuge – were unsuitable as they brought first-time mothers into contact with 'hardened sinners' including prostitutes and repeat offenders (Smith, 2007: 127). The welfare of unmarried mothers was later addressed by the Commission on the Relief of the Sick and Destitute Poor, Including the Insane Poor, who published a report on their findings and recommendations in 1927. Like the Catholic hierarchy, the commission (1927: para. 228) distinguishes between different categories of women, observing that 'in dealing with the problem of accommodation for unmarried mothers it must be recognised that there were two classes to be provided for, namely (1) those who may be amenable to reform and (2) those who for one reason or another are regarded as less hopeful cases'. It is suggested that the treatment for the former 'must necessarily be in the nature of a moral up building and, while requiring firmness and discipline, must be characterised by and blended with a certain amount of individual charity and sympathy' (1927: para. 230). The report calls for a series of newly funded residential institutions dedicated exclusively to 'first-offenders' (Smith, 2007: 52).

One of the more troubling aspects of the Commission's report is its recommendation that unmarried mothers be detained within institutions for specific periods of time, the length of which would depend on whether they were 'first time' or repeat offenders:

At present there is no power to detain a woman in any Poor Law Institution, even when it is clearly necessary for her protection. We suggest that if an unmarried woman who applies for relief during pregnancy or after giving birth to a child is willing, when applying for assistance, to undertake to remain for a period not exceeding one year there should be power to retain her for that period, in the case of a first admission. In the case of admission for a second time, there should be power to retain for a period of two years. On third or subsequent admissions the Board should have power to retain for such period as they think fit, having considered the recommendation of the Superior or Matron of the Home. All cases whose maximum period of residence is indeterminate should be reviewed annually. (*Report of the Commission on the Relief of the Sick and Destitute Poor, Including the Insane Poor*, 1927: para. 234)

The system of detention proposed here had no legal basis. It has been difficult for researchers to assess the extent to which women were detained because of difficulties in obtaining records for the twentieth-century Magdalen asylums (Smith, 2007: 24) and this is an area which requires more systematic investigation. The accounts of former inmates of asylums, mother and baby homes and similar institutions suggest that some women lived in prison-like conditions (Ryan Report, 2009). The (*Reformatory and Industrial Schools Systems Report* (1970: 39) also made the important point that because some girls and women spent many years within an institutional setting they became 'unfit for re-emergence into society'. In the past, the report notes, 'many girls have been taken into these convents and remained there all their lives' (*ibid.*). The rehabilitative function of various church-run institutions can therefore be called into question.

Concealment and containment

The Magdalen laundries, Smith (2007: 2) argues, formed part of Ireland's 'architecture of containment' which was based on an assortment of interlinked institutions, including mother and baby homes, reformatories, industrial schools, mental asylums and adoption agencies. All of these institutions were linked together in two important ways (Raftery and O' Sullivan 1999: 18–19; Smith 2007: 45). Firstly, many of the religious congregations who managed the reformatory and industrial schools also operated Magdalen laundries. Secondly, these institutions helped sustain each other – girls from the reformatory and industrial schools were sometimes sent to Magdalen laundries to boost their workforce (Raftery and O'Sullivan, 1999: 18–19). Similarly, the children of the 'Magdalens' (as inmates were sometimes called) ended up in the industrial and reformatory schools if no other home could be found for them. Thus a vast institutional network concealed women and children who appeared to belie the idealised picture of Catholic morality and family life which the Church and State wished to construct. The unmarried mother, above all, had to be concealed behind the closed doors of religious-run institutions: 'In a society where even the faint-est whiff of scandal threatened the respectability of the normative Irish family, the Magdalen asylum existed as a place to contain and/or punish the threat-ened embodiment of instability' (Smith, 2007: xviii). In addition to unmarried mothers, the Magdalen homes admitted a range of other unwanted women, in-cluding those deemed to be 'wayward', 'backward' or 'mentally defective', those on remand from the courts and those who were simply 'in the way' (*ibid.*).

The arbitrary nature of institutionalising girls and young women is also indicated in the *Report of the Commission to Inquire into Child Abuse* (2009) (Ryan Report). Young people (some as young as thirteen years) were admitted to 'residential laundries' for a whole range of reasons, including poverty, death of a parent and familial abuse:

> Three (3) female witnesses said they were transferred to residential laundries from Industrial Schools following confrontations with religious staff whom they challenged about abuse of themselves or of their co-residents. Another female witness stated that she was transferred to a laundry at 13 years to work. She stated that she was told by the Sister in charge that she was being sent to work in order to compensate the Order as her mother had been unable to meet the required payments for her keep in the Industrial School. Four (4) female witnesses stated that they were placed in residential laundries or other work settings with the knowledge or support of parents or relatives in the context of poverty, death of a parent and personal or family crisis including familial abuse. Two (2) of these witnesses stated that they or their relatives were told, prior to admission, that they would receive an education that never materialised as they were involved from the outset in full-time work within the institution. (Ryan Report, 2009, Volume 3: para. 18.13)

These witnesses describe a life of hard physical work, long hours and strict dis-cipline within the laundries:

> Seven (7) female witness reports related to continuous hard physical work in residential laundries, which was generally unpaid. Two (2) witnesses said that the regime was '*like a prison*', that doors were locked all the time and exercise was taken in an enclosed yard. Working conditions were harsh and included standing for long hours, constantly washing laundry in cold water, and using heavy irons for many hours. One witness described working hard, standing in silence and being made to stand for meals and kneel to beg forgiveness if she spoke. Another witness stated that she was punched and hit as a threat not to disclose details of her everyday life working in the laundry to her family. (Ryan Report, 2009, Volume 3: para. 18.25)

Two women who attended the mother and baby homes provided a similarly bleak picture of life within these institutions. Both described 'a regimented 'prison-like' atmosphere, where they were made to wear uniforms and punished for talking and laughing' (Ryan Report, 2009, Volume 4: para. 5.145). They described suffering humiliation at the hands of the nuns who were both verbally and physically abusive. Both women felt that they had been emotionally traumatised during their time in the home. Pre- and post-natal care was described as being non-existent. Maguire (2009: 88) has also noted the 'alarmingly high' rate of infant mortality in mother and baby homes, which inevitably raises questions about conditions in these institutions.

Not surprisingly many single mothers decided to leave the country. The Department of Local Government and Public Health, in its annual report for 1931/32, noted that several complaints had been received from the English Rescue Societies because of 'the number of girls who having got into trouble leave the Free State and go to England' (1932: 129–130). A conference was duly arranged between representatives of these societies and an Inspector from the department at which it was agreed 'that every effort should be made to discourage girls going to England in such circumstances and to bring them back where possible' (*ibid.*). Kornitzer (1952: 52) observed that efforts to repatriate Irish single mothers were not conspicuously successful, creating a surplus of Catholic babies available for adoption in Britain. Such a failure cannot have been wholly displeasing to the Irish authorities since it served to distort the nation's illegitimacy rate by artificially pushing it downwards. It was, therefore, possible for Church and State to take comfort in Ireland's relatively low official illegitimacy rate, which stood at 2.68% in 1925 (*Report of the Commission on the Relief of the Sick and Destitute Poor*, 1927, Appendix Table V). The statistics provided evidence (however spurious) of the virtuous adherence of the Irish to traditional sexual mores.

Raftery and O' Sullivan (1999: 19) have raised the issue of public silence within Irish civil society regarding the fate of the children and young women consigned to various church-run institutions:

> The sheer scale of the system has in part resulted in the strange public silence on these institutions for most of this century. While there were some courageous expressions of concern and dissent, the general absence of questioning was profound. Yet the majority of these institutions were not hidden away in remote areas. They were situated in prominent locations in towns and cities all over Ireland.

Since the 1990s this silence has been broken. The treatment received by the former residents of various church-run institutions became a public issue in the context of the deliberation of the Commission to Inquire into Child Abuse and the publication of the Ryan Report (discussed in Chapters 9–10). Public interest in the Magdalen asylums had been triggered some years earlier by the Channel 4 documentary *Sex in a Cold Climate* (1997) and the acclaimed film *Magdalen*

Sisters (2002). A series of books have also supported the search for truth and reconciliation. Mary Raftery and Eoin O' Sullivan in *Suffer the Little Children* (1999) first explored the issue of institutional abuse and exploitation in Ireland to a shocked public. It was followed by a number of more specific studies of Magdalen asylums, notably Frances Finnegan's *Do Penance or Perish: A Study of Magdalen Asylums in Ireland* (2001) and James Smith's *Ireland's Magdalen Laundries* (2007). Smith has since campaigned in the letters columns of the *Irish Times* for the rights of former inmates of these institutions and been critical of the Irish government's reluctance to engage with this group. An advocacy groups, called Justice for Magdalenes (JFM) has been formed and has called on the Irish government for an investigation and compensation. Their claims have been resisted on the (arguably spurious) basis that Magdalen institutions were under private management.

Conclusion

Organisations like the Girls Friendly Society, the Young Women's Christian Association and the various Catholic clubs and hostels tell us much about the position of girls and young women in Ireland and Britain at the end of the nineteenth and beginning of the twentieth century. These organisations both reflected and reinforced Victorian morality and were an attempt to police the sexual activity of the working classes. The extent to which these organisations actually achieved their objective is, of course, an entirely different matter. Cunningham (1990) has argued that members of voluntary organisations at the turn of the century were quite capable of resisting 'overt ideology' and some may have joined societies in a calculating spirit – to extract what they wanted and nothing else. While acknowledging that many members may have absorbed and internalised parts of the beliefs of these organisations (they may well have been predisposed towards them), Cunningham suggests that it would be quite wrong to see the influences flowing in one direction only. There was a tension between the desire to propagate certain beliefs and the need to maintain membership, and organisations had to respond to the needs of members if they were to survive. Indeed the post-war decline in GFS membership has been partly attributed to its intransigence regarding Rule III (Richmond, 2007). While attitudes to sexual morality were changing, the GFS continued to reflect the values of the Victorian era.

In conducting their moral mission women's organisations provided many practical supports to the young, including leisure, accommodation and travel. In a time when women from all over Europe were having to leave their home country to find work, organisations like the Travellers' Aid Society, the YWCA and the GFS provided much needed support (O' Connell, 1974). For domestic servants they were often the only source of recreation and opportunity for meeting other young women. In this sense these organisations could be described as philanthropic and even empowering. However the women who were most empowered by their involvement were those of the upper and middle classes who assumed positions of responsibility and leadership. Voluntary and philanthropic work, as noted earlier, was one of the few means by which women could enter public life. It is one of the contradictions of the GFS that while many prominent figures within the society opposed suffrage, they themselves held positions of influence, helping to push women more and more into public life.

The GFS and the YWCA, like many philanthropic organisations of the nineteenth century, were socially conservative. While they provided a range of services for working women they were largely inactive in areas which urged legislation regarding working and social conditions. These organisations (and others like them) certainly did not set out to change the world, though they may have helped to make life a little easier for some of the poorer women in Irish society at this time.

Another aspect of women's work in the moral sphere can be seen in the 'rescue' movement and the establishment of Magdalen asylums, which began in the eighteenth century. These institutions were concerned with prostitutes and other 'fallen' women and were initially provided by both lay women and religious congregations. In the twentieth century most of the Protestant-run Magdalen institutions were closed but those run by Catholic nuns entered a new phase of expansion, working with unmarried mothers and other categories of unwanted women in a society which was increasingly under the influence of the Catholic Church. The harsh conditions endured by inmates of the Magdalen laundries have only recently received widespread public attention. The only kindly explanation for the abrogation of the civil rights of single mothers in Ireland during the first half of the twentieth century is to attribute this policy to an excessive zeal for the ideal of chastity. But there was a chilling intolerance in this superimposed moral idealism. A society that did not tolerate education in birth control methods, abortion nor contraception could not, perhaps, be expected to treat this vulnerable minority with greater humanity. It did, however expose a dark side to the growing influence of Catholic ethics on the formulation of Irish social policy that was to become an established pattern (discussed in Chapters 9 and 10).

Notes

1 Public branding was also potentially libellous, as the Society discovered in 1908 when an associate in the Irish GFS suspended a member following rumours linking the girl's name with a married schoolmaster. The associate announced the dismissal at the Branch meeting and the girl then served her with a writ for slander, claiming £500 damages. The associate's Counsel thought the girl's action was justified and advised the associate to settle out of court, which she did (Richmond, 2007).

2   In the same year Mary Jane Kinnaird opened a house for girls coming up to London for the first time. Over the next twenty years both the Prayer Unions and the homes for girls extended their work to other areas, eventually combining to form 'The London Young Women's Institute and Christian Association' (soon to be known simply as the YWCA) (Graham 2004).

3   In 1887 the wording of the Objects of the Society was changed, removing the word 'working' before 'girls'. This change had been previously made by the Central Society in England (*GFS Annual Report* 1887).

4   The Industrial Department promoted instruction in what were termed the 'home arts' – cooking, laundry work, dressmaking etc.

5   Gothard (1992) argues that, through their involvement with the GFS, middle-class colonial women tried to secure privileged access to a valuable and limited supply of domestic labour. This conflict of interests is well-illustrated by a public scandal which engulfed the Sydney branch of the GFS during the mid-1880s. Women emigrating to the colony at this time would normally remain in accommodation at the Hyde Park Depot for the first few days and then attend a hiring day, where competition for domestic servants was often fierce. However the local GFS attempted to monopolise the small stream of GFS members by writing to them at the depot and ordering them not to attend hiring day but to wait until a GFS associate came for them. Prospective employers amongst the public soon realised that the GFS was interfering in the hiring process. Gothard (1992) notes that this involved not simply monopolising the supply of GFS emigrants but also following up non-GFS domestics in their new employers' homes.

6   According to the census of 1911, 73.9% of the population were Roman Catholic, 13.1% were Church of Ireland, 10% were Presbyterian, 1.4% were Methodist, with the remaining 1.5% made up of other denominations (Curtis, 1996: 146).

7   Eveleen Moore's report (1922) gives an indication of the services provided by the organisation: 'The two ladies attend in the Club on Club evenings, three nights a week, Wednesday, Thursday and Sunday, and get up concerts, etc. for the amusement of the girls. All Catholic Girls can become members of the Club by paying a subscription … Girls seeking situations in Dublin can have safe and comfortable lodgings in the Hostel for 4/- per week or 1/- per night; this provides bed in Dormitory, use of bathroom, hot and cold water, use of kitchen and utensils for cooking meals'.

8   In a breakdown of the inmates of seven of these asylums, Luddy found that overall they catered for a total of 10,674 women during the period 1800–1899 (Luddy, 1997: 497).

3

Constructing imperial man: uniformed youth movements in Britain and Ireland

> If Saint Paul was the prophet of manly Christianity and Dr Thomas Arnold its most famous public-school practitioner, then William Alexander Smith, the founder and first Secretary of the Boys' Brigade, must be credited with putting the idea into uniform, drilling it and providing it with a uniquely Scottish dissenting flavour. (Springhall, 1977: 22)

The last decades of the nineteenth century and the first of the twentieth saw the formation of various uniformed youth movements for both boys and girls, several of which have survived to this day. Their emergence has been explained in terms of a growing crisis of confidence within British society. The upper and middle classes, in particular, felt themselves to be under threat on two fronts: 'by the socialist enemy within from the mid-1880s and by the German enemy without from at least the mid-1900s' (Springhall, 1977: 14). The Boer War did little to inspire confidence in Britain's ability to defend her empire, sparking fears of national degeneracy and a decline in 'manliness'. Meanwhile concerns were also growing about juvenile 'restlessness' and delinquency, particularly in the urban squalor of overcrowded Victorian cities. This combination of internal and external threats led to a renewed emphasis being placed by the ruling elites on national unity and social conformity. The uniformed youth movements appeared to offer an antidote to at least some of the perceived social ills afflicting Britain and the Empire at this time. These organisations were deeply conservative, preaching class unity and promoting habits of discipline, respect for authority and selflessness amongst the young. However the need to appeal to different sections of society, and to both adults and young people sometimes resulted in multiple or even contradictory meanings and objectives. Alexander (2009: 42) notes, for example, that while Baden-Powell stressed the physical and disciplinary benefits of Guide camps, many of the girls themselves 'enjoyed a previously unknown degree of gender freedom during their company camps and hikes'.

A number of the uniformed youth organisations which originated in Britain spread to Ireland, including the Boys' Brigade, the Church Lads' Brigade, the Boy Scouts and the Girl Guides. In addition Catholic versions of uniformed groups would emerge, most notably the Catholic Boy Scouts and the Catholic Girl Guides. While the origins of Irish youth movements are clearly rooted in nineteenth-century Britain, Ireland was very different to its industrialised neighbour and this would have consequences in terms of their development. British youth organisations were often Protestant and urban in origin and so had a limited appeal in a country where the vast majority of the population were rural Catholics. An equally important challenge was Ireland's emerging sense of nationhood. The uniformed youth movements were introduced against the backdrop of the Celtic revival, a resurgent nationalist movement and growing tensions in Ulster over the issue of Home Rule. Nationalists resented the imperial rhetoric and ritual of Scouting and the Boys Brigade, and feared that these organisations were a covert means of recruiting boys into the British army. The challenges which the uniformed groups faced in Ireland were certainly not unique. The Scouts and Guides, both of which spread throughout the world, encountered problems in countries with serious political divisions based on race or religion (Proctor, 2002).

In this chapter we will chart the early history of uniformed youth movements, focusing in particular on explanations as to *why* they emerged and flourished in the late Victorian/Edwardian period. We focus on two areas in particular: social regulation and the development of 'manliness' amongst adolescent boys. The uniformed movements promised to curb certain tendencies (idleness, rowdiness, effeminacy) amongst urban youth, and to develop those traits which were seen as necessary for 'national efficiency' and military defence (manliness, patriotism and class unity). The debate over whether youth movements – particularly the Boy Scouts – had military objectives will also be considered. In the second part of this chapter we will consider the development of uniformed youth movements in Ireland, with particular reference to the Boy Scouts. We will seek to explain why the uniformed youth movements had such limited success in Ireland. It will be argued that religious sectarianism and the movement's imperial overtones would prove an obstacle to the development of scouting in Ireland, and became a particularly divisive issue following the war of independence. While claiming to be non-political, the rhetoric and ritual of Scouting conferred on its members a particular identity, which was in conflict with the sense of national identity which groups, such as Fianna Eireann, were constructing at the time. We will begin by briefly outlining the formation of the church-based brigades, the Boy Scouts and the Girl Guides.

Origins of the uniformed brigades

William Smith, founder of the Boys' Brigade (BB), is a little-known historical figure in comparison with Baden-Powell, the charismatic and publicity-conscious founder of Scouting. However it is worth noting that the Boys' Brigade pre-dates the Boy Scouts by almost a quarter of a century. Founded in Glasgow in 1883, it was the first mass voluntary youth movement in Britain and the forerunner of all the uniformed youth organisations. Smith was both a member of the Glasgow Volunteer Regiment (1st Lanarkshire Rifles) and a Sunday School teacher at the Free College Church. These different facets of his life would eventually be reflected in the Boys' Brigade, which was initially formed in order to improve Sunday School attendance and discipline. Smith was also concerned with the need to bridge the gap between leaving Sunday School and the age for joining the YMCA or one of the other young men's societies. His response was to form a brigade for boys based on the twin pillars of Bible class and drill, though other activities were gradually added.[1]

From the onset the movement had clear military overtones and connections. Many of the BB's officers were volunteer soldiers (like Smith himself) who were able to use their own experience to teach military-style drill to boys. The uniform consisted of a 'military-looking' pill-box hat, belt and haversack, while dummy rifles were used for drill (Wilkinson, 1969: 5). Various awards, decorations and medals were awarded to boys, including an 'Efficiency Badge' for attendance and good behaviour (Dublin Battalion *Annual Report 1908–09*: 26). Fundamental to the philosophy of this new organisation (and those which followed) was the fostering of an *esprit de corps*, a phrase often used to describe the morale and sense of camaraderie in male-only institutions, particularly the army and the Victorian public school. Thus one report explained that the object of the Boys' Brigade is attained 'by banding boys together in Companies' and 'by creating among them an *esprit de corps* which gives them a proper pride in their company, and a strong incentive to do nothing unworthy of it ...' (*ibid.*: 27).

While the military overtones of Smith's organisation were criticised by some commentators, the BB method also received enthusiastic praise as it was seen to cater for boys' interests while at the same time teaching them duty and discipline. In the coming years the Brigade would win a number of influential backers, including 'wealthy industrialists [who] embarked on conscience-salving expenditure on the Boys' Brigade as much as from a pervasive sense of social anxiety as from any other cause' (Springhall, 1977: 26). Support was also provided by church leaders, who saw the BB as an effective means of keeping boys off the street and within the church's sphere of influence. During the 1880s the movement spread all over Scotland and in the 1890s there was considerable expansion over the border, in England and Wales. In 1891 a number of different denominations were represented in companies across Scotland, England, Wales and Northern Ireland. However Presbyterian and Episcopalian churches accounted for the vast majority (75%), the remaining 25% included Wesley/ Methodist, Congregational, Baptist and 'others' (*ibid.*: 28).

The success of the Boys' Brigade led to the formation of other uniformed groups, including the Church Lads' Brigade, the Jewish Lads' Brigade and the

Catholic Boys' Brigade. It was also the inspiration for two of the earliest uniformed organisations for girls, the Girls' Brigade (which began in Dublin in
1893) and Girls' Guildry (founded in Glasgow in 1900).[2] Other uniformed youth
movements for girls at this time included the Church Girls' Brigade (1901), a
girls' equivalent of the Church Lads' Brigade and the Girls' Life Brigade (1902),
a sister movement to the Boys' Life Brigade (Springhall, 1977). The philosophy
and organisation of the Boys' Brigade would also be an inspiration to Robert
Baden-Powell, who went on to form the two most successful youth movements
of the twentieth century.

Baden-Powell and the formation of the Boy Scouts and Girl Guides

Robert Baden-Powell first gained fame for his role in the defence of Mafeking,
a town besieged during the Boer War. However it is as the founder of the Boy
Scouts and Girl Guides that he is remembered today. The Scouting movement
owes much to his early life, education and military career. Born into a professional middle-class family, Baden-Powell was educated at Charterhouse School
and throughout his life prized those qualities which he particularly associated with 'Public School Spirit': self-reliance, responsibility, loyalty and respect
for tradition (Jeal, 2001). He would later suggest that these qualities could be
engendered in 'less fortunate' boys, through the Scouting movement. Other traditions of the Victorian public school – athleticism, the 'cult of manliness' and
the demotion of intellectualism – would all inform Baden-Powell's views and
find expression in the Boy Scout movement.

Like many other Victorian men of his class, Baden-Powell went from one
male-dominated institution (the public school) to another (the army), serving
initially in India and later in Africa. In the course of his career he was to learn
much about scouting, reconnaissance and woodcraft. Elements from the 5th
Dragoon Guards' scouting system would eventually find their way into *Scouting
for Boys* (Jeal, 2001: 201). However the influence which army life was to have
on Baden-Powell went beyond mastering the art of scouting. The way of life in
Africa, and the people whom he met there, would also inform his outlook and
his ideas for a youth movement. He admired the toughness and self-reliance of
the 'white adventurers' in Rhodesia and the tribal societies in Africa, which – as
Jeal acknowledges – was ironic given that he was part of a force sent to destroy
them (*ibid.*). In the course of his career Baden-Powell would try to instil in 'city-
bred' soldiers and (later) Boy Scouts the tribal values of courage and resilience.

While the Victorian public school and army informed the philosophy
of Scouting, Baden-Powell was also influenced by the various youth movements which preceded the Scouts, including the Boys' Brigade, the YMCA,
the Woodcraft Indians (founded in the US by Ernest Thompson Seton) and
the Imperial Legion of Frontiersmen which, Jeal (*ibid.*: 374) argues, was much

closer to the ethos and atmosphere of the Scouts than the 'prayer-bashing' Boys' Brigade. Baden-Powell was undoubtedly impressed by the Boys' Brigade, though he considered that their programme, and that of similar organisations, laid too much emphasis on drill and gymnastics. He devised an alternative programme of activities – which were tested in the course of a nine-day camp at Brownsea Island in 1907 – and from January 1908 had his programme published in six fortnightly parts. The publisher of *Scouting for Boys*, Arthur Pearson, organised a successful publicity campaign, which was helped by Baden-Powell's standing as a war hero (Pryke, 1998; Warren, 1986). Existing youth organisations largely ignored Baden-Powell's programme, but boys bought the magazines and started to form themselves into 'patrols' (Gaughan, 2006: 4). While the movement started off almost spontaneously, a more formal structured organisation eventually emerged with Baden-Powell at the helm, as 'Chief Scout'. Despite some criticism over its alleged militancy and marginalisation of religion, the Scouting movement was an immediate success. The first census of the Scouts in 1910 indicated that the movement had more than 100,000 members in Britain (Proctor, 2002). Over the next decade Scouting spread throughout the Empire, Europe, the Balkans, North and South America, and even Japan (Jeal, 2001).

The Girl Guides owe their origin to a group of girls who turned up uninvited to the first big rally of Boy Scouts at Crystal Palace in 1909, demanding to be inspected (Springhall, 1977: 131). Baden-Powell, having originally conceived of Scouting as 'a masculine antidote to the feminizing influences of home and family' initially rejected the idea of including girls (Alexander, 2009: 40). Moreover, he reasoned that the presence of girls would act as a deterrent to male adolescent membership. He eventually agreed to a separate uniformed youth organisation to be called the 'Girl Guides', a name which had more domestic and feminine connotations than 'Scouts' (*ibid.*: 41). In the early years there were concerns about what constituted appropriate activities for girls, and the Guides had to demonstrate considerable skill 'in sitting on a far from stable fence, buffeted on one side by the suffragettes and on the other by reactionaries' (Jeal, 2001: 475). Despite these early difficulties, the Guides went on to become the most successful organisation for girls in the twentieth century, with numbers sometimes outstripping those for scouting (Proctor, 2002).

In the following section we will consider *why* these early youth movements met with immediate success, focusing in particular on the Boy Scouts and the Boys' Brigade. Two factors are particularly important in explaining this phenomenon: firstly the perceived need for 'social regulation' in the face of socialist threats and 'juvenile restlessness' (Springhall, 1977: 15); and secondly a crisis of masculinity which appeared to threaten Britain's national efficiency and defence.

Social regulation

The last decades of the nineteenth century and the first of the twentieth were a period of increasing economic and social uncertainty in Britain. The business and governing classes were beginning to feel nervous that their previously unassailable position in Victorian society might be threatened by the newly educated and enfranchised urban masses (Springhall *et al.*, 1983). Moreover the influence of socialism continued to grow and working-class interests were now represented through organised labour movements and the emerging Labour Party. Fear of an empowered working class and of an intensification of class conflict led to a renewed emphasis being placed by the ruling elite on cementing national unity. One strand of conservative thought – broadly known as social imperialism – suggested that this could be achieved through the promotion of patriotic feeling and a programme of moderate social reforms designed to appease a discontented working class (Springhall, 1977: 58).

The 'social imperialists' were to find willing allies in youth movements, particularly Scouting, which endorsed a common patriotism above class distinctions. At a time of growing unrest these organisations appeared to offer the prospect of stability by preaching class unity and promoting habits of discipline, respect for authority and selflessness amongst the young. Moreover Baden-Powell was to use his position as the 'hero of Mafeking' and later as Chief Scout to condemn various groups (trade unions, socialists, Bolsheviks) whom he believed were undermining national unity. The need for British unity to transcend class divisions was made repeatedly in the first phase of the movement, as the following extract from *Scouting for Boys* illustrates:

> If our empire is to stand Britain cannot be divided against itself. For this you must begin as boys, not to think of other classes of boys as your enemies. Remember that whether rich or poor, from castle or from slum, you are all Britons in the first place ... If you are divided amongst yourselves then you are doing harm to your country. You must sink your differences. (Baden-Powell, 1908: 278)

Trade unionists were denounced as 'paid professional agitators whose living depends on agitating (whether it is needed or not)' (Baden-Powell 1908: 337). Not surprisingly, some working-class parents opposed the Scouts and Guides because of the anti-trade union rhetoric expressed by Baden-Powell both in Scouting literature and in popular papers such as the *Daily Mail* and the *Telegraph* (Proctor, 2002). In the post-war period the Chief Scout appears to have been reconciled to the labour movement, and turned his attention instead to 'Bolshevism', which was allegedly threatening national reconstruction. In an article which appeared in the Dublin Boy Scouts' *Annual Handbook* (1919: 10) bolshevism is described in terms of madness, class hatred and hysteria, while the British people are characterised as 'quiet, steady-going citizens' who must nonetheless be on their

guard. The scouting movement pledged to counter the Bolshevik threat by training young people 'to be level headed and British, to give fair play to all and to be
unselfish in themselves, to be manly and responsible human beings' (*ibid.*: 11).

While the Scouts claimed to address various 'seditious' or revolutionary
elements in society, the movement also had more modest social regulatory objectives. All of the uniformed youth movements for boys at this time purported
to combat juvenile rowdiness, idleness and delinquency. The Boys Brigade, as
noted earlier, was initially formed in order to improve Sunday School attendance
and discipline. In scouting and brigade literature the boy is often constructed as a
threat, either as a juvenile criminal or, at the very least, a mischief maker. Thus Fr.
Ernest Farrell, one of the founding fathers of the Catholic Boy Scouts of Ireland,
claimed that 'if a boy is not at something good he is in real danger of being up to
something bad' (*Our Boys*, 1 October 1925: 53); while the B-P Boy Scouts noted
that 'if the growing boy is not occupied in healthy, exciting and sane work and
play he will nine times out of ten get into more or less serious mischief' (Dublin
Boy Scouts' *Annual Handbook*, 1919: 3). Similarly the Church Lads' Brigade asserted that: 'Left to themselves in their leisure hours they are apt to lounge about
the streets, idling and imitating the language and habits of men ten years their
senior' (cited in Springhall, 1977: 40). The prospect of young people 'idling', may
not only have been perceived as a nuisance, but also as an affront to a middle-
class work ethic. The uniformed groups would provide the necessary occupation
and moral training which, they claimed, was sometimes missing in the lives of
young people. As well as ascribing to themselves a preventative role, these organisations also claimed to act in a remedial capacity, reforming those who had
already committed some crime. The Boy Scout annual report of 1915 noted that
troops had been formed 'for the morally defective' in industrial schools around
the country (Boy Scouts Association *6th Annual Report*, 1915: xxiv). In a later
publication Baden-Powell claims that 'Scoutcraft is a means through which the
veriest hooligan can be brought to higher thought and to the elements of faith in
God' (Dublin Boy Scouts' *Annual Handbook*, 1919: 6).

The degree to which the Scouts succeeded in getting hold of 'hooligans'
(or as Baden-Powell once put it 'those of the worst class') has been questioned
(Pryke, 1998: 321). The movement, Pryke notes, was composed largely of lower-
middle and middle-class boys both before and after the war. Similarly Springhall
(1977: 25) points out that membership of the early Boys' Brigade was largely
drawn from the 'respectable' working classes, rather than the 'unwashed slum
boys' that some accounts suggest.

While social control was clearly important to the uniformed youth movements, the correct form and amount of that control was 'tricky', Lesko (2001: 50)
notes, because modern society demanded energetic, manly and strong citizens,
not docile or cautious boys. Thus those concerned with young people were faced
with a paradox: 'Their mission was to produce young, manly Christians who

were strong and responsible for their positions in society, but they knew, often from personal experience, that too much adult control over young men could break their wills and drain precious life-force resources. How could they carefully sculpt strong-willed boys without creating weak-willed, effeminate youth?' (*ibid.*: 59). The need to produce *manly* Christians, which Lesko refers to here, was a growing preoccupation in late Victorian society, and provided the context for the formation of the uniformed movements.

Masculinity and national efficiency

Ideas about masculinity vary over time and from culture to culture but by the second half of the nineteenth century, Sisson (2004: 17) notes, 'manliness' was to take on a particular meaning: 'Emphasis on the virtues of moral earnestness and purity of feeling made way for the values of athleticism, physical prowess and moral courage.' However, if athleticism and physical prowess were the benchmarks of manliness, the defeats of the Boer War suggested that many British men – particularly those from the working classes – were falling well short of expectations. Not only had the army suffered a number of unexpected defeats in the course of the war, but many would-be recruits had failed to pass medical tests. Consequently the government set up the Inter-Departmental Committee on Physical Deterioration, which reported its findings in 1904. Fears about the deterioration of manhood intensified over the next decade in the face of Germany's growing military power and competition from US businesses (Lesko, 2001: 70). As prices and profits declined, the ruling classes emphasised the need for 'national efficiency', seeing themselves as engaged in a Darwinian struggle to maintain Britain's military and economic supremacy.

Concerns about masculinity inevitably focused attention on teenage boys, the men of the future. Academics, reformers and various others concerned with children and adolescents ('boyologists') would enter into a debate about the nature of manhood, how it might be fostered in adolescents, and the factors which impaired its 'proper' development (Lesko, 2001). One of the main threats to masculinity – identified by commentators in the UK, the US and Germany – was the corrupting influence of modern cities, which sapped the boy's physical, moral and mental strength. If urban life was depleting the nation's manhood, then fresh air and outdoor activities were to be at least part of the solution. These views would provide further momentum for the uniformed youth groups, particularly the Boy Scouts. Camping expeditions became one of the defining features of the Scouting movement, with Baden-Powell extolling the benefits which a return to nature might have for boys:

> The outdoors is par excellence the school for observation and for realising the wonders of a wondrous universe. It opens to the mind appreciation of the

beautiful that lies before it day by day. It reveals to the City youngster that the stars are there beyond the City chimney pots, and the sunset clouds are gleaming in their glory far above the roof of the cinema theatre. (Dublin Boy Scouts' *Annual Handbook*, 1919: 6)

The Boys' Brigade did not have the same rural orientation of activity as the Scouts, though annual camps were organised (Pryke, 1998: 321). Nonetheless the organisation did offer physical training, encouraged outdoor activities (often in the streets but ideally in the countryside) and extolled the 'manly' virtues of discipline, loyalty and personal responsibility. Indeed the Boys' Brigade had (and still has) as its object 'the promotion of habits of Obedience, Reverence, Discipline, Self-Respect and all that tends towards a true Christian *Manliness*' (our emphasis). While the brigades placed 'manliness' at the centre of their mission, there were initially some concern that boys might regard religion as inherently effeminate and emasculating.[3] William Smith, founder of the Boys' Brigade, set out to dispel such notions: 'By associating Christianity with all that was most noble and manly in a boy's sight, we would be going a long way to disabuse his mind of the idea that there is anything effeminate or weak about Christianity' (Smith cited in Springhall, 1977: 22). The solution, Springhall notes, was to show boys the manliness of Christianity and to play down its more 'feminine' tendencies of compassion and turning the other cheek.

The uniformed movements were clearly part of a more general project to develop the manliness of Britain's youth. However some of the means by which they achieved this (drill, rifle exercises etc.), the symbolism and ritual (uniforms, marches) as well as the military background of many of their leaders, led to accusations that these movements were attempting to produce the soldiers of the future.

Good citizens or future soldiers?

The uniformed youth movements both reflected and helped to propagate a more widespread militarism in British society at the beginning of the twentieth century. Thus in 1910 William Smith declared that 'There can be no doubt that one individual result of the work of the Brigades has been to popularize the idea of military service among the people generally' (cited in Springhall, 1977: 18). However the military overtones of church-based brigades were not universally welcomed. When the Church Lads' Brigade became affiliated to the King's Royal Rifles Cadets, contemporary critics objected that this amounted to a distortion of the original purposes of a religious organisation (Summers, 1976: 120). The Scouting movement would also attract criticism for its alleged militarism, a charge which Baden-Powell consistently denied. Both the official *Headquarters Gazette* and Baden-Powell's papers maintained an opposition to military training, claiming instead to provide training in citizenship (Warren, 1986: 376). Nonetheless, critics at the time believed that, under the cover of informal education and outdoor activities, Scouting was preparing the next generation of soldiers. The strongest of these critiques in the Edwardian period emerged among trade-union leaders, working-class parents, and Labour Party leaders (Proctor, 2002). These groups considered Baden-Powell's pronouncements on national defence dangerous and felt that young people were being either directly or indirectly coerced into military service. Baden-Powell's military record (and that of many others associated with the movement) led to further suspicion as to his true motives (Wilkinson, 1969).

The question of whether Scouting was a quasi-military organisation is still disputed by historians today, with some arguing that Baden-Powell's motives were essentially military. Thus Hynes (1968) argues that Baden-Powell organised the Scout movement in order to prepare the next generation of British soldiers; while Rosenthal (1986: 226) wryly notes that *Scouting for Boys* 'must surely be the only handbook of peace Scouting that gives detailed advice on how to shoot a man'. However the military efficiency interpretation of scouting espoused by Springhall (1977; 1987), Rosenthal (1980; 1986) and others has been challenged, most notably by Jeal (2001) and Warren (1986). They argue that Scouting appealed to a diverse range of interests: some were concerned with the need for militaristic training, others with spiritual development, and still others with training for democratic citizenship. The movement was to become many things to many people, though critics often overlook this: 'whereas scholars have dwelled at great length upon the role of the militarists within the Movement, the role played by the philanthropists has been largely ignored' (Jeal, 2001: 414). Moreover the boys themselves could construct Scouting according to their own needs and interests, a point with which Springhall (1977) concurs.[4] While events such as the Boy Scout rally at Windsor Park in 1911 (at which the boys enthusiastically greeted the King) might be interpreted as a display of imperial sentiment, the boys themselves might not necessarily have experienced it in this way: to them it might simply have been 'the outing of a lifetime' (Jeal, 2001: 423).

Uniformed groups in Ireland

Several of the uniformed groups identified above spread to Ireland in the latter part of the nineteenth and early twentieth century, though their development was largely confined to the main cities or areas with a significant Protestant population. In 1888 the first Irish Boys' Brigade company was established in Belfast (Springhall et al., 1983). In the following years the organisation would expand rapidly in Ulster, thanks in part to the strong support of the Presbyterian churches. However the Brigade's presence in the rest of Ireland was confined mainly to Dublin, where the majority of companies were connected to the Church of

Ireland. Like their British counterparts, the Dublin Battalion also appears to have forged connections with the army. A booklet, produced to celebrate the twenty-first anniversary of the 1st Dublin company notes 'the great kindness and keen interest displayed by all officers of the Army who have been asked to act as Inspecting Officers or otherwise assist in the work'; the names of some of the most 'distinguished officers' are listed, including the Commander-in-Chief in Ireland (*The Boys' Brigade 1st Dublin Company (St. Matthias): Souvenir*, 1911: 2).

In 1908 the Boys Brigade (both in Ireland and Britain) faced a serious rival with the formation of the Boy Scouts. It is surely no coincidence that the Dublin Battalion's 1911–12 annual report refers, rather disparagingly, to unnamed 'newcomers, whose primary object is merely recreation or physical improvement' (Boys' Brigade Dublin Battalion *Annual Report 1911–12*: 1). Nonetheless figures for the Dublin Battalion suggest that the Boys' Brigade managed to hold its own in the city over the next few decades, with no major gains or losses (see Table 3.1). Although there are no remaining records of the socio-economic class of members of the Dublin Battalion, the annual reports suggest that those registered with the Brigade's Employment Agency included junior clerks, apprentices and assistants (Boys' Brigade Dublin Battalion *Annual Report 1908–9*). In the same report it is claimed that were it not for the BB summer camps, many of the boys would have enjoyed no holiday at all. Notwithstanding the obvious self-promotion, this comment suggests that the Brigade saw itself as catering for working-class boys whose parents would have been unable to afford a holiday.

Table 3.1 The Dublin Battalion of the Boys' Brigade, breakdown of membership

	1912	1922	1935
Companies	26	25	29
Officers	95	109	126
Staff-Sergeants	45	38	49
Non-commissioned officers		113	143
Warrant officers			20
Boys	870	831	747
Total	1,010	1,091	1,085

Source: Based on the *Annual Reports* of the Dublin Battalion for 1911–12, 1921–22 and 1934–35

As noted earlier, the Boys' Brigade led the way for other uniformed groups and by 1900 two of these (the Catholic Boys' Brigade and the Church Lads' Brigade) had branches in Dublin. *Dublin Charities* (Association of Charities,

1902: 248) describes the latter as 'semi-military, the boys of a parish being formed into companies, with commissioned and non-commissioned officers; the drill being strictly in accordance with the official infantry drill book'. The Church Lads' Brigade's programme of activities appears to have been remarkably similar to those provided by the Boys' Brigade, including physical drill, gymnastic, football, cricket and summer camps. In addition the organisation provided night schools, ambulance classes and social clubs. According to *Dublin Charities* (*ibid.*: 249) there were thirty-three companies in Ireland, 'as against 23 at the close of the last session'. The Catholic Boys Brigade (CBB), like other uniformed movements, emphasised its disciplinary role, having been formed 'to safeguard the rising generation from the evils and vices of the age, such as drinking, cursing, and evil-speaking; to encourage habits of obedience, discipline, and self-respect; and to promote the moral and physical welfare of the members' (*ibid.*: 248). To this end the CBB provided a range of activities (bands, night schools, gymnastic and dramatic classes) and claimed to help boys find employment. According to *Dublin Charities* (1902), between 700 and 800 boys were enrolled as members.

The Girls' Brigade is exceptional in that it actually started in Dublin and later spread to Ulster and England. The first company of the Girls' Brigade (GB) was formed in 1893 in the Sandymount Presbyterian Church, Dublin. Gradually other churches in the Dublin area followed. In the early years these companies appear to have operated independently of each other but in 1908 resolved 'to form a Central Organisation for work amongst girls in the city and County of Dublin' (Minutes of meeting 2/10/1908). The objective of the newly formed GB was identical to that of the Boys' Brigade (with the obvious exception of the words 'boys' and 'manhood'): 'The advancement of Christ's Kingdom among girls, and the promotion of habits of obedience, reverence, discipline and self-respect and all that leads towards a true Christian girlhood' (Girls' Brigade, 1983: 5). There were two main elements to the GB's work: religious education and physical fitness. Bible classes were held on a regular basis, underpinning the religious ethos of the organisation (*ibid.*: 5).[5] The Girls' Brigade was to remain a Dublin-based organisation until 1940 when a branch was opened at Enniskillen Presbyterian Church. Over the next twenty years membership in Northern Ireland would far outstrip that of Dublin (Girls' Brigade, 1983).

Scouting began in Ireland in 1908 and, like the Boys' Brigade, was most successful in Ulster and County Dublin. The movement was less evident in Munster and almost non-existent in Connaught (see Table 3.2). Clearly the development of uniformed groups in Ireland followed a particular pattern, which can perhaps be best explained by reference to the demographics, religion and nationalism of the time. While the origins of Irish youth movements are clearly rooted in nineteenth-century Britain, Ireland was very different to its industrialised neighbour and this would have consequences in terms of the development of these movements. The 1911 census indicates that the majority of the Irish population (57%) lived in rural areas; 6.1% in semi-urban areas; and 36% in urban areas (Curtis, 1996: 151). Even within the urban category there were comparatively few cities with more than 20,000 inhabitants. The three largest cities were Belfast (386,947) in the north, Dublin (398,235) in the east, and Cork (102,435) in the south-west. Demographics are important to a discussion of youth organisations because the majority of these organisations originated in cities and were in many respects a response to urban issues and problems. They were a means of controlling urban youth and keeping them 'safe' from the many temptations of the city. Ireland, however, had not had an Industrial Revolution and there were few urban centres. Given the demographics of Ireland in the nineteenth and early twentieth century it is not surprising that the cities and towns of Ulster (particularly Belfast), Dublin city and, to a lesser extent, Cork city became the strongholds of associational activity.

Another important factor in explaining the limited appeal of uniformed youth movements is the religious composition of Ireland at this time. British organisations were often Protestant in origin and so had a limited appeal in a country where the vast majority of the population were Catholic.[6] The Church Lads' Brigade, for example, was Anglican, a denomination which accounted for only 13.1% of the Irish population in 1911 (Curtis, 1996). Even the non-denominational Boy Scouts were often associated with Protestantism. Moreover the patriotic, imperialist and military overtones of the uniformed groups meant that they were often identified with the British ruling classes and the military. This not only limited their appeal but resulted in some groups (particularly the Scouts) becoming a focus for anti-British sentiment. These issues will now be explored, focusing on early Scouting history.

Table 3.2 Scouting membership in Ireland

Year	Ulster	Leinster	Munster	Connaught	Total for Ireland
1911	631	992	90	-	1713
1912	1319	919	247	20	2505
1913	1546	1064	293	-	2903
1922	4469	780	156	-	5405
1923	5034	751	108	-	5893
1924	5171	1060	44	3	6278
1925	5730	1158	63	2	6953
1926	5739	1191	34	2	6966

Source: figures shown here include both Boy Scouts and Cubs, and are derived from Boy Scout annual reports for the years shown.

Scouting in Ireland

In 1915 Baden-Powell acknowledged that 'Divided within itself by religious and political differences, Ireland has been a difficult field for the growth of our movement' (*Headquarters Gazette*, September 1915: 226). The objections to Scouting in Ireland were in many respects similar to those in Britain, particularly in relation to the movement's alleged militarism. But Ireland also presented a unique set of challenges for Scouting, in the form of a resurgent nationalism and long-standing divisions between the Catholic and Protestant populations. The first twenty years of the movement's existence were some of the most eventful in modern Irish history, including the outbreak of the First World War in 1914, the 1916 Rising, the War of Independence (1919–1921) and the Civil War (1922–1923). Baden-Powell claimed that Scouting was 'non-political, non-sectarian, non-class, [and] non-military' (*ibid.*: 226). However in Ireland, it came to be identified with 'a Protestant, Unionist and middle-class' minority (Gaughan, 2006: 16). There are three areas which are particularly important in understanding why the Scouts were perceived in this way: the leaders and religious affiliation; the alleged militarism of the scouts; and the rhetoric and symbolism of the movement.

Leadership and religious affiliation

The Scouting movement in Ireland was from the outset closely identified with the Anglo-Irish aristocracy, who provided camping facilities, assumed positions of leadership and even had troops named after them. Thus in 1911 the 3rd North Dublin troop became 'Lord Hompatrick's Own', while the 24th Dublin troop was named 'Pack-Beresford's Own' after a prominent County Carlow Anglo-Irish family (Gaughan, 2006). Of the movement's many titled patrons, the Earl of Meath was undoubtedly the most influential. Born in 1841 into the aristocracy of absentee Irish landlords, he served as a diplomat at British embassies in Frankfurt, Berlin and Paris. In 1912 he was appointed Boy Scouts' Chief Commissioner for Ireland. Meath's appointment to this post is particularly noteworthy because he was considered by his contemporaries to be an arch-imperialist, making him the subject of both praise and censure (see Springhall, 1970). In the early part of the twentieth century Meath embarked on a number of schemes to further the imperialist cause amongst young people including the Empire Day Movement.[7] This movement, Springhall suggests, was 'basically an imperial mutual admiration society' which campaigned for the celebration of Empire Day, particularly in schools.[8] Meath would later use his position as Chief Commissioner for Ireland to promote Empire Day amongst Irish Scouts.

As well as enjoying the patronage of the landed aristocracy, the Baden-Powell Scouts had close relations with the British forces in the country, with regard to leaders, facilities and rallies (Gaughan, 2006). One of the earliest troops was based at the Royal Hibernian Military School in Dublin, however this came to an abrupt end in 1922 when, following the formation of the new state, the school was closed and its staff transferred to England (Connell, undated: 72). The early troops in Cork also had military connections, consisting 'for the most part of sons of soldiers quartered there' (*Headquarters Gazette*, September 1915: 226). A report in the *Headquarters Gazette* (September 1915: 226) suggests that these troops were initially not popular with the local population, noting that 'their rally had to be carried on in private manner, out of the way of public criticism – and brickbats'. By 1915 Scouting seemed to have broadened its appeal, though ten years later the movement in Cork (and the province of Munster overall) had been substantially reduced (see Table 3.2), indicating the unstable foundations of Scouting outside Dublin and Ulster.

The Protestant churches also played an important role in providing meeting places and leadership: a list of the City and County of Dublin troops in 1917 indicates that at least eighteen out of the twenty-seven listed were based at Church of Ireland, Methodist or Presbyterian church halls, schools and (in one case) an orphanage (*Dublin Boy Scouts'*, 1917: 37).[9] Baden-Powell's reports on his visits to Ireland, and correspondence between the leaders, suggest that the movement was largely Protestant. As Scouting came to be associated with Protestantism, Roman Catholics were wary of joining. Thus religion became a significant obstacle to the development of Scouting in Ireland, as Baden-Powell reported in 1928:

> It should be remembered that the Protestants as well as the Roman Catholics are fanatical politicians. The Movement has been largely recruited among Protestants but some Roman Catholics are coming in inspite of the suspicions of it on the part of the priests, but lay RC have little influence with the hierarchy. (*Report to Imperial Headquarters by the Chief Scout*, 28 August 1928)

Mixed troops of Catholics and Protestants had been a failure, Baden-Powell reported in 1915, 'the religious antipathies being so strong between Irish boys' (*Report of Inspection Tour by the Chief Scout in Ireland*, August 1915: 2). He goes on to note that 'the ice had been broken' on the religious question by quietly getting Roman Catholics to start troops of their own. In 1927 it was even suggested (by some members of the Dublin Association) that separate *Associations* be formed under the respective direction of Catholic and Protestant Leaders. While Lord Powerscourt (Commissioner for Leinster) was angered by the idea of reorganising the movement on the basis of religious affiliation, Lord Meath took a more sanguine approach, appearing to think that it was almost impossible to get Catholics and Protestants to work together:

Although it is most annoying to find men so bigoted and narrow minded, all who have lived in Ireland know that Catholics and Protestants in that Country have never yet been able to live together in peace and amity, but have ever tried to obtain ascendancy in matters of religion and of politics. Of course we who desire peace should not relax our efforts in that direction, but I should not be astonished if ultimately it be found impossible to get the two religions to work together, and that Headquarters may ultimately find itself invited by both parties to form Sister Associations under the respective direction of Catholic and Protestant Leaders in connection with Imperial Head Quarters. (Letter from Meath to Lord Hampton, 27 January 1927)

Although this plan never came to fruition, the incident gives some indication of the difficulties and divisions over religion. While attempts were made to broaden the movement's appeal amongst the Catholic population, the perception that Scouting was both Protestant and pro-English would act as a deterrent to many Catholics. Powerscourt noted on several occasions that Scouting was 'looked upon as an English concern' and that 'the whole movement smacks of England' (Powerscourt to Meath 16 October 1923), a view which was shared by Lord Meath.[10] Although the Scouts were willing to make some concessions to Catholic and nationalist sentiments, there were limits to what they could do, without alienating their core supporters.

Scouting and militarism

Given the imperialist overtones of Scouting, and of the Earl of Meath in particular, it is not surprising that the movement stirred strong feelings in the nationalist community. Indeed the Baden-Powell Scouts appear to have been reviled by some of the most prominent nationalists of the time, including Patrick Pearse and Countess Markievicz. The suspicion that the Scouting movement was a covert means of providing future recruits for the British army, was cause for particular concern. An anti-enlistment campaign had been in existence in Ireland since the Boer War, attracting support from different nationalist groups (Benton, 1995; Denman, 1994). The alleged militarism of the Scouts was (as we saw earlier) criticised in Britain also, but had a particular significance in Ireland where the army had quashed a number of rebellions, one as recently as 1867. In Britain there was a sense that the Scouts might be preparing to fight *external* enemies (Boers, Germans etc.) but in Ireland there was also the possibility that they might be deployed on Irish soil, against Irish people. For some nationalists, then, Scouting represented a final capitulation to British rule and a betrayal of Irish history. It was in this spirit that Countess Markievicz described her feelings on reading an account in the *Irish Times* of a Boy Scout parade:

Reading this I realised vividly and suddenly that Ireland was being attacked at her most vital point, the minds of her children. The early impressions that a young mind receives become part of his subconscious self ... It was therefore horrible to me to read of regiments of little Irish boys learning to salute and to respect the flag that has been for so long the emblem of foreign rule, misery and oppression in Ireland ... I could see these children growing to manhood and gaily enlisting in the British army or Police forces, and being used either to batten their own class into submission in a class war at home or giving their lives in an Imperial war made to hold Ireland as slave State within the British Empire ...(*Eire*, 9 June 1923)

In one of the more ironic episodes of modern Irish history, Baden-Powell wrote to Patrick Pearse in 1909, inviting him to set up an Irish branch of the Boy Scouts. Baden-Powell would have been aware of Pearse's reputation as a headmaster and educationalist, hence the invitation. Pearse refused the invitation, declining 'to make potential British soldiers out of Irish boys' (cited in Sisson, 2004: 123). Pearse's comment appeared to reflect a more widespread suspicion of Baden-Powell's motives. Placards and leaflets were distributed in Dublin, warning the public that the Boy Scout movement was 'the latest recruiting device of England' (*The Irish Times*, 6 October 1910). Baden-Powell would defend Scouting in Ireland in much the same way that he had in Britain, claiming that the movement did not have military objectives but rather set out to control 'thoughtless' boys and turn them into productive adults who, 'instead of becoming loafers and drifting off to people other lands will make Ireland a rich and prosperous country' (*Headquarters Gazette*, June 1911: 2–3).

Regardless of whether Scouting did have military aims (the arguments for and against which were reviewed earlier) the movement was undoubtedly imperialist in sentiment, and this found frequent expression in Scouting publications and ritual.

Ritual and rhetoric of Scouting
Eric Hobsbawm (1983: 11) argues in *The Invention of Tradition* that a crucial part of British imperialism and patriotism involved the 'ritual occasions', practices and 'symbolically charged signs of club membership'. The youth of Britain and the empire were frequent targets of these symbols, Proctor (2002: 6) points out, as they were 'pictured as both the hope and the downfall of British imperial power in the early twentieth century'. The Scouting movement can certainly be understood within this framework of socialising young people to a certain idea of empire. On joining the movement boys pledged allegiance to the monarch; they participated in ceremonies such as 'Empire Day'; and they were on hand to greet the King at rallies in Dublin, Belfast, London and other cities. The movement's commitment to the British empire was most obvious at the discursive level as exemplified by *Scouting for Boys*, a publication which not only recalls how the empire was 'won', but also how it must be defended in the face

of national degeneracy and external threats. In Ireland, however, the rhetoric and ritual of Scouting conferred on its members a particular identity, which was at odds with the sense of national identity which other groups, such as Fianna Eireann, were constructing at the time (see Chapter 4).

During the Irish war of independence and the civil war the Scouting movement found itself in an increasingly precarious position, with activities suspended in many parts of the country.[11] Nonetheless Lord Meath regularly used Scouting publications to voice the movement's continued allegiance to king and empire. In 1920 *The Irish Scouts Gazette* reported that the Scouts and Cubs of the County Wicklow Association had held a rally to observe Empire Day. As part of the ceremony the troops and packs 'rallied round the Union Jack' and renewed their Scouting vow. A special message was read from Lord Meath, in which he explicitly linked Scouting and empire:

> I hope Scouts will always look on 'Empire Day' as one of the most important days which, as Scouts, they should annually observe. Let us on 'Empire Day' unite the mottoes of the Scouts and of the Empire Movement, 'Be Prepared!' and cheer for 'One King', 'One Flag', 'One Fleet', 'One Empire'. (*The Irish Scouts Gazette*, June 1920: 4)

In May of the following year Meath wrote to remind readers of the upcoming 'Empire Day', encouraging all those connected with Scouting in Ireland to commemorate the day. To help them do so, 'an empire cathecism' was provided, consisting of twenty-four questions, mainly on the empire and the monarchy. Despite the fact that Ireland was still engaged in a war of independence, Meath's cathecism locates the Scout firmly within the empire, owing his loyalty to the King and to his 'fellow-subjects of the King-Emperor':

> *Query*— What is your relation to the British Empire?
> *Answer*— I am a subject of King George V. and a citizen of the British Empire.
> *Q*— What are the duties of a citizen of the British Empire?
> *A*— To be a loyal friend of all fellow-subjects of the King-Emperor; so to live as never to bring reproach by word or deed on the Empire of which he is a citizen. To prepare himself by every means in his power to advance the welfare of his fellow-citizens, whether in peace or war, whatever may be their class, creed, or colour. (*The Irish Scouts Gazette*, May 1921: 2–3)

Meath's emphasis on imperial fellowship ('fellow-subjects', 'fellow-citizens') and on unity ('whatever may be their class, creed, or colour') is reminiscent of Baden-Powell's encouragement to British boys to unite and 'sink your differences'. Elsewhere in the same publication Meath sends an 'Empire Day Message', emphasising the internationalism and 'brotherhood' of scouting. His words indicate the Scouts' beleaguered status in Ireland at this time: 'it is most important in these troubled times that we should support and strengthen ourselves and each other by the remembrance of the solemn promises we all took when we entered our world-wide organisation and by renewing our vows in the presence of each other'. Although he is addressing the Scouts, Meath could be referring more generally to the precarious position of all those who remained loyal to the crown at this time. The message ends on a positive note, reporting Baden-Powell's 'distant travels', during which he met with 'our brother Scouts and sister Guides'. This idea of common bonds, regardless of country, was central to Scout and Guide philosophy in the 1920s and 1930s though, as Alexander (2009) has argued, the Scouting vision of 'a familial imperial internationalism' often obscured inequalities between countries.

In the same issue Meath commemorates those who died in the First World War, noting that 'the 'Union Jack,' which our enemies desired to trample in the dust, has emerged victoriously from the struggle, covered by fresh wreaths of honour and glory' (*The Irish Scouts Gazette*, May 1921). Later that year he reports on the King and Queen's visit to Belfast, to open the new Parliament in Ulster. In the following passage from that report Meath attempts to reconcile Scouting's claim to be non-political with his enthusiastic support for the monarchy and for Ireland's continued links (in some form) to Britain:

> As Scouts we have nought to do with politics, but, mindful of our promise and of our Scout law, we rejoice over the tempest of enthusiastic loyalty which greeted our beloved Sovereigns during their visit to the new Parliament of Ulster. May it not be long before Their Majesties open a similar Parliament in the capital of Ireland, and receive an even more enthusiastic welcome from the responsive hearts of Southern Irishmen! We may, indeed, then hope that peace, prosperity, and happiness shall reign over our dear country ... and we shall all be able with one voice to cry 'Long live Ireland! Long live Their Majesties, the King and Queen of Ireland!' (*The Irish Scouts Gazette*, July–August 1921: 1)

Meath's various pronouncements may not, of course, have represented the range of views from different sections of the movement at this time. Private correspondence between Powerscourt, Meath and Baden-Powell indicate that there were internal divisions, based on the issue of where the Scouting movement's loyalties should lie. In a letter to Meath (16 October 1923) Powerscourt outlined the quandary which scouting faced following the formation of the Irish Free State:

> The Scouts that exist at present are strictly divided into two camps. One all for the Free State and for nationalising the movement into something really Irish and at the same time respectable. The others are violently 'Union Jack' and nothing else,

which to my mind is a quite hopeless policy if the movement is going to extend at all. This is all very fine, but if I move as seems to me necessary, I automatically shatter our nucleus from top to bottom and a very large proportion, say about one third, will resign. Now if I was sure that the Catholics will come in when we have nationalised it, I would not hesitate, but the whole movement smacks of England and will always, I fear in the minds of most, hence the extreme improbability of making that a success.

Powerscourt's fears that the movement might split proved unfounded. Ultimately their policy during this period was to 'go on as before' and maintain a low profile for fear of antagonising republican opinion (Letter from Powerscourt to Meath 27 October 1923).[12] The Scouts did make some efforts to court Catholic favour, for example by inviting prominent Catholics to take the review of the annual rallies of the Dublin City and county Scouts (Gaughan, 2006: 17). However the formation of the Catholic Boy Scouts of Ireland (CBSI) in 1926–1927 was seen as a serious challenge to efforts to encourage more Catholics to join the Baden-Powell Scouts. Moreover the Baden-Powell Scouts continued to be seen as pro-English and pro-monarchy, a fact which the CBSI were able to use in promoting their own movement.

While some voices were raised at grassroots level on the need to meet nationalist sentiment, Gaughan (2006) argues, there was little enthusiasm for this at Scouting headquarters. The Scouting promise of allegiance to the King would prove particularly controversial. According to Scouting law, each boy on joining the movement must pledge allegiance to the king. There were some who felt that this should be changed to 'country', while others thought that there was no need for alteration as, according to the Constitution of the State, the King was head of the British Commonwealth of which the Irish Free State was a member. The issue of the promise came to a head in 1937 when it was debated at length by the Executive Committee, consequent to the refusal of a parent to allow his son to take the 'promise' as it stood. On this occasion, and again in 1939, the call for change was rejected. However by 1941 many Scout leaders wished to have the wording altered. Lord Powerscourt intervened and stated that the matter should not be submitted to the Eire Scout Council, that the country was still a part of the British Commonwealth of Nations and that a change would alienate the support of people who had helped to maintain the movement in the country (Gaughan, 2006: 22). It was not until the 1950s – after Ireland's link with Britain and the Commonwealth had been severed – that the pledge of allegiance to the King was finally dropped for Irish Scouts.

Nationalism would become an issue for the Boy Scout and Girl Guide movements in other countries, the 'promise' again proving to be particularly contentious. Afrikaans Scouts in South Africa, for example, did not want to pledge allegiance to the British king (Proctor, 2002). Similarly in 1928 students at the Brahmo Girls School in Calcutta refused to make the Guide promise of loyalty to the King-Emperor (Alexander, 2009: 51). Tensions also arose as a result of religious differences, particularly in countries with 'nonhomogenous populations' including the United States, the Caribbean and British/French colonies (Proctor, 2002: 144). In Canada, like Ireland, distinctions between Catholics and Protestants were of paramount importance because of the political resonance of religious identities. Religion was tied to culture, politics and language, Proctor notes, and so separate Scout and Guide groups were the norm. Similarly in Malta, where Guiding began in 1918, trouble arose between the Maltese Roman Catholics and the English Protestants; eventually two divisions were formed that reflected the religious and racial division of that country (ibid.). In other countries – particularly South Africa and the southern states of America – race and colour would become divisive issues for the Scouting movement (Jeal, 2001). Far from being a unifying force in these countries, Scouting often reflected or helped to solidify existing divisions based on race, colour, religion and politics.

Conclusion

The uniformed youth movements which developed in the last decades of the nineteenth and first of the twentieth century were hugely popular with young people of both genders: the Scout and Guide movements, as noted earlier, began almost spontaneously as a response to the publication of *Scouting for Boys*. In the course of this chapter we have, however, focused on the motivation of the *adult* leaders and patrons of these movements. Organisations like the Boys' Brigade and the Boy Scouts enjoyed the support of some of the most influential groups in society, including industrialists, land owners, church leaders and the military establishment. For these patrons, youth movements represented a form of social control, providing 'wholesome' activities and teaching habits of duty, discipline and obedience. Moreover these organisations warned young people of the dangers of trade unionism, socialism and communism, encouraging them instead to be 'level headed and British' (Dublin Boy Scouts' *Annual Handbook*, 1919: 10). The origins of the youth movements must also be understood within the context of a growing crisis of masculinity, with some fearing that British men were no longer up to the task of defending the empire or maintaining Britain's industrial competitiveness. A number of contemporary commentators (as well as later historians) argued that the Boy Scouts went beyond developing 'manly' attributes, and were in fact preparing the soldiers of the future. While there is much in Scouting literature to suggest that the movement was concerned with social regulation and military preparedness, there were also a number of internal contradictions. For example, while Baden-Powell emphasised the disciplinary aspects of the Scouts and Guides, the hikes and camping trips provided young people (particularly girls) with a previously unknown amount of freedom. Moreover the movement enjoyed the support of a wide range of people including educationalists and philanthropists. Scouting was in some respects a rather mercurial movement, as Jeal (2001) has noted, it transcended the intentions of its founder from the earliest days and came to have different meanings for different groups.

The Scouts and Guides were also, Proctor argues, 'identity-forming institutions'. In Ireland they came to be associated with Protestantism and imperialism. While Baden-Powell maintained that Scouting was for everyone (regardless of class, creed or politics) Powerscourt's comment that 'the whole movement smacks of England', clearly indicates that it had not acted as a great leveller or unifier. On the contrary the Scouts became a target for anti-British sentiment, attracting criticism from some of the most prominent nationalists of the time. Moreover the perception that the Boy Scouts was a Protestant organisation aroused the suspicions of the Catholic Church and alienated much of the Catholic population. Ireland's experience of Scouting was not unique. Similar issues arose in other parts of the empire, where the Scout and Guide movements often reflected, or even helped to reinforce, existing divisions based on race, colour, religion and politics.

Notes

1 The annual reports of the Dublin Battalion provide a glimpse of the range of activities on offer to members. These included drill meetings, company Bible classes, ambulance classes, athletic and swimming clubs, instrument bands, various classes (shorthand, writing, wood-carving, etc.), 'boys' rooms', employment agencies and summer camps (Dublin Battalion *Annual Report* 1908–09).
2 The link between the Girls' Brigade and their brother organisation is clear from existing records. It was decided to 'adopt the scheme of the Boys' Brigade so far as applicable to girls'; help in training and assessment of standards was initially provided by officers of the Boys' Brigade (Girls' Brigade, 1983: 5); and the wording of the two organisations' objectives was virtually the same.
3 The connection between gender and religion in the nineteenth century is important, though it is not possible to consider this in detail here. Obelkevich (1990: 341) argues that religion 'was much less 'feminised' (or demasculinsed) in Britain than in some Catholic districts on the Continent, where no self-respecting man set foot in a church'. However, within the British working classes (who made up a large part of the Boys' Brigades' membership) it was generally the wife who attended chapel; the gender gap was narrower in the middle and upper classes where it was expected that husband and wife would attend church as a couple. Although men controlled the churches both nationally and locally, women were the majority in most congregations. The perceived link between religion and femininity, which is implied in

Smith's words, may therefore be based partly on the differing levels of participation by women and men in the church at this time.

4   Many of the surviving reports on Scouting offer the point of view of those in author-ity rather than that of the boys themselves. Over-reliance upon these materials have, Springhall suggests, 'tended to conceal the more evasive and often potentially sub-versive methods that boys could adopt to deflect and undermine well-meaning, if maladroit, middle-class attempts to maintain order and discipline in a youth move-ment. It oversimplifies an undoubtedly much more complex relationship to assume that the membership received the doctrines of its adult leadership quite passively without first transmuting their "message" through an adolescent's set of cultural as-sumptions derived from social class and normative reference groups' (Springhall, 1977: 122). Scoutmasters also interpreted Scouting in their own way.

5   Press reports at the time suggest that there were other clubs and classes providing physical instruction for girls. The Dublin Working Girls' Drill Association ap-peared in various reports on drill and gymnastic competitions (*Weekly Irish Times*, 4 May 1907; 23 May 1914). In 1907 the Dublin Ladies' Physical Culture Society was formed and was, according to the *Irish Times*, 'composed mostly of young ladies engaged during the day in the various business houses throughout the city' (*Weekly Irish Times*, 4 May 1907: 23). In 1910, under the auspices of the National Physical Recreation Society, teams composed of working girls competed in drill exercises (*Irish Times*, 22 April 1910: 4). Some of the drill classes which existed before 1908 appear to have been amalgamated into the Girls' Brigade when the central organisa-tion was formed (Girls' Brigade, 1983: 4).

6   According to the census of 1911, 73.9% of the population were Roman Catholic, 13.1 were Church of Ireland, 10% were Presbyterian, 1.4% were Methodist, with the remaining 1.5% made up of other denominations (Curtis, 1996: 146).

7   Meath founded the Lads' Drill Association which 'attempted to arouse the British nation to the serious nature of the problem of Imperial Defence' and advocated 'the systematic physical and military training of all British lads, and their instruction in the use of the rifle' (Meath cited in Springhall, 1970: 101). In addition he cam-paigned for military training in schools and was involved in the Duty and Discipline Movement. The objects of the Duty and Discipline Movement were stated as being to 'combat softness, slackness, indifference and indiscipline and to stimulate dis-cipline and a sense of duty and alertness throughout the national life, especially during the formative period of home and school training …' (cited in Springhall, 1970: 104).

8   In 1908 the House of Commons turned down a proposal for official recognition of Empire Day, the announcement 'being received with loud Irish Nationalist and Labour cheers' (Springhall, 1970: 105).

9   In some instances no address is given for the troop or it is unclear from the address where they were based.

10 In a letter from Meath to Green (18 November 1922) he notes that 'The real objec-tion to the Scouts in the minds of both Free Staters and Republicans, as well as those of the reforming Scouts themselves, is, as Powerscourt says in his letter, 'that at present the movement is looked upon as an English concern'.

11 Meath's correspondence during the 1920s often refers to the precarious nature of the Scouting movement. In a letter to Lord Hampton (27 January 1927), for example, he describes the position of the Scout Movement in the Free State as 'one of very delicate character', going on to note that 'any unwise action might easily lead to an explosion and wreck the Movement'.

12 This policy seems to have been pursued partly because of advice given by William Cosgrave, with whom the Scouts appear to have had good relations (Letter from Meath to Powerscourt, 29 October 1923).

4

Building national identity: youth movements and nationalism in twentieth-century Ireland

> It is to the young that a nation must look for help; for life itself – and this is our message to those who are young in Ireland to-day. Ireland wants you, Ireland is calling you. Join Na Fianna Eireann, the young army of Ireland, and help to place the crown of freedom on Her head. (Countess Markievicz, 'Introduction', *Fianna Handbook*, 1914: 8)

> No single political doctrine has played a more prominent role in shaping the face of the modern world than nationalism. Millions of people around the world have willingly laid down their lives for their 'fatherlands' and this almost ritualistic mass self-sacrifice continues unabated. (Ozkirimli, 2000: 1)

From the late eighteenth century nationalism became a powerful political ideology, with nationalist movements emerging in countries across Europe. In Ireland there were failed rebellions against British rule in 1798, 1848 and 1867. By the latter part of the nineteenth century the Irish Parliamentary Party had become the dominant force in Irish political life, its energies centred on persuading the British government to grant Home Rule (Ward, 1983). However in the 1890s the party disintegrated into factions, following the very public scandal which engulfed their leader, Charles Stewart Parnell, over his affair with a married woman. Disillusioned by the 'seamier side of politics', a new generation of Irish people would turn their energies into regenerating a national identity that had almost been destroyed by the increasing anglicisation of Irish society (Lyons, 1973; Ward, 1983: 40). A range of associations and societies – most notably the Gaelic League and the Gaelic Athletic Association – were formed in the latter part of the century as part of the Celtic Revival. Children and young people were seen as central to the success of this revival and to the assertion of a distinctly Irish identity. As Condon (2000: 168) has pointed out: 'nationalists and loyalists competed for the control of the cultural allegiances of Irish children because they were primarily perceived and valued in the generational sense of their being the 'future citizens' of the State, or the 'Irish nation of the future''. Some of the most prominent nationalist leaders and commentators of the period – Patrick Pearse, Countess Markievicz, Arthur Griffith, Maud Gonne and Bulmer Hobson – were critical of an anglicised educational system and popular culture, and set out to provide nationalist alternatives. This Gaelicisation was partly to be achieved through movements such as the Gaelic Athletic Association (GAA) and the Gaelic League, but also through organisations which were targeted specifically at children and young people.

In the course of this chapter we will consider two of these nationalist organisations: Inghinidhe na hEireann and Fianna Eireann. Both set out to engender a sense of national identity through the promotion of the Irish language, history and mythology, and other traditions which were held to be distinctly Irish. Despite its fervent nationalism, we shall argue, Fianna Eireann had much in common with the imperialist Baden-Powell Scouts (see Chapter 3). In the final part of this chapter we will consider another nationalist movement, the Blueshirts, which was open to all Irish people but had a special appeal to the young. Although the Blueshirts was formed in post-independence Ireland, the project of fostering national identity and unity was still important in the fragile and divided Free State. While the Blueshirts had some features in common with European fascist movements – extreme nationalism, appeal to youth, preoccupation with physical fitness and 'manliness' – they also drew on earlier nationalist and imperial discourses.

Constructing Irish national identity

Before considering the means by which Irish identity was constructed it is important to distinguish between two broad approaches to understanding the concept of nationhood, one favoured by nationalists themselves and the other by scholars of nationalism. Nationalists often believe that their nation is something natural and eternal: 'it has always been there in one form or another' (Kornprobst, 2005: 404). On the other hand, there is a broad consensus in the scholarly community that nations are constructed or 'invented' (*ibid.*: 405). One of the most influential exponents of this theory has been Benedict Anderson (1991: 6–7) who suggests that the nation is an 'imagined political community':

> It is *imagined* because the members of even the smallest nation will never know most of their fellow-members, meet them, or even hear of them, yet in the minds of each lives the image of their communion ... it is imagined as a *community*, because, regardless of the actual inequality and exploitation that may prevail in each, the nation is always conceived as a deep, horizontal comradeship. Ultimately it is this fraternity that makes it possible, over the past two centuries, for so many millions of people, not so much to kill, as willingly to die for such limited imaginings.

Studies of Irish nationalism have identified three important processes by which national identity was constructed or 'imagined' in the nineteenth and twentieth century: the promulgation of Irish history and mythology, the revival of Irish language (and a consequent idealisation of the Irish-speaking West) and the popularisation of Irish sports. Nationalists hoped that by 'rediscovering' their ancient history the people, particularly the young, would be brought to a new awareness of themselves as 'Irish' and as heirs to a noble heritage. The notion of a glorious past (or 'golden age') has an important purpose in nationalist discourse, Coakley (2004) argues, as it inspires a sense of national pride and solidarity in the present, and provides an impetus for future action. Irish nationalists of the late nineteenth and early twentieth century derived comfort and inspiration from Irish mythology (particularly the epic tales of the warriors Cuchulain, Fionn MacCumhail and the Fianna); from the achievements of early Christian Ireland; and from various 'myths of struggle' against external rule (Coakley 2004; Smith 1997).[1] These accounts of past greatness and heroic struggle would provide much needed strength and inspiration at a time when Irish independence seemed more illusive than ever. Nationalist accounts of Irish history were made increasingly available to children when writers and educators began to perceive that children's culture was 'a crucial territory to be repossessed for the nationalist cause' (Condon, 2000: 176). Inghinidhe na hEireann and Fianna Eireann (who were named after the ancient Fianna) would also play a part in nationalising the youth of Ireland, through the teaching of history, mythology and the Irish language.

The saliency of language to issues of national identity came to the fore in nineteenth-century European nation-building. Inspired by the Romantic movement, language came to be seen as 'an expression of both individual and collective identity' (Johnson 1997: 177). However the Irish language had been on the decline throughout the nineteenth century, due to famine, emigration and a system of primary education modelled on that of England (Lyons, 1973). Various language preservation societies were formed in the latter part of the century but the real push towards a revival occurred with the founding of the Gaelic League in 1893. Branches of this organisation were set up throughout the country providing classes in the Irish language for adults and children. By 1902 it had succeeded in introducing the teaching of Irish into 13,000 national schools (Ward, 1983: 41). The League officially professed that it was both a non-sectarian and non-political organisation, and many Ulster Protestants were among its members. Nonetheless, by raising popular consciousness about the Irish language, the League provided further impetus for the Irish independence movement. As harbingers of cultural nationalism, Johnson (1997: 180) notes, the Gaelic League and the Literary Revival 'both played significant roles in articulating an Irish 'imagined community' and in allowing the [native-speaking] West of Ireland to act as synecdoche of Irish identity'.[2] The battle to revive the language entered a new phase during the 1920s and 1930s when successive governments made Irish a fundamental part of the primary school curriculum. Children and young people were central to the new state's plans for the promotion of national solidarity and identity through the teaching of Irish language and history.

The revival of Gaelic sports was another central feature of the construction of national identity (particularly male identity) in the late nineteenth and twentieth century. The Gaelic Athletic Association (GAA) was founded by Michael Cusack in 1884 to increase access to sport, particularly for working-class and labouring men, and to encourage the playing of games which were held to be traditionally Irish (Sisson, 2004). After a turbulent start, the organisation spread throughout the country, benefitting from its close links with the Gaelic League. Sport was seen as important to the nationalist cause for a number of reasons. First, it provided a sense of cultural unity and an all-important connection with Ireland's past. The game of hurling was held in particular esteem as it linked to an ancient and aristocratic sporting tradition: Cuchulain himself had famously played the game. Second, the revival of Gaelic games provided an alternative to 'imperial' sports, such as cricket, which were encouraged by local gentry and patronised by members of the community loyal to the Crown (Sisson, 2004). Finally, sports were important for building physical strength in young men and promoting values associated with masculinity: competitiveness, team spirit, endurance and courage. A preoccupation with masculinity and a belief in the redemptive power of sport was, of course, a feature of late Victorian/Edwardian thought (see Chapter 3). Ironically, Sisson notes, the motivating force behind the foundation of the GAA owed much to imperial discourses on the moral and physical health of men. From the outset the GAA 'successfully mapped an imperialist sporting ethos onto a nationalist model' (*ibid.*: 115).

While Baden-Powell attributed the perceived decline in masculinity of British men to urbanisation and 'over-civilisation', Irish nationalists had reasons of their own to be anxious about physical and moral degeneration. It was feared that Irish men had been emasculated by centuries of British rule and had internalised a form of self-hatred. Moreover the 'Irish-Irelanders' argued that certain aspects of the Celtic revival, and of Victorian literature on Celticism, had further exacerbated this process, producing an image of the 'enervated, emotional, feminized Celt' (Sisson, 2004: 11).[3] Prominent nationalists such as Patrick Pearse and D.P. Moran would search for more robust models of Celtic masculinity, often finding them in bardic and pagan Ireland. The discourse of manliness would find its way into the speeches, letters and publications of a number of nationalist organisations in the late nineteenth and early twentieth century (Benton, 1995: 152). However as the nationalist movement became increasingly militarised after 1910 notions of manliness would be associated more and more with armed struggle. The ultimate assertion of manhood was the blood sacrifice, a view which Patrick Pearse famously articulated: 'bloodshed is a cleansing and a sanctifying thing and the nation which regards it as the final horror has lost its manhood' (cited in Benton, 1995: 155).

This section has considered the construction of national identity, focusing on Irish history, language and sport, though undoubtedly there were other cultural forms (including music and literature) which were also important (see Lyons, 1973). While organisations like the GAA and the Gaelic League spearheaded the Celtic revival of the late nineteenth century, smaller groups – such as Inghinidhe na hEireann – would also play a role. This society not only promoted the study of the Irish language and history, but also attempted to counteract 'anglicising' influences in Irish society, particularly those targeted at children.

Inghinidhe na hEireann (Daughters of Ireland)

The origins of Inghinidhe na hEireann can be traced to a committee of women formed at Easter 1900 to organise a children's event, known as the 'Patriotic Children's Treat' (Ward, 1983). This event was effectively a response to an earlier 'treat' provided during Queen Victoria's 1900 visit to Ireland. The work of the committee, and the controversial royal visit which preceded it, are worth recalling here as they illustrate how children's culture was politicised during the late nineteenth and early twentieth century. A seemingly innocuous event became the focus for a struggle between competing identities, one imperial and the other nationalist.

In April 1900 Queen Victoria, after an absence of almost forty years, paid a three-week visit to Ireland. Her arrival was greeted with hostility amongst members of the nationalist community who saw the visit as politically motivated and designed to boost the ranks of the British army. Nationalist opinion was particularly incensed by one aspect of the royal programme of events – a 'treat' organised for thousands of Irish children. According to an article published in the *United Irishman* (and probably written by Arthur Griffith) there was 'no more regrettable feature' of the royal visit than 'the exploiting of the children of our city and country to swell the chorus of interested enthusiasm which the toadies had succeeded in arousing' (cited in Condon, 2000: 173). The author goes on to assert that 'many of the children were too young to understand the nature of what was asked of them, for, thanks to our glorious system of National education, they are as ignorant of their country and its needs as any government official'. Inghinidhe na hEireann would later publish an equally disparaging account of the event:

On the occasion of Queen Victoria's last visit to Ireland, the flunkeys and place-hunters of Dublin, unable to get up any popular demonstration of welcome for her, tried to make use of the innocent children, and in the English Queen's name, invited all the School Children of Ireland to attend a demonstration in the

Phoenix Park ... To the credit of our brave little ones let it be said, they resisted the inducements of cakes, sweets, and oranges held out by the jingo proselytisers, and of the 35,000 children on the attendance rolls of the Dublin Schools, only 5,000 allowed themselves to be dragged to the Phoenix Park and paraded before the English Queen; and these 5,000 children were mostly from the Union or Workhouse Schools, Masonic Schools, and such institutions where the children had no choice in the matter. (Inghinidhe na hEireann *First Annual Report* 1900–1901: 2)

A committee of nationalist women, led by Maud Gonne, was formed to organise an event of their own. The Patriotic Children's Treat which was held in Clonturk Park on 1 July 1900 was, Condon (2000) argues, a decidedly political and counter-hegemonic gesture. On arriving at the park, after a procession through the city, the children received sweets and other refreshments, and participated in various amusements and games, a hurling match being one of the highlights of the day. However the primary motivation for the day was 'nationalist edification', and the children were also 'treated' to some lessons in nationalism which were delivered by Gonne and the Reverend Fr. Kavanagh PP (*ibid.*: 175). In addition children were given copies of a nationalist, anti-conscription pamphlet which instructed them on the nature of patriotism. Subsequent police intelligence reports wryly noted that the children 'were treated to moderate refreshments and unlimited treason' (cited in Denman, 1994: 227). While this event was clearly intended as a nationalist response to Queen Victoria's visit, it can also be seen as part of a wider nationalist campaign to counter-act the anglicising influences of school and popular culture, and to build a distinctly Irish sense of identity. These concerns were carried over into Inghinidhe na hEireann which held its inaugural meeting in October 1900, with Maud Gonne as President. The new society's founders were mainly members of the Irish Classes connected with the Celtic Literary Society. The principal objects of Inghinidhe na hEireann were 'to encourage the study of Gaelic, of Irish Literature, History, Music and Art' and to 'discourage the reading and circulation of low English literature, the singing of English songs, the attending of vulgar English entertainments ... and to combat in every way English influences' (*First Annual Report* 1900–1901: 1–2). The society was also pledged to support and popularise Irish manufacturers.

Much of the new society's efforts were directed towards the education of children and the provision of cultural activities. Classes were held for the teaching of Irish, history, singing and drill (*ibid.*: 3). Ward (1983) notes that these classes were very popular, partly due to the fact that they were able to call on the services of a large number of talented people. The poet Ella Young, for example, agreed to teach history by retelling the sagas and hero tales. Moreover the children's education sometimes extended beyond the classroom. At Christmas the Society organised a 'treat' which, like its predecessor, incorporated historic and contemporary themes including 'Magic Lantern Views of Irish Historical

Subjects' and 'scenes from the Boer War, explained by Miss Gonne' (*First Annual Report* 1900–1901: 3). Commemorative events were organised including a trip to the grave of Wolfe Tone, leader of the 1798 Rebellion. In their account of this trip, Inghinidhe na hEireann combine several issues which were close to their heart, including the commemoration of Irish heroes, the revival of the Irish language, hostility to the British army and support for the Boers:

> On Sunday, June 23rd, forty of the children attending the Irish Classes, who had the best record for attendance and application to their studies, were taken to Bodestown to visit the grave of Wolfe Tone … They sang Irish songs and talked in Irish to the great delight of the people along the roads who received them most cordially. The children carried Irish flags and Boer flags and loudly booed and hissed every English soldier they passed. They arrived back at Abbey Street at 8.30 p.m., having had a very pleasant day. (*ibid.*: 7)

As part of their aim of reviving Irish traditions, and providing an alternative to 'vulgar English entertainments', the society instituted monthly *ceilidhes* (dances), at which papers on Celtic heroines were read. The form of entertainment prevalent in Dublin at the turn of the century, Ward (1983: 55) notes, infuriated many nationalists, being wholly British in character and consisting mainly of 'music hall frolics'. Consequently Inghinidhe na hEireann supported W.B. Yeats in his bid to establish an Irish theatre which would both 'form a new identity for Irish people and provide the impetus for a new generation of Irish writers' (*ibid.*). Members of the society participated in various dramatic productions, which led to the formation of a professional theatre group, out of which came the Abbey Theatre.

    While education and support for the Celtic Revival were key aspects of the society's work, members were also involved in more overtly political issues, including the anti-recruitment campaign and open support for the Boers in their conflict with British forces in South Africa.[4] In addition all the children attending Inghinidhe na hEireann classes and entertainments were pledged never to enlist in the 'English' army or navy (*First Annual Report* 1900–1901: 4).

    Although Inghinidhe na hEireann was relatively short-lived (by 1910 the Society was effectively a spent force) it was nonetheless significant for a number of reasons. Firstly it formed part of the Celtic revival of the early twentieth century, which was of vital importance to the nationalist cause in helping to build a distinctly Irish identity. Secondly the society recognised the importance of targeting children and young people as the future citizens of the State or the 'Irish nation of the future' (Condon, 2000: 168). And finally the society provided women with the opportunity to become involved in nationalist politics, an arena from which they were largely excluded. Moving into the second decade of the twentieth century, however, nationalist politics became increasingly militarised, further limiting the scope for female involvement (Benton, 1995). It was within this context that another nationalist youth movement, Fianna Eireann, was formed.

Origins and objectives of Fianna Eireann

Founded in 1909, Fianna Eireann was a uniformed youth movement which provided training in scouting and military exercises, Irish history and the Irish language (*Fianna Handbook*, 1914). Membership was open to all boys, 'no matter what class or creed or party they or their fathers belong to' (*ibid.*: 23). The Fianna, or National Boy Scouts, was the outcome of a collaboration between Countess Markievicz and Bulmer Hobson, both staunch republicans. In 1902 Hobson had formed a rudimentary boys' movement in Belfast, also called Na Fianna Eireann, mainly to promote hurling and the Irish language (Lyons, 1973). After a promising start the organisation ran into difficulties, largely due to lack of funding and Hobson's various other commitments (Hobson, 1968). Seven years after the original Belfast Fianna had been formed, Hobson mentioned his venture to Countess Markievicz, who suggested that they start a national organisation to train boys to work for the independence of Ireland. Markievicz hired a hall at 34 Lower Camden Street, Dublin and about one hundred boys turned up to an inaugural meeting in August 1909 (Lyons, 1973). However her presence at the meeting was not universally welcomed, reflecting a more general antipathy to women's involvement in nationalist politics at this time. Hobson (1968: 16) later recalled that 'When the election of officers was taking place at the meeting, there was a certain reluctance among the boys about the election of the Countess to office, on the grounds that she was a woman, and I had on many occasions to point out privately that they could not accept her financial help and refuse her membership or office.' The organisation was even more reluctant to admit girls as members, although a girls' branch was formed in Belfast (Hay, 2008).[5]

During the first seven years of its existence, Fianna Eireann developed branches in at least nineteen Irish counties – mainly in the cities and larger towns of Leinster, Munster and Ulster – as well as Glasgow and Liverpool (Hay, 2008). Although it was named after the mythical warriors of pagan Ireland, the Fianna owed much to the late Victorian/Edwardian uniformed groups, particularly the Boy Scouts. Both organisations shared a concern for the physical fitness and moral character of boys, which was in turn part of a more general preoccupation with 'manliness' at the time. Many of the qualities or attributes which the Fianna claimed to instil – self-reliance, self-respect, obedience, thoughtfulness, independence, self-sacrifice, service to country and good citizenship – are almost identical to those claimed by the Baden-Powell Scouts (*Fianna Handbook*, 1914: 23–24). Fianna boys participated in elementary drill and route marching, and learned signalling, first aid and various scouting skills. The instructional content of the *Fianna Handbook* (which included camping, outdoor cooking, knot-tying and survival techniques) differed little from contemporary manuals used by the Boy Scouts. Like the GAA before them, the Fianna appear to have adapted imperial forms for nationalist ends (Sisson, 2004). Indeed Markievicz claimed that the inspiration to form a youth movement came to her after reading in the paper of a march of Scouts and brigades through Dublin (see Chapter 3). While she was repelled by the idea of Irish boys being indoctrinated into imperialism, she had no qualms about forming a similar group of her own, for nationalist purposes. Like Baden-Powell, Markievicz believed that character and allegiances are formed in youth: 'The grown person is moral or unmoral according to the emotions and principles that moved his youth ... The same love of country and the same respect for laws and rulers inspire him as those which inspired the people amongst whom he grew up and the teachers by whom his impressionable mind was first cultivated' (*Eire*, 9 June 1923). It was therefore seen as imperative for nationalists to secure the allegiance of boys from an early age.

While there were some similarities with the Boy Scouts, Fianna Eireann was formed with a much more military and ideological agenda than its British counterpart. Each boy, on joining, promised 'to work for the independence of Ireland [and] never to join England's armed forces' (*Fianna Handbook*, 1914: 167).[6] Fianna Eireann's object was 'to re-establish the independence of Ireland' by means of 'the training of the youth of Ireland, mentally and physically' (*ibid.*: 167). The training referred to here was partly military and each boy was encouraged 'to become so proficient that when Ireland needs soldiers he can take an important place in the fighting line' (*ibid.*: 15). Thus while Baden-Powell consistently denied that the Scouting movement was intended to produce future soldiers (see Chapter 3), Fianna Eireann openly claimed this as one of their objectives. Moreover the language of war, militarism and martyrdom pervades Fianna Eireann texts. In the introduction to the *Fianna Handbook*, for example, Countess Markievicz describes the organisation as an 'army of young people', whose path to freedom may lead them 'the same road that Robert Emmet and Wolfe Tone trod' (*ibid.*: 6, 8). Even if they should die their 'self-sacrifice' would not be in vain because it 'keeps the spirit of a nation free' and lights 'the torch of Freedom to guide a nation's steps'. Death was something to be faced without fear or even hesitation: 'and if we must die as they died we will not flinch' (*ibid.*: 8). The first issue of the *Fianna* journal (February 1915: 3) opened on a similar note, reminding readers: 'You have a cause to fight for, be prepared to die for your cause, and keep before you always "Ireland First"'. As well as the prospect of an early death, the young Fianna member could look forward to much suffering along the way: 'the price of Freedom is suffering and pain. It is only when the suffering is deep enough and the pain almost beyond bearing that Freedom is won' (*Fianna Handbook*, 1914: 7). The relish with which death and pain is described here is reminiscent of Patrick Pearse's notion, referred to earlier, that bloodshed is a cleansing thing. Irish 'martyrs' such as Emmet, Tone and the Fenian leaders were held out as models. Fianna members were clearly being primed for a possible armed conflict. While the Boy Scouts and other uniformed groups promised to control 'unruly' boys (see Chapter 3), this claim is not made in Fianna texts. The great fear for Irish nationalists was that young people would become 'anglicised' and resigned to their fate as subjects of the empire. Marchievitz and Hobson therefore set out to radicalise youth people.

Lessons of history: the 'golden age' and the 'age of struggle'

One of the noteworthy features of Fianna Eireann – which again distinguishes them from other uniformed youth groups of the time – is that their training was partly academic, including Irish history and the Irish language. The revival of the Irish language and history were, as we saw earlier, an important part of the nationalist agenda at this time, helping to create a sense of national identity and solidarity. For many nationalists, political independence was not enough, Ireland also had to have a distinctive character and heritage, as Markievicz explained with reference to Fianna Eireann:

> Their minds were to be trained in the true principles of Nationality ... As Pearse put it: to vision an Ireland 'not free merely, but Gaelic as well, not Gaelic merely, but free as well.' They should be Irish in their knowledge of Ireland's history; Irish in their use of her language; Irish in their adoption of the fine code of honour of the old Fianna, and Irish in their prowess in arms and in their attitude of honourable soldiers waiting faithfully for the hour to come when they too should serve Ireland with all the passion of their glorious youth. (*Eire*, 9 June 1923)

The notion that the past should act as a model and inspiration for the present ('adoption of the fine code of honour of the old Fianna') is symptomatic of Fianna Eireann rhetoric at this time. Not only did Fianna Eireann encourage the teaching of history, but the organisation's own literature is suffused with historical references, to the degree that the present is interpreted through events of the past. Of course, as Coakley (2004) and Smith (1997) have argued, nationalist history often has ideological purposes, it addresses current needs and can be an impetus to future action. It is significant that the *Fianna Handbook* – which sets out the philosophy, structure and methods of the organisation – also includes chapters on Irish history written by Patrick Pearse and Roger Casement. Both chapters are concerned with the exploits of the mythical Fionn and the Fianna of pagan Ireland – part of the 'golden age' of nationalist history referred to earlier. Pearse describes how the young Fionn fought to win back his birthright, became a great leader and ushered in what is described as 'the golden age of the Fianna'. While the contemporary significance of Fionn's story is largely implied in Pearse's chapter, Roger Casement is more direct in the lessons which he wishes to draw from Irish history and mythology. In a chapter entitled 'Chivalry', he argues that Ireland must revive the chivalric code of behaviour of the ancient Fianna. In order to shape the future, Ireland must look to her glorious and noble past: 'we must go back to the national life when it was untouched by foreign influence and uncorrupted by foreign thought. We must teach the youth of Ireland of to-day what Fionn and the Fianna taught the youth of Ireland in the dawn of Irish story' (*Fianna Handbook,* 1914: 79). The spirit of 'ancient chivalry' is later linked to more recognisably nationalist objectives. It was this spirit which called Fionn MacCumhail and his Fianna to guard the coasts of Ireland against the 'imperial conqueror' [the Romans] nearly two thousand years earlier; and it was the same spirit that inspired the Fenians of the nineteenth century. Casement concludes by urging his young readers to take up the cause of Irish independence.

The 'freedom struggle' is one of the most powerful components in nationalist historiography, Coakley (2004) notes, and is a recurring theme in the *Fianna* journal.[7] From its inception in 1915 this journal ran regular features on rebellious movements of the eighteenth and nineteenth centuries (the Fenians, Young Ireland and the United Irishmen) and rebel leaders, particularly Robert Emmet and Wolfe Tone. While Tone and Emmett both presided over failed campaigns, and were ultimately executed, they are elevated to the status of heroes and national martyrs in the pages of *Fianna*. Again, the significance of their short lives (and deaths) are spelled out for twentieth-century boys:

> Robert Emmet gave his boyhood to Ireland. Only 23 when he died, his whole boy's life was given to prepare himself to do his share in the great struggle. At 18 he was already a leader. It was his mind, his courage, his devotion that inspired and organised the United Irish Societies in Trinity College ... This, then is what Robert Emmet tells us, the Fianna, train yourselves to work for Ireland. You are never too young to do your share in the good work. No danger is so great that you cannot surmount it; no death is so hard that you cannot face it nobly. It is only by surmounting difficulties and by dying nobly that Ireland's children can get the Crown of Freedom on her brow. (*Fianna*, March 1915: 5)

History is used here (and in other articles) to argue that young men are both capable of leadership and have a duty to act. In May 1915 the issue is addressed in an editorial, with the authors suggesting that boys must be prepared as one day they will be men and will have to 'take on their shoulder the burden of their country's troubles' (p. 4). But action need not necessarily be deferred until adulthood: 'it is worth while remembering that boys can win battles, as was proved by a little drummer boy, who won the day at the Battle of the Bridge of Lodi, for Napoleon' (*ibid.*). The *Fianna* journal also describes 'great victories', though these are usually achieved by *other* countries. The American War of Independence is described, as is the story of Zaragoza, in which the Spanish defeated Napoleon's forces. The implied 'message' of these accounts is that ordinary people – often untrained and ill-equipped – can win against superior forces.

Armed conflict

Fianna Eireann's militaristic rhetoric and military training suggest that members were being prepared for an armed conflict, which soon came. The fifteen years following the formation of Fianna Eireann were some of the most significant in modern Irish history (including the 1916 Rising, the War of Independence and the Civil War) and members, or former members, of the Fianna were to play a part in these events. One of their first forays came when they were asked to assist with the landing of arms for the Irish Volunteers at Howth in 1914. Bulmer Hobson later recalled that the Fianna 'were the only body on whose discipline I could rely' (Hobson, 1968: 62). Given Hobson's connections with the Irish Republican Brotherhood (IRB) it is not surprising that a number of the Fianna graduated into the ranks of that organisation, or joined the Irish Volunteers (Hay, 2008; Hobson, 1968; Lyons, 1973). In 1912 Hobson started a special 'Fianna circle' of the IRB with Con Colbert as head. Hay (2008) argues that by the fourth annual *ard-fheis,* in July 1913, Fianna officers who were IRB members had effectively gained control of the organisation, making all major decisions regarding policy behind the scenes. Although Countess Markievicz continued to act as president of Fianna Eireann, records suggest that she had little real influence over the direction of policy during this time.

Many former and current members of Fianna Eireann were involved in the 1916 Rising: as commanders, fighters, dispatch carriers and scouts (Hay, 2008). Seven were killed in action while two others – Sean Heuston and Con Colbert – were later executed for their part in the Rising. Markievicz, who had been one of the commanders at Stephen's Green and the College of Surgeons, was spared execution because of her gender. The Fianna reorganised after the Easter Rising and by June 1917 claimed to have attracted an all-time high of over 30,000 members (*ibid.*: 69). The organisation later played a role in the War of Independence and on the anti-Treaty side during the Civil War. Following the formation of the Irish Free State the organisation tried to emphasise its educational (rather than military) role; it also continued to operate in Northern Ireland despite having been outlawed there in 1923 (Hay, 2008).

In the final section of this chapter we will turn to the Blueshirts, an organisation which emerged in the early years of the Irish Free State. Although formed in a very different political climate, the Blueshirts had much in common with Fianna Eireann, particularly in their nationalist rhetoric, support for the Irish language, concern with physical fitness and appeal to young people.

The Blueshirts

During its lifetime the Blueshirts were to have four separate identities beginning
with the formation of the Army Comrades Association (ACA) in February 1932.
The aims of the movement were initially uncontroversial: to uphold the State
and to honour Irish Volunteers who had died during the Anglo-Irish conflict.
The ACA claimed to be non-political and attracted little attention at the time.
However over the next few years the association would undergo a change of
leadership and policy, transforming itself from 'a benevolent group protecting
the interests of ex-Army men, into a shirted and increasingly involved political group' (Cronin, 1997: 20). The Blueshirts were increasingly identified with
the fascist movements of 1930s Europe, partly because of the wearing of the
coloured shirt and other outward trappings of fascism. Under the leadership of
Eoin O'Duffy the organisation (which he renamed as the National Guard) also
adopted some of the corporate ideals and fervent opposition to communism
which typified European fascism at this time.

The lasting political legacy of the Blueshirts, Cronin (1995) notes, was
their central role in the formation of Fine Gael. After the National Guard was
banned by the Fianna Fáil government in 1933 it amalgamated with Cumann
na nGaedheal and the Centre Party to form Fine Gael. This was soon followed
by the formation of the Young Ireland Association (YIA), which had the same
constitution and leadership as the National Guard. The Blueshirts had effectively
re-formed under a different name.[8] By 1934 the Blueshirts had become a mass
movement with a membership of 47, 923, approximately one-quarter of whom
were women (Cronin, 1997: 115).[9] Manning (1970) has argued that the organisation derived much of its support from prosperous farmers who opposed the
economic war which de Valera and the Fianna Fáil party were waging against
Britain.[10] While Cronin agrees that the movement derived much of its support
from rural Ireland, he argues that this was not confined to the middle classes.
There was one demographic group which the movement was particularly keen
to attract: the young. In the following pages we will look at how the Blueshirts
represented themselves as a movement of youth and vigour, and extolled the
virtues of manliness, physical strength and discipline. We will argue that while
Blueshirt rhetoric reflected aspects of fascist ideology, it can also be traced back
to earlier Irish nationalist movements and, beyond this, to the imperialist discourse of uniformed youth movements such as the Boy Scouts. While a detailed
analysis of their political policies is beyond the scope of the current study, the
nationalist rhetoric of the movement will be considered, again highlighting the
links with earlier youth movements.

Youth, masculinity and sport

The concept of a youthful membership was at the core of the Blueshirt ethos: 'Though it is open to every Irishman who will share in its work and accept its discipline, it seeks particularly to recruit the young. To them it gives a golden opportunity of rendering active and manly national service' (Blythe Papers P/24/ 649a: 1). In 1934 O'Duffy claimed that Blueshirt membership was 'drawn largely from those who have barely reached the age of manhood', adding that it was 'no wonder that the older generation recognises the glory and significance of the new movement' (*United Ireland*, 2 June 1934: 5). Another prominent Blueshirt leader, Ned Cronin, insisted that 'we must have the help of the rising generation' and invited 'the young men of today, and of all walks of life, to come forward and shoulder their civic responsibilities' (NIJUS 93/3/17). The Blueshirts were equally keen to recruit women 'who are young and active, and consequently certain of being in sympathy with the rising generation' (*United Ireland*, 20 January 1934: 4). Recruiting youngsters into the ranks of the Blueshirts was a definite policy that succeeded, Cronin (1997) argues, not least because it provided the young with a much-needed sense of purpose and excitement: 'O'Duffy appealed to the youth of Ireland as the group that could sweep away all entrenched belief, and take Ireland into a brave new world' (*ibid.*: 121). In this respect the rhetoric of the Blueshirts is similar to that of Fianna Eireann which, as we have seen, represented the young as the nation's saviour.[11] Of course by the 1930s the foreign 'tyrant' had been replaced by what O'Duffy termed the 'native tyranny' of de Valera and the Fianna Fáil government. Writing in *United Ireland* (16 December 1933: 1) he constructs Irish history as an on-going fight against tyranny in which young people have played a key role in the past, and must do again: 'To-day let the youth of Ireland prove equally steadfast to the sacred trust of national freedom and regeneration ... Where every other tyrant, from Cromwell to Hamar Greenwood, failed, de Valera too will fail.'

In policy documents and Blueshirt newspapers the young are praised for their spontaneity, resourcefulness, enthusiasm, intelligence and receptiveness to new ideas.[12] However, juxtaposed with these images of empowered young people is a more authoritarian discourse concerning discipline and duty to one's country. O'Duffy repeatedly referred to the movement, and its members, as being 'disciplined' and self-reliant.[13] The first issue of *The Blueshirt* (5 August 1933: 5), for example, reminds readers that there 'can be no real cohesion, none of that unity of purpose and action which is the personification of strength, nor any really useful personal service and self-sacrifice without the tempering of discipline'. Members are exhorted to make it a cardinal point of personal pride to behave to their superior officer with respect and to obey their orders unhesitatingly. Statements such as these indicate that while the Blueshirt leaders admired the idealism and energy of youth, they also felt that these qualities had to be harnessed and channelled in the 'right' direction. The language of order and discipline would also find its way into various policy documents: according to their constitution, the National Guard was pledged 'to make organised and disciplined voluntary public service a permanent and accepted feature of our National life' (Blythe Papers P/24/658: 1).

Manliness was another attribute which the Blueshirts looked for in their youthful membership. In his speeches and statements to the press, O'Duffy addressed 'virile young Irishmen', encouraged them 'to step out manfully ... in their blue shirts' (*United Ireland*, 2 June 1934: 5) and to participate in 'manly outdoor sport'. This preoccupation with the ideals of manliness and discipline may have reflected O'Duffy's fear of national decline in Free State Ireland. According to a recent biography (McGarry, 2005: 162), O'Duffy believed that the temptations of modern society were contributing to the physical and moral degeneration of the population. His reports as Garda Commissioner (Police Chief) reveal a growing concern about immorality and the decline of civic spirit. In his public statements O'Duffy complained of falling participation in sport, asserting that it would lead to national and racial decline. Modern forms of transportation and entertainment were seen as partly to blame. O'Duffy looked back nostalgically to previous generations of Irish men and women who did not lounge at street corners or 'go into dance halls and jazz until morning' (cited in McGarry, 2005: 159). He was not, of course, alone in voicing these concerns. The idea that Ireland was in a state of moral decline, whether attributed to the experience of the revolution or the infiltration of foreign influences, was shared by many cultural nationalists, politicians and the Catholic clergy in the 1920s and 1930s (McGarry, 2005; Whyte 1980). For O'Duffy sport represented one means of national regeneration. Like Baden-Powell before him, the Blueshirt leader believed that exercise not only built physical strength but also character.

Under O'Duffy's leadership team sports, athletics and drill were to form a central plank of the Blueshirt programme for young people. The promotion of athletics and sports is included in the various Blueshirt constitutions. Thus, the Constitution of 1933 specified: 'All forms of athletics, physical drill, gymnastics, boxing, etc. shall be practiced by its members in the interest of health and character, and for the purpose of inculcating discipline and to ensure proper deportment in public' (*United Ireland*, 23 December 1933: 5). In 1934 the Blueshirt Athletic Association was formed. Meanwhile the Blueshirt newspapers included regular features on 'physical culture' and reported on sporting events and victories.[14]

There are obvious parallels between the Blueshirt ethos and that of fascist movements in Germany and Italy. The exaltation of youth, manliness and physical strength were key elements of fascist ideology (Mosse, 1997; Paxton 2005). However, as McGarry (2005: 252) has argued, these ideas were not simply 'borrowed' from 1930s Europe, but 'rooted in the militaristic masculinity of Victorian and Edwardian Britain'. As we saw in Chapter 3, the cult of manliness was particularly associated with British public schools but would gradually extend to other institutions in both Britain and Ireland. The ideal of manliness was central to the uniformed youth movements of the late nineteenth and early twentieth century, particularly the Boys Brigade and the Boy Scouts. The GAA and other Irish nationalist movements would later appropriate an imperialist sporting ethos for their own purposes. So while the Blueshirt preoccupation with youth and masculinity may have drawn on fascist ideology, it was also embedded in earlier imperialist and nationalist discourses. In preaching the virtues of duty, discipline, manliness and physical exercise, O'Duffy was reflecting ideas which Baden-Powell had articulated over twenty years earlier. Indeed O'Duffy himself likens the objectives of the Blueshirts to those of the Scouts. However, it is to the *Catholic* Scouts that he pays tribute, not the earlier Baden-Powell movement: 'I hope to see most harmonious relations existing between the National Guard and that splendid organisation the Catholic Boy Scouts whose aim and objects have so much in common with ours, the uplifting of Irish youth; and I hope that as boys grow up and leave the ranks of the Scouts many of them will decide to take their part in the labours of the National Guard' (Blythe Papers P/24/657a: 7).

As well as inculcating certain values, Blueshirt sporting events had an important social and political function, bringing young people together and helping to recruit new members to the movement (Cronin, 1997). Indeed in some parts of economically depressed rural Ireland Blueshirt events were the *only* source of recreation, a point which the movement used to its advantage. A varied recreational programme was provided for members, including picnics, excursions, and, most popular of all, dances. O'Duffy, as noted above, was sometimes critical of commercial dancehalls (particularly those which featured 'foreign' music such as jazz) and so the Blueshirt dance was presented as a wholesome alternative: 'There is all the difference in the world between this kind of thing and entertainments run by strangers for their own profit. The one is part of the community life and the other is just an extraneous growth'(*United Ireland*, 7 April 1934: 5). In 1934 O'Duffy even promised to make the provision of sport and recreation a responsibility of the State, under a Fine Gael government: 'It will be the function of the State to promote by means of the various resources at its disposal – school teachers, civic guards, army instructors, etc. – the organisation of parish clubs with local halls where the young may come together and engage in healthy competitive effort, acquiring a higher physical standard and giving to the life of rural Ireland some of the colour and variety which it so sadly needs' (O'Duffy 1934: 25). O'Duffy's plans never came to fruition of course – he soon parted ways with Fine Gael and the party spent many years in opposition – but this proposal is nonetheless indicative of the General's commitment to organised sports and recreation programmes for young people.

Again there would appear to be some parallels with fascist Germany and Italy where complete working and recreational programmes were developed for citizens (Cronin, 1997). However, Cronin argues, the impetus for the Blueshirt sporting and social programme came not from Europe but from the previous hundred years of Irish history. During the nineteenth and early twentieth century various organisations, including Young Ireland, Daniel O'Connell's repeal movement, the Fenians and the GAA, used sport and social events to gain popular and political support. In post-Famine Ireland this would take on particular significance as the populace had lost their traditional forms of entertainment, most notably the three-day fair. By the end of the nineteenth century the Irish people were not only receptive to any group preaching nationalist political ideas, but also to any group providing a social life. Those who could offer both were ideally placed to attract members. What was true for the political movements of the nineteenth century, Cronin argues, was also true for the Blueshirts. In the 1930s people were bereft of any real form of organised recreation and the Blueshirts filled that need. In doing so the organisation took inspiration from its predecessors, particularly the GAA. The similarity between many of the GAA's tactics and those of the Blueshirts owed much to O'Duffy's earlier involvement with that organisation. Cronin (1997: 187) concludes that the relative success of the Blueshirt recreation programme may be explained by its origins in Irish history, while less familiar ideas and policies (such as corporatism) failed. The patronage of sport and recreation was also important in asserting the nationalist credentials of the movement.

The Blueshirts, cultural nationalism and fascism

Nationalism, 'usually of a very extreme variety' is one of the defining characteristics of fascism (Manning, 1970: 234). Devotion to country was certainly a key aspect of Blueshirt rhetoric and could be taken as an indicator that the movement was fascist in outlook and intent. However, Manning argues, nationalism was so much a part of the general consensus of Irish politics at this time that the differences between the various groups on this question were merely of degree and emphasis. The nationalism of the Blueshirts was 'moderate', he asserts, and certainly less extreme than that of Fianna Fáil and the IRA (*ibid.*). On the other hand, McGarry (2005) has suggested that Blueshirt propaganda reflected a 'zealous nationalism' which was influenced by fascist ideology. Fervent rhetoric may have been partly motivated by the desire to wrest the patriotic high ground from de Valera and Fianna Fáil. The Blueshirts' nationalist credentials were suspect, in some people's eyes, because of O'Duffy's and Cumann na nGaedheal's pro-treaty past. The speeches and writings of prominent Blueshirts suggest that they were taunted as 'traitors', a claim which they bitterly resented. Thus in 1932 Ned Cronin wrote: 'We are no traitors ... We are *men*, not white-livered curs, accommodating enough to cower before the antics of every Wrap-the-Green-Flag-round-me-type-of warrior who, perhaps, was wetting his cradle in the days and the nights when many of our members were fighting the BRITISH OCCUPATION' (NIJUS 93/3/17). O'Duffy was equally keen to assert his nationalist credentials insisting that Fine Gael would 'not play second fiddle to anybody in the matter of Nationality' (cited in McGarry, 2005: 235).

The movement was pledged to promote the reunion of Ireland (Blythe Papers P/24/658: 1) which of course had been divided under the terms of the treaty. Cultural nationalism was also a significant element of the Blueshirt programme with the constitution of the National Guard (and subsequent constitutions) pledging to 'preserve the Irish language and all that is best in the National tradition' (Blythe Papers P/24/658: 1). Like the nationalists of the late nineteenth and early twentieth century, O'Duffy (1934: 23) argued that language was central to Irish identity:

> We recognise that Ireland, situated as she is, cannot retain her national individuality if the historic language of her people is suffered to disappear ... There is nothing in the conditions in any other country that would lead one to believe that Irish nationality could for long survive the death of the Irish language. I believe that if the Irish language is lost the fruit of all the sacrifices that have been made for Irish freedom will be thrown away.

O'Duffy goes on to assert that a Fine Gael government would apply themselves 'to the preservation and extension of all elements of custom and culture which tend to give Ireland distinction as a nation'. The Gaeltacht was seen to be of particular importance in reviving the language and was, moreover, inhabited by 'intelligent, hardy, industrious and patriotic' people' (*ibid.*: 22). The idealisation of the West of Ireland which, as noted earlier, began in the late nineteenth to early twentieth century, was continued into the 1930s by both the Fine Gael and Fianna Fáil parties. It was also reflected in popular culture. The rural West was celebrated and romanticised through the medium of painting, travel-writing and the revival of folk arts (Cusack, 2001). So while it is possible to argue that there were some aspects of Blueshirt/Fine Gael rhetoric which were 'anti-modern' in its romanticisation of the rural West, they were certainly not alone. As McGarry has pointed out, O'Duffy's outlook reflected the anti-modern sentiments of the post-revolutionary language movement in general. However despite the efforts of successive governments the Irish language continued to decline.

The Blueshirts would also draw on Irish history and mythology as a means of firing their youthful members with patriotic feeling. The boys' units were encouraged to study the history of Ireland and make themselves familiar 'with all the great deeds of our ancestors' (*United Ireland*, 19 May 1934). Cuchulain was held up as a model 'for our young Blueshirts' to emulate: 'His heroic deeds should inspire every one of us to learn and practice all manly exercises from our earliest days' (*ibid.*). Ireland's Christian tradition was also acknowledged, with the Flag of St Patrick adopted as an emblem (O'Duffy, 1934: 26). The events of the previous fifty years provided more recent heroes and martyrs for Blueshirt propagandists to reference, including Arthur Griffith, Kevin O'Higgins and, above all others, Michael Collins. The memory of Collins was celebrated by rallies at Beal na Blath (site of his ambush and assassination) and features in the Blueshirt press. The Blueshirts, and O'Duffy in particular, were presented as Collins' successors: 'Collins went forth to his death at Beal-na-Blath – but O'Duffy continues his work faithfully and well' (*The Nation*, 27 July 1935: 4).

The use of historical mythology and hero-worship were important aspects of fascist ideology (McGarry, 2005: 249) although, as we have seen in the course of this chapter, these were also features of earlier Irish nationalist youth movements, and of national identity-building more generally (Coakley, 2004). Other aspects of Blueshirt policy and rhetoric, particularly in relation to corporatism, may have been more directly inspired by developments in 1930s Europe. The two main studies of Blueshirt history (Cronin, 1997; Manning, 1970) address the question of whether or not the movement was fascist. While acknowledging the difficulties of defining fascism, Manning identifies certain key traits (extreme nationalism, appeal to youth, corporatism, anti-semitism, etc.) and assesses the degree to which these were in evidence in the Blueshirt movement. He concludes that the Blueshirts had origins similar to many fascist movements, that they had many of the external trimmings of fascism (uniforms, salutes, etc.) and exhibited some fascist characteristics such as a strong emphasis on youth, attachment to some form of corporate policy and a fanatical opposition to communism. On the other hand, he argues, not all of these characteristics were the exclusive preserve of fascist movements and the Blueshirts lacked some of the basic features of fascism – opposition to democracy, a commitment to violence almost as an end in itself, and a belief in dictatorship. Moreover the majority of Blueshirts probably never saw their movement as a fascist one. Cronin (1997) also makes an important distinction between the leaders, some of whom (particularly O' Duffy) could be described as fascists, and the ordinary members who probably had little interest in, or understanding of, fascist ideology. He concludes that the Blueshirts 'undoubtedly possessed certain fascist traits, but they were not fascists in the German or Italian sense' (*ibid.*: 68). McGarry (2005) agrees that ordinary members knew little about fascism – they were motivated by the legacy of the Civil War and their concerns about the IRA and the economic war. 'Despite much hysterical propaganda, and some wishful thinking, Ireland was not Weimar Germany or post-war Italy: in retrospect, it is difficult to see how intelligent politicians persuaded themselves otherwise' (*ibid.*: 269).

Connolly Youth and internationalism

As Ireland modernised from the late 1950s, Irish youth began to rethink their attitude towards the world in a spirit of internationalism. The Student Revolution in Paris during May 1968 inspired many young Irish people with a new consciousness of the possibility of radical social change. The nationalist ideals of previous generations took on a jaded tone. Irish youth not only looked outwards for popular entertainment, epitomised by rock bands like The Beatles and The Rolling Stones, but also imbibed revolutionary socialist and anarchist political ideas. While middle-class youth expressed this idealism through the student movement, working-class youth had to look elsewhere since they were largely excluded from Ireland's universities.

The Connolly Youth Movement (CYM), founded in 1963 by young republicans (revolutionary nationalists), linked itself to the Communist Party of Ireland and the Dublin Housing Action Committee. The latter espoused direct action on behalf of Dublin's homeless population. Sometimes the CYM clashed with militant nationalists, accusing Sinn Fein of 'fascist tactics' in Connacht, resulting from a dispute over territory (Hanley and Millar, 2009: 249).

The militant nationalist legacy was also part of the Connolly Youth Movement's tradition. Its inspiration had come from the iconic leader of Irish socialism, James Connolly, who was executed for his part in the 1916 Rising. The links between socialism and nationalism in Ireland have not been easy to rupture. However, following the collapse of communism in 1989, the CYM disbanded due to falling membership. It reformed in 2002, inspired by the anti-globalisation/anti-capitalist movement and continues to play a role in Irish politics, mainly centred on Dublin but embracing national campaigns, such as Shell to Sea and US Military Out of Shannon.

Conclusion

Nationalism, Ozkirimli (2000) argues, has played a central role in shaping the face of the modern world. In the Ireland of the late nineteenth and early twentieth century nationalism took a number of forms: party political, militant republicanism and cultural revival. Securing the allegiance of young people was seen as key to the success of the nationalist cause (whatever form it took) as they represented the next generation of Irish men and women. For republicans like Countess Markievicz and Bulmer Hobson, young men had to be prepared for a possible military confrontation, which eventually came. Moreover young people were seen as central to the project of cultural nationalism. Independence from Britain was not enough for Patrick Pearse and many of his contemporaries, a free Ireland had to have its own distinct identity: 'not free merely, but Gaelic as well; not Gaelic merely, but free as well'. Civil society organisations, including the GAA, the Gaelic League, Fianna Eireann and Inghinidhe na hEireann were instrumental in fostering this distinctly Irish identity through the promotion of the Irish language, culture and sports, and the promulgation of a nationalist version of Irish history and mythology. Constructing a sense of national identity was equally important in post-independence Ireland, with the Irish language forming a central part of the primary school curriculum. The patriotic rhetoric of the youthful Blueshirts was part of the general consensus of Irish politics at this time, and may also have been a means of deflecting accusations of treachery in the bitter aftermath of the Civil War.

While women played some part in nationalist politics, they were nonetheless often marginalised in this male-dominated area of public life (Ward, 1983). In the early part of the twentieth century women could not vote and nationalist movements did not always welcome their involvement. This point is well-illustrated by events at the inaugural meeting of Fianna Eireann when, as noted earlier, even the organisation's founder was asked to step down because of her gender. Some women may have been further disadvantaged by their background: Maud Gonne and Countess Markievicz had both been born into the Anglo-Irish ruling class, leading some nationalists to question their loyalty. As nationalist politics became increasingly militarised after 1910 the role accorded to women was further limited. Rather than having an active part themselves, women were often cast as the 'wives and mothers' of the fighting men (Benton, 1995).

Notes

1   Martin Williams' (1983) analysis of nationalist poetry and prose indicates that the national struggle was, from the late nineteenth century onwards, consistently represented in mythical terms. Nationalist leaders were compared with the Red Branch Knights; the heroic figure of Cuchulain was held up as a model of courage, self-sacrifice and military prowess, for other young men to emulate.

2   Cusack (2001) has also looked at the idealisation of the West of Ireland in the Irish Free State. She notes that the new Irish Free State (and the Catholic Church) retained an 'ideology of the rural', even as it engaged in limited modernisation. During the 1930s and 1940s the Irish cottage landscape became an expression of 'authentic' Irish culture and a national emblem.

3   Victorian perceptions about the emotive and feminine aspects of Celtic culture were popularised through the books of Matthew Arnold who, in one influential study, described the Celtic races as 'keenly sensitive to joy and to sorrow' and who 'aspire ardently after life, light, and emotion' (cited in Sisson 2004: 11).

4   Maud Gonne played a significant role in the anti-recruitment campaign during and after the Boer War (Denman 1994). In 1899 the Irish Transvaal Committee was formed by Gonne and Arthur Griffith. One of the committee's objectives was to organise meetings all over the country against recruitment. The Boer War appears to have captured the imagination of Irish nationalists. As well as campaigning against recruitment into the British army, an Irish brigade was formed in the Transvaal to fight on the side of the Boers, with John MacBride as major.

5   At the 1912 annual congress a resolution was carried (by one vote) to allow girls to join the organisation (Hay 2008). However a plebicite was subsequently held among the *sluaighte* (or troops) in which a majority (12 to 5) voted in favour of changing

the constitution back to its boys-only condition. Calls for a separate girls' organisation to be established nationally were not acted on. A girls' branch of the Fianna had existed in Belfast since 1911, although it faced considerable opposition before it was affiliated with the Belfast district council.

6   As well as pledging not to join the British army, the Fianna boys also distributed anti-recruitment material, a subject raised in a number of police reports (National Archives, Kew, CO 904/119; CO 904/14).

7   The *Fianna* journal began publication in February 1915 and included features on the organisation (objectives, events, etc.), fictional stories, poetry and accounts of historical events. The latter were mainly concerned with Irish history, though there were also features on international history, usually with some relevance to Irish nationalism. In one issue, for example, the editor introduces a new series of short stories, which will 'give boys ideas of how other countries run revolutions' (April 1915: 3). Historical themes appear in a number of forms, including poetry and historical fiction and non-fiction. Initially *Fianna* was a monthly journal for boys, though it later broadened its audience.

8   The movement would undergo a further name change in December 1933, becoming the League of Youth (LoY). As with the transformation from the National Guard to the YIA, the formation of the LoY hardly changed the substance of the movement (Cronin 1997).

9   O' Duffy claimed a membership of 100,000, though Cronin (1997) disputes this figure.

10 The economic war began in June 1932 when the Fianna Fail government withheld the payment of land annuities from the British government (Cronin, 1997: 135). The British retaliated by placing a 20% duty on all trade in live animals, butter, cream, eggs, bacon, pork, poultry, game and other meat. This policy was to have serious consequences for the farming sector and was bitterly opposed by the Blueshirts.

11 Cronin notes that there are also some parallels between O' Duffy's rhetoric and that of Mosley, Salazar, and others, who constantly made pleas for the youth to rebel against the 'Old Gang' in politics.

12 See for example 'Blue Flag Notes' in *United Ireland* (16 December 1933: 9). Youth are presented as forming the vanguard of various national movements of the past, including the Fenians, the Land League, the Gaelic League, Sinn Fein and The Irish Volunteers. The author ('Onlooker') argues that in the next Parliament, youth must be more strongly represented as the country needs more deputies 'with fresh and open minds'.

13 See for example, O'Duffy (1934).

14 For example, in one *United Ireland* article (28 April 1934) men are rated in terms of their physical fitness and manliness: the fit and healthy individual is judged to be '100 per cent man', while 'the puny and sickly ... fall below 10 per cent' in the manliness scale. The first issue of the *Blueshirt* journal announced that articles on physical training would be featured every week.

PART II

YOUTH POLICY AND PRACTICE

5

The co-production of a service: active citizenship, youth work and the State

> Co-production offers a rich narrative about the myriad small-scale acts of participation that improve the way we and others around us experience the public realm and that enable us to actively reshape it for ourselves. (Skidmore and Craig, 2005: 37)

In this chapter we seek to explore the relationship between youth work, active citizenship and the State in contemporary Ireland in the co-production of the youth service. Co-production envisages the active engagement of citizens in service delivery. When discussing active citizenship as it relates to youth policy, youth work and young people, a distinction arises between the mode of delivery of youth work, and the status of young people within society. The prior may be analysed through the prism of active citizenship, expressed within and through youth organisations that associate in civil society predominantly or partially through the voluntary involvement of its 'workforce' (there are some reservations to referring to volunteers as a 'workforce', hence the inverted commas), whether these be adults or young people. The latter may be analysed through the recognition – whether partial, whole or differentiated – of young people in terms of their citizenship within Irish society. In this chapter we concentrate on active citizenship and its relationship with the State as it pertains to contemporary youth policy expressed through the co-production of youth work. In contextualising this discussion of youth work, co-production and active citizenship, the chapter begins with a discussion of the historical relationship between Irish youth work and voluntarism. This is followed by a contextualisation of contemporary youth work practice in relation to social policy, and the purported importance of voluntarism through active citizenship is contrasted with the emergence of state-interventionist youth work that has emerged in recent years in an increasingly co-produced service. The impact of this intertwining of a historical reliance on voluntarism built on the Catholic social principle of subsidiarity with the professionalising tendency brought about by reforms in

governance promoting a 'developmental Welfare State' that places emphasis on
the state management of civil society in the co-production of social services is
examined empirically, by using survey data to explore the contemporary reality
in relation to voluntarism in youth work. Original, primary empirical data relating to the status of volunteering in youth organisations collected for this study
is presented. This analysis is then contextualised within a discussion on citizenship, identity and funding in youth policy.

Youth work, religion and voluntarism

Historically speaking, as we have seen in previous chapters, most organised engagement with young people has occurred through associational activity in civil
society, often in partnership with the State or the Catholic Church, or with the
express sanction of these parties. Youth work, as an activity defined approximately as the personal, social and cultural development of young people that is
offered as complementary to the formal education that they receive, has been
no different in this regard (see Chapter 6 for a discussion on the nature of youth
work). As Devlin (1989), Hurley (1992) and Jenkinson (1996) have all pointed
out, embryonic youth work in Ireland and the UK began with volunteers, but
it is hard to pinpoint the exact genesis of this in practice as they were not 'voluntary associations' as we would identify them today. Rather, women and men
undertook 'youth work' in their neighbourhoods, often based on their religious
beliefs. This type of 'youth work' began to transform into organised association
from the 1840s onwards, with the development of the Young Men's Christian
Association (YMCA) (founded 1844); Catholic Young Men's Society (1849);
Boys' Brigade (1883); Girls' Brigade (1893); Scouting Association of Ireland
(1908); Irish Girl Guides (1911); Catholic Boy Scouts (1927); Catholic Guides
of Ireland (1928); and An Óige (Youth Hostel movement) (1931) (Devlin, 1989;
Jenkinson, 1996). The Society of St Vincent de Paul and the Legion of Mary also
coordinated youth clubs in the 1920s and 1930s (Devlin, 1989: 17). The post-
independence flourishing of Catholic civil society youth associations, and the
tacit – yet relatively remote – support of the State is notable, as the social policy
paradigm it promoted enabled the growth of such associations. This policy
paradigm was framed by and through Catholic social principles. These social
principles were enunciated in the seminally influential papal encyclicals *Rerum
Novarum (Of New Things)* (1983, [1891]) and *Quadragesimo Anno* (Forty Years)
(1936, [1931]), which had become cornerstones of Irish social policy, particularly under Taoiseach Eamonn de Valera's Fianna Fáil party, first elected to office
in 1932. In particular, the concept of subsidiarity (i.e. the State should be the last
resort in social provision) was crucial.

  This gave license for the Irish state to effectively abrogate its welfare responsibility for young people. What emerged was a problematising discourse, where

young people were seen as a potential threat to the social order. An embryonic example of the problematising orientation of the relationship of the State to young people was in the development of *Comhairle le Leas Óige* (CLLO) (in English, Council for the Welfare of Youth) within the City of Dublin Vocational Educational Committee (CDVEC) in 1942, established under provisions in the 1930 Vocational Education Act. While ostensibly about the 'Welfare of Youth', the Youth Training Centres that emerged as the practical expression of CLLO were largely to avoid the spectre of 'undisciplined conduct by young persons – all too common in recent years' (CDVEC, cited in Devlin, 1989: 18). Though the existence of CLLO demonstrates that there was some perfunctory statutory involvement in youth work in the 1940s, great attempts were made to not undermine the principle of subsidiarity and the pre-eminence of the Church or, indeed, the policy of institutionalising youth in industrial and reformatory schools. For example, *Comhairle le Leas Óige* released a document in 1944 that stated that its activities were aimed at 'influences detrimental to their [young people's] character as citizens of Dublin and Eire' (CLLO, 1944: 5) and 'does not ... presume to take the place of a good home life ... and it does not claim to be a Youth Movement'. Furthermore, CLLO was endorsed by the Catholic hierarchy, its first Chairperson being Fr. D. Vaughan. So, taken in aggregate, the pre-independence influence of religious-inspired 'volunteers', the post-independence influence of Catholic social principles, and a state and government heavily influenced by those principles (to the point of introducing a new Constitution in 1937 that reflected them more overtly), the stage was set for the primarily voluntary production of youth work.

This reliance on the voluntary sector to provide youth work has been one of the central features of social policy relating to youth and youth work since the period following the 1937 Constitution and the consequent Catholicisation of social issues. The 1951 report by the Commission on Youth Unemployment reflected this, saying, 'The Commission is of the opinion that the following features are essential to any Scheme formulated to deal with the problem of unoccupied youth: (a) Cooperation with the Ecclesiastical Authorities, including adequate provision for religious instruction and exercises; (b) Preservation of the family unit; (c) Voluntary cooperation on the part of youth; (d) Incentive of opportunity to earn; (e) Attractiveness of activities; (f) cooperation with the appropriate voluntary organisations ...' (Commission on Youth Unemployment, 1951: 70). Less than two decades later, this recognition of the role of voluntary organisations in the delivery of youth work was further recognised by the state with the formation of the National Youth Council of Ireland (NYCI). In 1967, Donagh O'Malley, then Minister for Education, invited representatives of voluntary youth organisations to form the NYCI as an umbrella body that the State could then relate to on youth policy matters. Hurley characterises this as 'the first official recognition of the need to support the work of voluntary organisations' (Hurley, 1992: 15). The NYCI was officially established in early 1968.

The 1960s produced a volunteer boom in Western society. The welfare state had made a major contribution to tackling poverty and inequality. But major social problems remained, including homelessness, marginalisation and the isolation of many vulnerable citizens. While there was no longer a need for 'Lady Bountiful' style stereotypical traditional charities or working-class mutual associations and friendly societies, many citizens were not covered by the safety net provided by the welfare state. This led to a revival of volunteering but based upon a new and more democratic conception of the volunteer, as an active citizen, albeit the term had not yet come into popular usage. Voluntary organisations placed themselves in an ancillary relationship with the welfare state. Instead of seeking to displace the welfare state, voluntary organisations sought to supplement and support it. In Sweden, where the world's most advanced welfare state was created, voluntary organisations were called 'the idealistic sector'. While many of these organisations were in receipt of financial support from the State, their independence became essential to their identity, as more and more citizens began to question the benevolence of the statutory sector towards the poor and marginalised (Sheard, 1992).

A second influence was also vital in the emergence of the 1960s boom in volunteering. Sheard (1992: 12–13) comments that the 'generation gap' was also a factor in the volunteer boom:

> Changing attitudes towards the welfare state, however, were not the only reason for the revival of interest in volunteering in the 1960s. The other main factor was concerned with changing attitudes towards young people. From the late 1950s onwards, the problem of the generation gap began to enter the popular consciousness and established adult society began to be increasingly alarmed at what it perceived as anti-social behaviour by a succession of youth cultures. The Teddy Boys and Beatniks of the 1950s gave way to the Mods, Rockers, Hippies, Hell's Angels and student revolutionaries of the 1960s. The newspapers and television regularly gave prominent and sometimes sensational coverage to scenes of violence and disorder involving groups of young people … It was against this backdrop that volunteering began to be perceived in a new role: as a safe, constructive outlet for the otherwise unpredictable and destructive energies of disaffected young people.

Clearly there were precedents for civic engagement with youth. What was new about the 1960s breed of youth organisations was their empowering emphasis on the social education and personal development of marginalised youth. And, what was distinctive about the new breed of youth organisations that emerged from the moral panic about youth in the 1960s was a different way of engaging with disaffected youth.

The American youth icon, singer and poet Bob Dylan famously proclaimed: 'Your sons and your daughters are beyond your command'. Several of Dylan's songs such as 'Blowin' in the Wind' and 'The Times are a-Changin' became anthems of both the US civil rights movement and the anti-Vietnam War movement, in which idealistic youth sought to engage with the great public issues of the day, as active citizens. The emergence of a radical counter-cultural youth movement had challenged the hierarchical structures of modern society in an unprecedented way. In May 1968, the students of Paris started a revolution that echoed around the Western world, articulating young people's discontents with the traditional social order.

Civic engagement with youth became an urgent and pressing public priority across the developed world. Ireland was no exception. The foundation of the National Youth Council of Ireland (NYCI) in 1968 symbolised the growing recognition of youth as a public priority in Irish society. Public policy began to respond with a series of official enquiries into the role and task of youth work, reflecting its prioritisation on the political agenda. The voting age was reduced from twenty-one to eighteen years, reflecting a new and more inclusive attitude towards youth citizenship.

Youth work and the State

In 1977 the report *A Policy for Youth and Sport* (known as the Bruton Report), began to elucidate the statutory interpretation of the meaning of youth work, describing it as the 'education of young people in an informal setting' (*A Policy for Youth and Sport*, 1977: 9). It too reiterated the pre-eminence of the voluntary sector in delivering youth work. This is perhaps best exemplified in a question Mr Bruton answered in the Dáil from an opposition TD, 'I would like to ask the Parliamentary Secretary why sufficient emphasis was not placed on the employment of full-time professional youth leaders to train voluntary youth leaders? … Why was money not made available in the policy document?', to which Mr Bruton replied: '… The whole idea of employing full-time youth leaders, as outlined in the policy is that *they should act as a support to the adult voluntary worker and should not take over responsibility from him*' (Dail Eireann, 1977, emphasis added).

In 1980 the report *Development of Youth Work Services in Ireland* (colloquially referred to as the 'O'Sullivan Report') was published (*Development of Youth Work Services*, 1980). As its name intimates, this focussed explicitly on youth work, and it too reinforced the voluntary delivery of youth work. By now though, the State was entering into a more formalised relationship with the youth work sector, with several of the O'Sullivan report's recommendations being in relation to the financial support of voluntary youth work organisations (Forde, 1995: 30). What is perhaps of greatest interest in the O'Sullivan Report is how it began to implicitly include and exclude certain voluntary organisations as constituting 'youth work'. Its terms of reference excluded uniformed groups, and its recommendations for funding were only to non-uniformed groups. Here we find the continuing problematisation paradigm within which Irish youth work and youth policy in general has been constructed – in this case the underlying assumption appeared to be that uniformed groups represented embryonic 'good citizens' whose development, under the principle of subsidiarity, was to be entrusted to their family and local community (albeit that uniformed organisations do not emanate from the local community as such – rather they are the lowest units on a hierarchical ladder, with a centralised national structure), and therefore not in need of state support. On the other hand, the 'non-uniformed' e.g. youth clubs – almost exclusively the preserve of the working class and the rural poor – were deemed worthy of support by dint of their engagement with potentially problematic young people, whose parents and communities were, we are left to assume, not viewed as being up to the task. The inculcation of values was central to this endeavour, as can be seen from the definition of youth work that it adopted: 'Youth work is essentially concerned with the provision of strategies, opportunities and services to meet the developmental and other needs of young people. Its aim is to help young people towards a more secure, independent, creative and active role in society, by enabling them to formulate values and goals, to plan for the future and accept responsibility for their decisions, to develop relationships with individuals and society, and to make their own contribution to the community at large' (*Development of Youth Work Services*, 1980: 11).

While the Bruton and O'Sullivan reports were undoubtedly of significance, the most comprehensive and ambitious policy document to emerge in this period was the *National Youth Policy Committee Final Report* (known as the 'Costello report' after the committee chairman), which was published in 1984. The continued emphasis on voluntarism as the dominant mode of production of youth work was again in evidence, as was the general emphasis on youth work as an expression of dealing with potentially problematic young people. In its terms of reference, the policy was to 'make recommendations for the improvement and better co-ordination, development and delivery of youth services having regard to the *traditional voluntary* nature of Irish youth work provision' (1984: 8, emphasis added). However, unlike its predecessor policy documents, it gave explicit consideration to the pluralist philosophy underpinning this approach (*ibid.*: 14–24), which aligned voluntarism as vital to the reproduction of liberal representative democracy. In this regard, the report is remarkably prescient of a political zeitgeist that would not fully mature in many Western democracies until the 1990s, as it championed the introduction of the notion of 'social capital' as the foundation for 'active citizenship'.

The Costello Report is in many ways a fascinating, if paradoxical, document. It acknowledges that any positive youth policy where young people are valued and regarded as having potential, if contradicted by shortcomings in other policies (for example, in relation to employment), would be completely ineffective. In this context, it goes so far as to say, 'the needs of young people are so important, indeed urgent, that a planned response to them is required' (1984: 25). This, one would imagine, would imply a strong state welfare effort. Yet what the report goes on to propose is a youth policy that promotes the 'self-reliance, responsibility and active participation [in society]' of young people (*ibid.*: 15). The same can be said of its attitude to the development of youth work, which it ambitiously states should be recast as a 'National Youth Service', again implying a strong state effort – if even only at the level of funding of a range of developmental services to young people – but then reinforces the Catholic social principle of subsidiarity (*ibid.*: 22–23) and the primacy of voluntarism as the 'cornerstone' of the youth service (*ibid.*: 100–112).

It would seem reasonable to conclude that the Costello Report favoured the 'Big Society' over the 'Big State' model of social development. The largest section of the report, Chapter 13, is concerned exclusively with identifying and discussing problematised young people: 'disadvantaged' (i.e. poor) young people; those with poor school attendance; the homeless; Travellers; the disabled; substance mis-users and young offenders. This view of youth work was internalised by many youth work organisations themselves, exemplified in the recommendations of the 1983 report *Youth Services 2000* by the National Federation of Youth Clubs (which claimed a membership in excess of 35,000 at the time of its writing). It listed unemployment, poverty, educational disadvantage, urban housing, the 'handicapped', alcohol and drug abuse, the undermining of traditional values and sexuality as the main issues facing young people. In this paradigm, the young person as a positive active agent is rarely present. It is a telling insight into Irish youth policy and its view of youth work that such a diverse range of young people are subsumed into an overarching problematised category, with that category being the 'target group(s)' of youth work – itself regarded as a vehicle for the inculcation of values deemed necessary to the success of a liberal democracy. That uniformed groups are excluded from this necessity implies that these 'disadvantaged' groups represent a threat to the social order through their location at the margins of society. And so, in summary, we have the general orientation of the Irish state to youth work up to the mid-1980s: an overarching framework dominated by Catholic social principles; a reliance on voluntarism as a mode of production, derived from those principles; the exclusion of 'mainstream' (i.e. generally middle-class) young people from youth work; and the problematisation of those defined as being recipients of youth work.

The origins of co-production

The period between the mid-1980s and the late 1990s saw little change in the general orientation of the State towards youth work, although there were many programmatic developments. These included Youth Diversion Programmes, designed to direct young people 'at risk' of criminal behaviour away from such outcomes; the Special Project to Assist Disadvantaged Youth, designed to engage with 'disadvantaged' (i.e. working class) young people; and the provision of the Young People's Facilities and Services Fund, largely targeted at drug misuse (see Chapter 6). However there was little sense of the development of a coherent policy towards youth work beyond the long-established problematisation paradigm. Indeed, Devlin (2008: 45) characterises this interregnum as 'the long march towards legislation', where the gap between the Costello report, published in 1984, and the enactment of legislation governing youth work in the Youth Work Act 2001 was finally bridged. However, while policy toward youth work was effectively made 'on the hoof' during this period, and regularly in reaction to moral panics around drug use, youth crime etc., the period does have one significant characteristic – the apparent move towards professionalised youth work via the range of state-funded initiatives listed above (and therefore, following policy-makers' views of what youth work should be concerned with, rather than emanating from youth work organisations themselves). As a result, youth work in Ireland is currently, and has been for some time, in an unusual, paradoxical and perhaps even contradictory position in relation to the notion of voluntarism. As a sector, it finds itself in a vortex of variant influences where the meaning of and emphasis on voluntarism in relation to youth work – and indeed within youth policy more broadly – is increasingly dictated by public policy objectives that seek to problematise youth.

This tension occurs both between the State and civil society, and also within civil society itself. The Irish state's agenda towards voluntarism was first codified in its relationship to the 'community and voluntary sector' (effectively a synonym for civil society, thereby including youth work) in the 2000 White Paper, *Framework for Supporting Voluntary Activity* (Department of Social, Community and Family Affairs, 2000). The White Paper can be seen as part of a broader strategy of the co-production of social services often described as the 'rolling back' of the welfare state: 'a parallel development, both internationally and nationally, is a trend in recent years away from State Welfareism towards a more pluralistic system of provision, with many governments looking to the voluntary sector and to volunteers to play a larger role in the direct delivery of welfare services' (*ibid.*: 14). The White Paper concluded that changes in governance 'require a philosophy reflecting what is sometimes an *enabling state* or *assisted self-reliance* where local mobilisation is assisted through the provision of external resources and technical assistance' (*ibid.*: 43, emphasis original). This approach to welfare pluralism through state-resourced voluntarism was further articulated, reinforced and advocated with the publication of the National Economic and Social Council's (NESC) *Developmental Welfare State* (NESC, 2005). This document proposed a programme for welfare reform that had in many ways been actual state practice for some years in relation to voluntarism and the provision of social services, particularly during the much vaunted years of the Irish social partnership policy paradigm, of which youth work was a prime example:

> The Developmental Welfare State (DWS), therefore, regards the radical development of services as the single most important route to improving social protection ... This requires it [the State] to harness the characteristic contributions of non-profit organisations and the commercial sector ... Social protection that is paid for by the state does not have to be provided by the state. (NESC, 2005: xix)

As part of this policy, unprecedented resources flowed into civil society organisations during the period from approximately 1990 to 2005 (see Powell and Geoghegan, 2004 for the extent and impact of this in relation to community development groups). The increasing accountability to the State that was required of civil society groups and therefore by youth work organisations was an associated feature of this set of circumstances. This requirement for accountability gave rise to the need for youth work organisations to begin a process of professionalisation that some youth work groups welcomed and others did not. However, the increasing importance attached to youth policy and youth work by the State during this period, coupled with the accountability imperative arising from resource allocation, and the drive from some quarters within youth work towards professionalism, gave rise to an array of developments. These included the enactment of legislation governing youth work's provision and delivery in the Youth Work Act 2001; the development of a National Youth Work Development Plan (Department of Education and Science, 2003); the development of professionally accredited youth work courses in several seats of higher learning such as University College, Cork and the National University of Ireland, Maynooth; and the establishment of a North-South Education and Training Standards Committee for Youth Work (a cross-border Committee with ministerial backing in both Northern Ireland and the Republic of Ireland). There was also an increase in the range, scope and ambition of a wide array of state-funded but civil society-delivered project-based interventions which focused on the negative impacts of material disadvantage, for example Special Projects to Assist Disadvantaged Youth (see Chapter 6). Taken aggregately, these developments demonstrate a shift towards 'professional'[1] youth work during a period of exchequer largesse. Quite how these developments have impacted on youth work in terms of its voluntary delivery remained an open question until the empirical research carried out for this book. In the next section we detail and review the empirical evidence in relation to voluntarism and youth work.

Voluntary organisations and youth work provision: a national survey

The findings reported here are derived from a national survey of youth work provision. The survey was conducted in 2008/2009 and of the 3,194 questionnaires sent out, 662 were returned. Questionnaires were sent, in the main, to youth clubs, youth cafés, uniformed groups, youth information centres and various targeted projects (e.g. Garda youth diversion projects, special projects to assist disadvantaged youth, neighbourhood youth projects). Whilst providing an important outlet for young people, sports clubs (e.g. GAA clubs), music and drama clubs and so on were excluded on the grounds that they specialise in the activity itself, rather than using the activity as a resource for informal education. Moreover to have included these clubs would have multiplied the sample to an unmanageable size and the focus of the survey would have been lost. For further details on the survey methodology and findings see Powell *et al.* (2010).

Based on our national survey, Table 5.1 clearly demonstrates that youth work in Ireland remains overwhelmingly delivered by voluntary agencies, with 90% of respondents indicating their youth work organisation is a voluntary organisation.

Table 5.1 Voluntary or statutory status of organisations

Organisation status	Number of groups	Percentage of total responses
Voluntary	589	90
Statutory	64	10
Total	653	100

Number of respondents: 653, Non-response: 9

The vast majority (88%) of youth work groups indicated that they were part of larger regional or national organisations, listed in Table 5.2. Foróige accounted for 26% of youth work organisations, followed by Youth Work Ireland (YWI) with 25%, Scouting Ireland (13%) and the Irish Girl Guides and Catholic Guides of Ireland (11%). Interestingly, these five organisations constitute three-quarters of the total number of youth work groups, suggesting that a relatively small number of parent/umbrella organisations dominate the sector. However, it is also interesting to note that 12% of respondents to our survey work under an additional thirty-five parent/umbrella organisations (listed collectively in Table 5.2 as 'others'), providing an indicator of the wide remit of youth work across a broad range of organisations. Examples of these include the City of Dublin Youth Services Board (CDYSB), Club4You and the Irish Wheelchair Association.

Table 5.2 Names and frequency of parent/umbrella organisation

Parent organisation	Number of groups responding	Percentage of total responses
Foróige	141	26
Youth Work Ireland	132	25
Scouting Ireland	68	13
Irish Girl Guides/Catholic Guides of Ireland*	60	11
Catholic Youth Care	13	2
Macra na Feirme	11	2
Church of Ireland	10	2
Girls' Friendly Society	9	2
Girls' Brigade	8	1
Ogra Chorcai	8	1
No Name Club	7	1
Boys' Brigade	6	1
Others	64	12
Total	537	100

Number of responses 537; 45 did not respond to this question
*Both organisations are categorised together here because many respondents simply replied with 'Guides', without specifying the organisation.

While dominated by voluntary organisations, the question remains as to the extent of voluntarism within youth work organisations during the recent period where programmatic youth work expanded significantly. As was pointed out earlier, the late 1980s and 1990s saw an influx of funds that produced external imperatives towards specific policy-driven programmes. In a similar piece of research on community groups (Powell and Geoghegan, 2004), it was found that while there had been a significant increase in the levels of 'professional' community workers during the same period, the number of volunteers in community work had, if anything, marginally increased (Powell and Geoghegan, 2004: 129–142). Table 5.3 provides empirical evidence of the relative number of volunteers to paid staff in youth work.

The evidence is compelling. Notwithstanding the programmatic tendencies within Irish civil society as a whole, which may accelerate a professionalising process, youth work remains a predominantly voluntary activity, with some 69% of the people involved in our respondents' groups participating on a voluntary basis. If we are to include Board members (who are almost always volunteers), then this rises to 84%. This is a remarkable figure given that in youth work's closest 'family resemblance' – community work – paid members of staff came to *outnumber* volunteers after the influx of funds during the period of economic expansion and relative exchequer largesse during the 1990s and early 2000s (see Powell and Geoghegan, 2004: 130). While this is the first study to provide base-line data in relation to volunteering in youth work and is therefore without a basis for comparison,[2] it appears that youth work has retained attractiveness as a form of voluntary work in a period that has seen a general decline in volunteer-ing in Ireland. Ruddle, a leading researcher on levels of volunteering in Ireland has engaged in several research projects (Ruddle and Donoghue, 1995; Ruddle and Mulvihill, 1999; Ruddle and Mulvihill, 1994), all of which measure voluntary activity, and all of which point to a slow but inexorable decline in volunteering during the 'Celtic Tiger' years. Ruddle and Mulvihill's (1999) survey in particular discovered that levels of volunteering dropped continuously during the 1990s, with 33% of respondents to their research having volunteered in the preceding month, compared to 35% in 1994, and 39% in 1992. Powell and Guerin (1997: 116), on the basis of a national opinion survey, found a similar decline, noting that 32% of the population had given services without pay to a voluntary organi-sation. Within this general picture, they discovered significant socio-economic variations in participation, with 43% of middle-class members of the population (ABC1) having volunteered their services to a voluntary organisation, in con-trast to 25% of working-class members of the population (C2DE), and relative under-representation of young people aged fifteen to thirty-four years, of whom 27% volunteered. They found no major gender differences in levels of volunteer-ing – 31% of men and 33% of women had given their services to a voluntary organisation (Powell and Guerin, 1997: 28). This downward trend appears to have continued into the new millennium, being broadly confirmed by the Task Force on Active Citizenship (2007: 7), which concluded that 29% of the adult population (860,000 people) are 'active citizens' as they defined them. Similarly, a recent study, carried out by the Central Statistics Office (CSO), indicated that 28% of the population over fifteen years of age were active in voluntary and community groups (CSO, 2009: 8). It remains to be seen if this downward trend will change in the unemployment-ridden times Ireland finds itself in at the time of writing. The Task Force on Active Citizenship (2007: 8–9) also noted a vari-able level of participation amongst the population:

> Lower rates of engagement were found among those over the age of 65, those not in the labour force or at study (especially homemakers), people on low income (less than €300 per week), persons living in urban areas and those who left school early. Lower rates of volunteering were also found among newcomers (those who stated their nationality as other than Irish) compared to the rest of the popula-tion (24%).

Table 5.3 Numbers of volunteers, paid staff and board members

Description	Number of staff	Percentage
Volunteers		
full-time male volunteers	657	8
full-time female volunteers	1,325	16
part-time male volunteers	1,335	16
part-time female volunteers	2,335	29
Paid staff		
CE workers (male)	107	1
CE workers (female)	149	2
full-time paid employees (male)	245	3
full-time paid employees (female)	353	4
part-time paid employees (male)	147	2
part-time paid employees (female)	308	4
Board members		
board/management/steering (male)	568	7
board/management/steering (female)	668	8
Total	8,197	100%

Number of responses: 641, missing: 21

While nearly one-quarter (24.8%) of all volunteers in 2006 were active in sporting organisations, only 4.3% were engaged in youth work (Task Force on Active Citizenship, 2007: 8). This statistic suggests that youth work is a minority form of voluntary engagement with young people. However, within its own context, volunteering remains the dominant mode of engagement. Indeed The Task Force on Active Citizenship noted that while volunteering in sport fell slightly between 2002 and 2006, there was a slight increase in volunteering in youth work. Anecdotal evidence also suggests that the recent economic downturn has generally encouraged volunteering activity (Duncan, 2009). One of the youth work organisations interviewed in the course of our research reported on the 'positive side' of the economic downturn:

> We are getting more volunteers (increase over 10%) over the last year ... and we are getting more young people ... I think young people are scared about their future and I think part of our work is to reassure young people.

Some others argued that the current economic crisis will have long-term impacts on the youth work sector:

> I do think we will be seeing greater changes in the sector. More volunteers, less dependence on state funding. Maybe we will be going back to the original roots – a youth movement rather than a youth service.

Other youth work organisations, however, reported continuing difficulties with finding sufficient volunteers to run youth clubs in certain areas and at times such as evenings and weekends. Some also indicated that the increasing demands on volunteers through child protection guidelines, but also the general professionalisation of the sector, was posing a challenge for volunteers.

Notwithstanding that the overwhelming majority of people involved in youth work do so in a volunteer capacity, and that it has maintained this profile during a period where voluntarism has been in general decline, this feature is not spread evenly throughout different types of youth work interventions. Our survey and interviews with heads of youth work organisations suggest that while youth clubs and uniformed youth groups are largely run by volunteers, targeted projects (such as neighbourhood youth projects, Garda youth diversion projects) employ paid youth workers and other professionals (see Chapters 6 and 7). Targeted projects also attract significantly higher levels of government funding, much of which is made available in order to employ professional youth workers.

Table 5.4 provides a ratio analysis of the gendered nature of voluntarism within youth work. As is abundantly clear, women outnumber men in every facet of youth work, whether voluntary or paid. What is perhaps of most significance in these figures is that while women outnumber men in every category, the ratio in which they outnumber men is at its highest in voluntary positions (2.02 women for every man for full-time volunteers, and 1.75 women for every man for part-time). This is also true of part-time employees, where women outnumber men by in excess of over two to one. However, when involvement is on a full-time paid basis, while women still outnumber men, this figure drops to 1.44 women for each man employed. The increased presence of men in these positions of relative power and influence is not limited solely to paid positions: the most striking figure of all is that women and men are almost equally represented on Boards of Management, where there are 1.17 women for each man.

Table 5.4 Gender of volunteer and paid staff

Description	Number of females	Number of males	Female/male ratio
full-time volunteers	1,325	657	2.02 : 1
part-time volunteers	2,335	1,335	1.75 : 1
community employment (CE) workers	149	107	1.39 : 1
full-time paid employees	353	245	1.44 : 1
part-time paid employees (but not CE)	308	147	2.10 : 1
board/ management/ steering group members	668	568	1.17 : 1

Number of respondents: 641, missing: 21

Interestingly, while men are well-represented in paid positions (relative to their involvement in voluntary work), the data seems to suggest that they are less qualified than their female counterparts in a number of areas, including youth work, social work and teaching qualifications (see Table 5.5).

Beyond the issue of gender, the statistics suggest that youth work has a significant amount of untrained or unqualified volunteers and paid staff. This is not necessarily a criticism of the sector: youth work's position outside of the formal education sector, as a 'semi-profession', on the margins of state concern and of funding opportunities, and its historical provenance in the free association of citizens, are all characteristics that lead to a paradoxical contemporary situation, where professionalism – whether conceptualised as the preserve of paid staff, or as an indicator of quality provision – sits somewhat uncomfortably within the broader terrain of a free civil society where association is a fundamental human freedom.

Table 5.5 Qualification of paid staff by gender

Highest educational qualification of staff	Frequency	Percentage
Male		
Secondary education	44	19.5
Third level (general qualification)	60	26.5
Third level youth work qualification	19	8.4
Third level community work qualification	14	6.2
Third level youth and community work qualification	27	11.9
Third level social work qualification	16	7.1
Third level teaching qualification	33	14.6
Female		
Secondary education	78	34.5
Third level (general qualification)	87	38.5
Third level youth work qualification	37	16.4
Third level community work qualification	22	9.7
Third level youth and community work qualification	54	23.9
Third level social work qualification	36	15.9
Third level teaching qualification	49	21.7

Number of responses for each of the above questions varied from 220–225.
(The response rate is low largely because many clubs and uniformed groups did not have paid staff and therefore these questions were not applicable to them.)

Youth policy and bifurcated youth work

While the overwhelming majority of youth organisations claim voluntary status, a distinction arises between those that might be termed *voluntary agencies* and those that may be termed *volunteer organisations* (cf. Powell and Guerin, 1997). Voluntary agencies are those that might be described thus in terms of their provenance in civil society and their historical reliance on the voluntary association of their members, but which have transformed into partly professionalised entities due to internal and external forces. In contrast, volunteer organisations, as their name suggests, are associations in civil society that rely almost exclusively on volunteers, in almost all aspects of their operation. Voluntary youth work agencies, through a combination of their recognition by the State since the inception of the NYCI and subsequent policy formulations, and their willingness to work with young people most marginalised in Irish society have taken on the task of working with problematised young people. It is at this particular interface that we find Youth Work Ireland, Foróige, Catholic Youth Care and the like. To them goes the lion's share of state funding, even piecemeal as it tends to be. While volunteers still clearly play a significant role in these organisations, the role of the paid professional youth worker is crucial. There are differences from voluntary agency to voluntary agency on what that role entails (for example, as a generalisation, Foróige places significant emphasis on the notion of the professionalised, skilled youth worker; whereas many of the regional youth services within the federalised Youth Work Ireland often use professional youth workers to support volunteers who then do the frontline youth work), but the professional youth worker is recognised as an integral part of their organisation.

Volunteer organisations, in contrast, receive little state funding, and primarily work with 'mainstream' young people. There is little sense of a 'professional' youth worker in uniformed groups and these organisations rely almost entirely on volunteers. Moreover these organisations tend not to undertake targeted youth work and so are less dependent on state funding. In contrast, voluntary organisations are increasingly involved in targeted initiatives (such as the Garda Youth Diversion Projects), with the result that they may be influenced by political agendas that are all too often subject to the whim of moral panics. The State promotes its welfare reform agenda by harnessing such groups into a governance project that semi-professionalises 'voluntary' youth work agencies, where problematised young people are engaged with through a raft of programmatic interventions which, it is arguable, such voluntary youth agencies may not have arrived at if left to their own devices. This must of course be tempered by the acknowledgement that the support offered to these young people in the programmatic interventions that arise are often of great benefit to them; however, it leaves voluntary agency youth work with precious little room to manoeuvre outside of the 'deficit model' of intervention in young people's lives. Moreover, as we shall see below (and in Chapter 6), state funding of youth work is increasingly directed into targeted youth work, to the detriment of more 'mainstream' provision.

These differing views of voluntarism, of active citizenship, are significant above and beyond who provides what youth services to whom. They go to the very heart of what youth work thinks it is, or thinks it can be as it moves forward into the twenty-first century. As there is such variety in orientations, rather than suggesting a youth work sector with pluralistic approaches, it actually provides an 'uneven surface' onto which the State can project particular policy agendas. To compound this, youth work agencies are then pitted against one another through funding applications. It arguably makes the youth work sector all the more vulnerable to political and state control, and is in effect a constraint on active citizenship, and the 'Big Society'. It also, arguably, runs contrary to both the philosophies of voluntary youth agencies and purported pluralism of youth policy. This is significant, as it potentially leaves Ireland neither with the 'steady state' youth work or youth policy of the Scandinavian countries, but neither does it allow the voluntary youth sector to unify as a coherent actor within civil society. Were the many youth groups a reflection of a pluralist civil society this would be a sign of a healthy democracy, but when organisations are pitted against one another in the search for scarce resources, it leads to a potentially fractured youth work landscape that could easily be controlled from the centre, counter-intuitively through local VECs. An example of the weakness of the youth work sector that arises from such a structural relationship with the State can be found in the overturning of the original 1997 Youth Work Act, which envisaged a more independent youth work sector. Many of its provisions were widely welcomed by voluntary youth agencies. However, the 'rainbow coalition' of Fine Gael, Labour and Democratic Left that promoted this Act fell from office, and when the Fianna Fáil/Progressive Democrat coalition took over, the Act was dropped. The Youth Work Act 2001 that replaced it took away that independence, and gave the governance of youth work to VECs. This was widely and vociferously questioned by many voluntary youth agencies on the grounds that many VECs (with the important exception of Dublin, and a small number of VEC projects across the country) had little experience or knowledge of youth work. Notwithstanding, the youth work sector, for the reasons outlined above, were powerless to stop this change. In broader social theoretical terms, what has occurred through the 'partnership' policy years was a blurring of the lines between state and civil society. This would be a potentially positive development were the State to be resocialised in the process. However, it is arguable that the current Irish state does not envisage allying itself with civil society, but arguably is more interested in harnessing civil society in a project of reinvented governance, which hollows out the welfare state. While welcomed by international investors as a sign of Ireland's 'seriousness' in tackling the barriers to international investment, it is likely to be a concern for all active citizens (of whatever hue) who value associational freedom and the future of the youth generation.

The welfare state and youth work: a Cinderella service?

There are approximately fifty youth organisations in Ireland, which are affiliated to the National Youth Council of Ireland. They are all voluntary. Youth policy has historically been a branch of the education system in Ireland, but as noted above has recently been transferred to the Department of Health and Children, in the form of the Office of the Minister for Children and Youth Affairs. It was a highly neglected part of governance prior to the Youth Work Act 2001. The Irish state has traditionally preferred to leave responsibility for youth with third-sector organisations. But, as already noted, there has been significant evidence of growing state interest in the co-production of youth services in the period 2000–2010, in terms of new legislative structures, and funding relationships. However, there is still a pervasive sense amongst youth organisations that they are cast in a Cinderella role in the Irish welfare state. On the positive side, the National Youth Work Development Plan (NYWDP) (Department of Education and Science, 2003) indicates a shift in the State's youth policy towards more active engagement with youth organisations. Co-production between the State and the voluntary and community sector is internally paradoxical, with limitations such as those set out above, while also bringing real benefits to young people.

While many government departments and agencies are involved in funding youth work organisations, the principal financial responsibility resides with the Office of the Minister of Children and Youth Affairs, established in 2005, under the aegis of the Department of Health and Children. Most of the funding for youth work since 1988 has been drawn from the National Lottery. While this source of revenue has greatly benefited youth work organisations, it has declined as a priority of National Lottery funding over the years. However, under the new policy framework and the NYWDP increasingly responsibility is falling on the Irish Government to fund the sector. A commitment by government to provide €37m towards funding the legislative framework and NYWDP has only been partially achieved. According to an NYCI Budget Submission in 2007 only €12m of the €37m was allocated by 2007 – the end date for the NYWDP.

The role of the National Lottery in youth services funding has proven to be somewhat contentious. However, in 2008, funding for youth services had risen to €52.6m. The then Minister for Children and Youth Affairs, Barry Andrews, reported to the Dáil 'steady progress' in the implementation of the National Youth Work Development Plan (Dáil Eireann, 2008). But a report in the *Irish Times* (30 November 2008) questioned the government's commitment to funding the youth service and particularly the use of National Lottery funding in the light of a cut in the 2009 budget allocation to €48.2m. These suggestions of underfunding the youth services have been consistently disputed by the government. The Minister for Education and Science, Mary Hanafin, stated in the Dáil on 3 November 2005, that the government was fully committed to the implementation of the National Youth Work Development Plan (Hanafin, 2005).

However, the computation of expenditure on youth work is a difficult and complicated task. There are a variety of funding sources and targets (discussed in Chapter 6). The sector can be broadly divided into mainstream youth work (including youth clubs, uniformed groups and youth cafés) and targeted projects which focus on particular types of youth people deemed to be 'at risk' (e.g. special projects for disadvantaged youth). The budgets for targeted interventions are significantly higher than those for mainstream work. As Table 5.6 indicates, the vast majority of mainstream groups responding to our survey operated with budgets of less than €10,000 per year. Targeted youth work provision presents a very different picture: only 24% of projects have budgets of less than €10,000 while 41% have budgets of over €80,000. While this represents a welcome injection of funding into the sector it also reinforces the impression of a state agenda of problematisation and social control, which is not easily compatible with the ideals of a voluntary youth service. The implications of this growing divide between targeted and mainstream youth work will be explored in Chapter 6.

Table 5.6 Budget size mainstream/targeted youth groups

Budget figure (€)	Mainstream		Targeted	
	Number of groups responding	Percentage of all groups	Number of groups responding	Percentage of all groups
less than 10,000	309	85.6	42	24.2
10,001–40,000	36	9.9	14	8.0
40,001–60,000	4	1.1	23	13.3
60,001–80,000	5	1.4	22	12.8
80,000–100,000	2	0.5	28	16.1
100,001–150,000	0	0	18	10.4
150,001–200,000	1	0.3	7	4.0
More than 200,001	4	1.1	19	10.9
Total	361	100	173	100

Total responses: 534, non response: 128

Conclusion

This chapter has sought to focus on the complex meanings of active citizenship in the co-production of the Irish youth service. What has emerged is a bi-furcated service in which volunteer-led services, such as uniformed groups and youth clubs, operate within civil society largely beyond the reach of the regulatory state. But many of the large voluntary organisations that dominate the youth work landscape have been drawn into a partnership with the State. Increasingly, the State sets the agenda of youth policy by problematising disadvantaged youth. There are profound policy dilemmas at stake. We have looked at the concept of active citizenship and its potential for empowerment. However, the pursuit of empowerment is challenged by the regulatory agenda of social control. How can these conflicting imperatives be reconciled in Irish youth policy? Is it possible to move it towards a Scandinavian model that focuses on a positive welfare model based upon the resource potential of young people? We are left with searching questions at the end of this chapter. Undoubtedly, there has been real progress in building an Irish youth service. The concept of the co-production of the Irish youth service in a partnership between the voluntary and community sector and the State has much to recommend it. But it must address questions of shared values and common strategies that are youth-centred and based upon welfare rather than regulatory principles. That is the challenge that both youth organisations and the State need to address, if youth policy is to be built upon empowering principles of positive welfare in the form of social education and personal development.

Notes

1   We use the term 'professional' and 'professionalisation' in their sociological sense. The concepts appear in a large and complex literature, but they essentially acknowledge that professionalisation is an accumulation of attributes (Millerson, 1964) such as 'theoretical knowledge as the basis of skill, the development of specialised training and education, the testing of competence of members by formal examinations, the development of a professional organisation, the emergence of a professional code, and finally the development of an altruistic service' (Turner, 1995: 132). Many youth work organisations in Ireland regard the label of 'professional' differently to this sociological concept, and view it as a pejorative term used to devalue volunteers and valorise paid staff. We make no such assumption, and our use should be seen as describing a social process in which a social activity is 'professionalised' by forces both internal and external.

2   Hurley (1993) carried out extensive research on volunteering within Youth Work Ireland (then the National Youth Federation). This research concentrated primarily on volunteer frequency, perceived (dis)advantages; activities undertaken, etc., but did not enquire into the absolute number of volunteers within organisations.

6

Mapping the contemporary youth work landscape: models, objectives and key issues

> Over the years youth work in Ireland has struggled to develop an identity of its own; an ethos and conceptual framework that is particular to that discipline, as opposed to being seen as an offshoot of social work, probation work or even sport and recreation activities. There is a need to clarify what is central to youth work as there is much confusion, even within youth organisations, as to what it entails. (Jenkinson, 2000: 107)

> Has youth work ever been so fashionable – or at greater risk? (Davies, 2005: 7)

Youth work in Ireland emerged from a number of diverse traditions, each with its own distinctive values, priorities and styles of working. As we saw in Chapters 2 to 4, imperialism, nationalism and religion (both Protestantism and Catholicism) were important influences in the development of the early uniformed groups and other youth movements. Several of these, including the Scouts, the Girl Guides, the YMCA and the YWCA, are still in existence today and are part of worldwide movements. In the course of the twentieth century other forms of youth work would emerge in Ireland, often in response to urban poverty or rural isolation. Much of contemporary Irish youth work is implemented and coordinated by a few large organisations, which have their origins in the youth club movement of the 1950s and 1960s (Hurley, 2002). These include Youth Work Ireland, which is a federation of independent regional youth services, and Foróige, a national organisation with regional offices throughout the country. Catholic Youth Care and Ogra Chorcai are two of the other main providers, though a survey conducted in 2008 found that more than forty organisations are involved in youth work, indicating the considerable diversity of the sector (Powell *et al.*, 2010).

From the outset the provision and delivery of youth work in Ireland has been led by voluntary organisations. Although the State has become more involved, providing much of the funding that supports the sector and enacting legislation in the form of the Youth Work Act 2001, youth work continues to be located predominantly in the voluntary sector. In this respect Irish youth work differs from that in Britain, where the State is the main direct provider of youth services (O' hAodain, 2010). Irish governments do nonetheless exert an important, if indirect, influence through their funding of the sector. Over the last few decades increased support has been provided for initiatives 'targeted' at certain groups of young people, particularly those who are perceived to be disadvantaged or 'at risk' of involvement in crime or drug abuse. This has led to concerns that a two-tier youth service is developing in which the 'mainstream' is underfunded while targeted projects take on a compensatory role, making up for the shortcomings of statutory services, including justice, education and health (Kiely, 2009).

As this brief overview suggests, there is considerable diversity within Irish youth work; and a complex relationship between state funders and voluntary sector providers. In the course of this chapter we will trace the changing youth work landscape, identifying established and emerging models of youth work and exploring some of the issues and challenges facing the sector. We will begin by looking at how youth work is defined in the literature and policy documents before going on to identify different models associated with 'mainstream' and 'targeted' provision. While there is a certain consistency across different forms of youth work (for example a concern with 'personal and social development' and informal education) there are also contradictions and tensions within the sector. In the second part of this chapter we will consider these commonalities and con-tradictions, focusing in particular on whether youth work is moving away from its remit as 'complementary to formal education' towards a 'compensatory' role. While this chapter is intended to provide a broad overview of the youth work sector, some of the issues raised here will be explored in detail in Chapter 7 by means of a case study of the Garda Youth Diversion Projects.

The findings reported here are derived from a national survey of youth work provision (see Chapter 5 for details), an analysis of policy documents and a series of interviews held during 2010 with volunteers, project workers, support workers, heads of national and regional organisations, VEC youth offic-ers and officials from the Office of the Minister for Children and Youth Affairs (OMCYA).

What is youth work?

The term 'youth work' encompasses a wide range of practice and is provided by a diverse group of organisations, from independent local clubs to large inter-national organisations like the YMCA. New forms have emerged over the last decade, often in response to government policy and priorities, further stretch-ing the boundaries of what can be described as 'youth work'. Moreover youth workers themselves have sometimes found it difficult to articulate what it is that makes their practice distinctive. Commenting on the European context, Coussee (2009: 6) suggests that youth work suffers from 'a perpetual identity crisis' in which it seems hard for youth workers 'to put their work into words'. Kiely (2009) reaches broadly similar conclusions in her analysis of Irish youth work, pointing to a lack of clarity in many of the terms used to communicate the values and objectives of the sector. Members of the public, on the other hand, tend to think of youth work in rather narrow terms as a form of recreation provided in a particular place (a club, 'den' or centre), oblivious to the more ambitious goals which the sector sets for itself, including relationship-building, personal development and social education (Devlin and Gunning, 2009).

Notwithstanding these difficulties in trying to define youth work, it is possible to extrapolate from academic and policy documents a number of key features. Youth work is generally described in terms of informal education which is based on the voluntary participation of young people. While some 'learning situations' are planned (such as discussion groups or structured programmes) the majority arise in the everyday encounters between members, and between members and youth workers (Hurley and Treacy, 1993:1). The educative purpose of youth work is often seen to be personal and social development, as the Youth Work Act (2001) makes clear:

> 'youth work' means a planned programme of education designed for the purpose of aiding and enhancing the personal and social development of young persons through their voluntary participation, and which is (a) complementary to their formal, academic or vocational education and training; and (b) provided primarily by voluntary youth work organisations.

A concern with personal development and social education is evident in government reports from the 1970s onwards, signalling a move away from the 'character-building' philosophy of earlier forms of youth work (Hurley and Treacy, 1993; Treacy, 2009). Of course, as Kiely (2009) has rightly pointed out, 'personal development' and 'social education' are open to interpretation and we will explore their meaning in the Irish context later in this chapter.

Voluntary participation is generally agreed to be another defining feature of youth work (Davies, 2005). Young people have traditionally been able to freely join youth organisations and leave when they choose. This has important implications for the content of youth work and the interaction between adults and young people. Youth workers must develop programmes and ways of working which are attractive to participants and which they perceive to be of value in the 'here and now', and not just at some indeterminate date in the future (ibid.: 13). The voluntary principle also ensures that young people possess and retain a degree of power which they may not experience in other areas of their lives. Negotiation, 'openness to a real give-and-take' and greater parity of esteem are therefore important elements of the youth worker/young person relationship, as Davies (*ibid.*) points out: 'any youth worker who patronises, rides roughshod over or simply ignores them is liable to find her or himself without a clientele to work with'.

A related point is that membership of a youth club can be an empowering experience as young people have the opportunity to make decisions, take on new responsibilities and have their views represented: experiences which are often denied them in other areas of their lives, particularly within formal education. Indeed Jeffs and Smith (2002) have argued that most people only encounter 'genuine democracy' in autonomous organisations, clubs and associations, where profit is not the prime objective, strong leadership is mistrusted and dialogue is nurtured. A range of other objectives and ideals of youth work are asserted in the literature including: promoting social inclusion (Devlin and Gunning, 2009; Morgan and Kitching, 2009); 'starting where young people are starting' (Davies, 2005: 15); fostering association, relationships and community (Jeffs and Smith, 2008); being 'friendly, accessible and responsive while acting with integrity' (*ibid.* 278); and being available to all young people and not just those who have been allotted 'adult-imposed labels' (Davies, 2005: 15).

While there is a certain consistency across the different definitions of youth work there are also, as O'hAodain (2010) points out, a number of contradictions. Youth work can be empowering, but it can also be an instrument of social control, regulation and conformity. Gilchrist *et al.* (2003) reach similar conclusions with regards to youth and community work, arguing that it is at its best when motivated by ideals of justice, democracy and equality; and at its worst when motivated by 'fear and insecurity' to become an 'unquestioning servant' of the forces of 'repression and control'. From the outset youth and community work has been 'constrained to negotiate the tension between domestication and liberation' (*ibid.*: 7). Tensions within the youth work sector are perhaps most evident in relation to targeted projects, with some commentators arguing that these initiatives undermine the ethos and objectives which the youth work sector has traditionally claimed for itself (Kiely, 2009). We will return to these issues later in this chapter, following a profile of both mainstream and targeted youth work provision.

Mainstream youth work

The definition of mainstream youth work used in our research is closely adapted from what Davies and Merton (2009: 9) describe as 'open access' youth work in which admittance is not dependent on the young person 'having a prior label attached'; does not lay down eligibility criteria; and is not only voluntary but allows 'considerable freedom of choice within the relevant facilities'. Targeted provision, on the other hand, comprises programmes and/or facilities for specific young people – particularly those identified as 'at risk' and/or with 'special needs' – and which are meant to offer dedicated and often intensive support (*ibid.*: 8).

On the basis of these definitions we classified uniformed groups, youth clubs and youth cafés as 'mainstream' while various other initiatives which identified a particular group (for example Special Projects to Assist Disadvantaged Youth) were classified as targeted provision.

Uniformed groups

The uniformed groups represent one of the oldest forms of youth work – most have their origins in nineteenth or early twentieth-century Britain – and are today part of international networks. Several uniformed youth movements currently operate in Ireland, including Scouting Ireland, the Irish Girl Guides, the Catholic Guides of Ireland, the Girls' Friendly Society (GFS), Boys' Brigade and the Girls' Brigade. The majority of these are single-sex organisations. Scouting, which began as an all-boys movement, now admits girls although our research suggests that boys continue to outnumber girls.

Jeffs and Smith (2008) have argued that association and commitment to the group have traditionally been central elements of youth work. An *esprit de corps* underpinned the work of the early uniformed groups and to this day these organisations (perhaps more so than any other youth work providers) are concerned with fostering the young person's sense of belonging to the group and committing to its ethos. Young people are required to wear uniforms, immediately signalling their membership of a particular organisation. In some cases new members make a promise and agree to a set of rules concerning their actions not only within the group but also outside of it. Girls and young women joining the GFS, for example, promise 'to be regular in public and private prayer, and to promote friendship and purity of life' (Girls' Friendly Society, 2010). Similarly those wishing to join Scouting Ireland take the Scouting promise and agree to follow Scout law (to be loyal, trustworthy, considerate and helpful, respectful of self and others, respectful of nature and the environment, and so forth). In this instance the young person is not only joining an organisation but committing (in principle at least) to a particular ethos and code of behaviour. This is quite a different proposition to joining a youth club, where new members are normally only required to agree to specific rules concerning their behaviour on the premises (e.g. no smoking or drinking). The structure and membership policies of some uniformed organisations may also encourage a sense of commitment or longevity of membership. Members of Scouting Ireland, for instance, work in small groups (patrols) which are intended to 'build a sense of community, responsibility and loyalty' (Scout Leader). In addition uniformed groups accept members at a much younger age than clubs – some as young as five – so that there is potentially a longer period of membership with young people progressing from one stage to the next.

Because the Scouts and Guides have such a long history and an international standing, members of the public are likely to have certain perceptions of what it means to be a Scout or a Guide. While having an instantly recognisable 'brand' is certainly an advantage, it can also have its drawbacks as uniformed groups become pigeon-holed into certain categories. In recent years both the Scouts and Guides have expressed concern about their public image, particularly the perception that they are rather old-fashioned, staid and excessively virtuous (Brophy, 2009). As one Scouting Leader told us:

> Young people have said to me that they wouldn't be seen dead walking past their school in their scouting uniform, in case their friends see them. In France or Switzerland scouting is seen as cool but in Ireland and the UK it's seen as pansy-ish, it's associated with helping old ladies across the street – regardless of whether or not they want to be helped. Our members think that this view couldn't be more wrong – scouting can involve rock climbing, abseiling and other adventurous activities, but that's not what its seen to be about by people outside the organisation. Image perception is important, but it's very difficult to change. The best that we can hope for is that by providing these activities the word will go out that it's more interesting.

Our survey suggests that the uniformed groups provide a range of different activities – similar in many cases to those provided by youth clubs, though with some notable exceptions. Sports are important to both groups with just over 80% of uniformed and 92% of clubs playing sports regularly or very often (see Table 6.1). On the other hand the proportion of uniformed groups undertaking activities involving music, dance and DJ-ing is noticeably lower than for clubs. This pattern is reversed for arts and crafts and environmental projects which feature much more prominently in uniformed provision. Table 6.1 also reflects the continuing popularity of traditional Scouting/Guiding activities including outdoor pursuits (camping, walking) and summer camps. (For a more detailed list of activities undertaken by youth organisations see Powell *et al.* 2010.)

One area where there appears to be a considerable difference between the uniformed groups and other forms of youth work is in relation to faith development. Most youth clubs (77%) indicated that they never undertake faith development work, 6% did so occasionally and only 17% (as Table 6.1 indicates) did so regularly or very often. On the other hand, 50% of uniformed groups reported that faith development work was undertaken regularly or very often, 27% occasionally with only 24% indicating that this was not part of their work. As we saw in Chapters 2 and 3, the founders of the uniformed brigades and the Girls' Friendly Society were motivated by a concern for the spiritual and moral development of young people, and had close connections with the Church.

Table 6.1 Activities undertaken by uniformed groups and youth clubs

	Uniformed groups		Youth clubs	
	Activities undertaken regularly or very often %	Number of responses*	Activities undertaken regularly or very often %	Number of responses*
Sports	81	157	92	189
Outdoor pursuits	87	163	62	174
Arts and crafts	93	163	56	171
Summer programmes	55	150	41	164
Dance/music	57	153	78	180
Summer camps	64	157	22	157
Badge work	98	163	5	149
Environmental projects	77	154	42	166
Drama/theatre	45	150	54	168
After school clubs	7	143	16	160
DJ (music)	16	140	50	167
Citizenship education	44	138	32	158
Photography/ video/film	23	146	32	163
Faith development	50	149	17	157
Youth exchanges	25	148	19	160
Homework clubs	3	143	3	156
VJ (audio-visuals)	6	135	20	154

*The number of responses refers to the number of respondents who answered the question, which varied for each activity.

While these organisations have changed considerably over the years, religion continues to be a guiding principle in their work. The central role of religion is made clear in the Boys' Brigade Mission Statement which promises to 'care for and challenge young people for life through a programme of informal education underpinned by the Christian faith' (Boys' Brigade 2010). This objective is to be achieved in part by 'delivering Christian teaching in partnership with the church in which the company is based and encouraging the development of a personal Christian faith'. The Brigade's original objective of promoting 'habits of obedi-ence, reverence, discipline, self-respect and all that tends towards a true Christian manliness' has been retained into the twenty-first century (Boys' Brigade 2010). Moreover formal religion is central to the structure and operation of the Boys Brigade, which currently works with around 1,600 churches in Ireland and the UK. Similarly the Girls' Friendly Society has close connections with the Church of Ireland, and its stated purpose also appears to have changed little since the nineteenth century: 'To unite for the glory of God in one fellowship of prayer and service, girls and women throughout the world, to promote friendship, and to uphold purity in thought, word and deed' (Girls' Friendly Society, 2010).

While religious objectives are clearly part of the rhetoric of these organi-sations, further research would be needed to explore the extent to which this informs practice. However, it is worth noting that all members of the GFS and the Boys' Brigade who participated in our survey indicated that promoting religious values was an important or very important aspect of their work. Interestingly the Catholic Guides of Ireland – the only group to actually identify a religious de-nomination in its title – make no mention of religion in their mission statement. A history of the organisation, published in 2009, suggests a gradually distancing of the organisation from the Catholic Church:

> From the start the Catholic church has played a formative and dominant role in the organisation. However, by the twenty-first century this position had weak-ened considerably. It could be said that the spiritual aspect of the organisation was now pursued independently. Some members of CGI express regret at what they perceive as the church's abandonment of them and the distancing of the local chaplains who had once played an important role in the spiritual direction of the organisation. (Brophy, 2009: 175)

A fall in the number of priests over the last decade appears to have placed further strain on this relationship as chaplains have less time to devote to the organisa-tion. For various reasons, then, the links between the Catholic Church and the CGI were gradually weakened. Like the Irish Girl Guides and Scouting Ireland, the organisation now describes itself as non-denominational, but with a com-mitment to the 'spiritual development' of its members (interview 2010).

Youth clubs and youth cafés

In contrast with their uniformed counterparts, youth clubs tend to be Irish in origin and to have been formed over the last seventy years. One of the main providers, Foróige (originally Macra na Tuaithe) was founded in 1952 in response to the needs of young people living in rural Ireland. While Foróige is a national organisation, there are also a number of regional organisations, such as the Kerry Diocesan Youth Service, which are affiliated to Youth Work Ireland (YWI). The majority of the clubs participating in our survey were either Foróige or YWI affiliates, indicating their importance to the youth work sector. Some of the other main providers include Catholic Youth Care, No Name Club, Macra na Feirme and Ogra Chorcai.

The defining features of the youth club, according to those interviewed in our research, is that it is open to all young people and run by volunteers, with minimal involvement by paid staff. The club model is especially associated with rural youth work, as one respondent pointed out:

> Traditionally youth clubs were a kind of model of youth work that would have been run in rural areas. What's a youth club? I suppose a youth club is generally run in rural areas by a group of trained volunteers and supported by a youth service but it's the volunteers in the local area that do all the work. So they set it up, they open the doors, they recruit the young people, they manage the programme, they manage the funding, they do every aspect of it. It generally runs from September to May, that's the youth club season. So it's run by local volunteers for young people. It's very much a social outlet for people. And it's entirely run by volunteers ... A youth club generally happens one night a week in a local community hall, whereas a youth café could be open every night of the week in an urban area.

The survey findings would seem to confirm this perception of the youth club as rural based: 67% of respondents said that all or some of their members come from rural areas. The majority of those attending youth clubs are in the eleven to fifteen age range, and the proportion of males and females attending is almost identical. A range of activities are normally on offer (see Table 6.1) and this rather eclectic mix is seen to distinguish youth work from other activities for young people, such as football or rugby clubs.

One relatively recent and innovative model of engaging young people in youth work settings has been the establishment of youth cafés. In *Teenspace, National Recreation Policy for Young People* (Office of the Minister for Children 2007: 123) youth cafés were identified as 'a key need'. The Child and Family Research Centre, NUI Galway, were subsequently commissioned to undertake research into current youth café provision in Ireland and to produce a best practice guide (OMCYA, 2010a) and 'toolkit' on how to set up and run a youth café (OMCYA, 2010b). In 2010 the government also announced plans to provide

€1.5 million to fund a network of youth cafés across the country. This funding scheme is to be administered by Pobal.

While noting that there is 'no set model for a youth café', the *Youth Café Toolkit* (OMCYA, 2010b: 2–3) nonetheless identifies three main categories:

> *Type 1:* The first type of youth café is simply a safe meeting place where young people can hang out with their friends, chat, drink coffee or soft drinks, watch TV or movies, or surf the Internet. This kind of café is normally what you would expect to find when a café first opens.
>
> *Type 2:* The second type of youth café includes all the things offered above plus a variety of recreational and educational activities, chosen by the young people themselves, plus information on State and local services of interest to young people. The activities or programmes in this kind of café are usually developmental and/or community-focused. This kind of set-up would normally emerge after a café has been open for some time and has found its feet.
>
> *Type 3:* The third type of café is the most developed and usually takes a few years to reach this stage. In this kind of café, all the things on offer above in Types 1 and 2 are available, plus a range of specific services, directly designed for young people. These might include, for example, education and training, healthcare information (both physical and emotional) and direct targeted assistance. When functioning effectively, this kind of café allows young people to identify their needs, establish their desired outcomes and, therefore, determine the most appropriate level of service provision for themselves.

While the report makes clear that youth cafés should be available to all young people, 'type 3' above opens the way for more targeted provision. This point is reiterated elsewhere in the Youth Café Toolkit: 'the rationale for establishing a café may be based on the need to address specific deficits, such as, for example, drug use among young people' (OMCYA, 2010b: 23). Moreover the reference to 'specific services' – including education, training and healthcare information – seems to indicate an inter-agency approach. This was confirmed by a senior official in the OMCYA who informed us: 'what has emerged is very much a multi-disciplinary model, a venue for all sorts of activities ... Some of the youth cafés already have a very wide range of practitioners involved in them, for example a nurse in health education' (interview 2010). She went on to note that while youth cafés are 'going to be guided by youth work principles' they were 'not coming at it purely from the youth work perspective'. What this will mean in practice remains to be seen, though in adopting an inter-agency approach the cafés may attract some of the criticisms currently directed at targeted projects, namely that they have a compensatory role, making up for the shortcoming of various statutory services.

Interviews conducted with youth workers on the ground (shortly before the publication of the OMCYA reports and the announcement of government funding) suggest that the café model offered a number of opportunities and challenges for the sector. They reported that the youth café model allowed for a more casual, less structured form of provision, compared with the traditional youth club. This was particularly appealing to older teenagers, or those who were new to youth work services, as one youth worker pointed out:

> When you get to the older teenagers they do just want a place to hang out, they do just want a place to chat, they don't want organised activities, they don't want recreational programmes, they don't want to do woodwork or arts and crafts. They don't want any structure at all.

On the other hand a few respondents questioned whether there was anything truly distinctive about the youth café model, suggesting that this form of provision 'has been around for ages' and that 'youth café is just the latest buzz word'. Another youth worker felt that there were significant differences between the youth café and earlier forms of provision, however, this could give rise to certain difficulties as no one was quite sure how it 'fitted in' with existing youth work and what the proper procedures were. In addition, the role of the volunteer (a key element of the youth club) became less clear in a café setting. If the purpose of the café is to provide a place for young people to simply 'hang-out', what purpose does the volunteer fulfil? In this context the project worker or volunteer may inadvertently take on a supervisory role:

> It is sometimes unclear what the role of the volunteer is in the youth café. Our leaders in youth clubs would be involved in activities, but it's a different role in the youth café. Leaders might end up in a supervisory role. In one of our youth cafés the leaders were there very much in a sort of supervisory capacity, providing drinks and that sort of thing, rather than interacting with them.

Clearly the youth café model is still evolving and the recent reports commissioned by the OMCYA (as well as the promise of government funding) will no doubt shape their future development.

Targeted youth work

The idea of targeting certain young people is not new: as we saw in Chapter 3 the early uniformed groups set out to reform 'loafers' and 'wasters' (typically perceived to be working-class) who drank and smoked, hung around street corners, and avoided playing games. What is new, however, is the role which consecutive Irish governments and policy-makers have assigned to youth work as a means of addressing social issues such as early school leaving, juvenile crime, under-age drinking, substance misuse and so on. The recent *National Drugs*

Strategy (interim) 2009–2016 report, for example, emphasises the importance of youth work services in preventing drug abuse, particularly targeted interventions such as those provided through the Young People's Facilities and Services Fund (YPFSF) (Department of Community, Rural and Gaeltacht Affairs, 2009). Similarly the *Report on the Youth Justice Review* notes that various initiatives – including Neighbourhood Youth Projects, Special Projects for Youth and YPFSF-funded projects – can be used to 'address strong risk factors which can contribute to potential youth offending' (Department of Justice, Equality and Law Reform, 2006: 20).

In the following pages we will outline some of the main targeted youth work initiatives identified above, including Special Projects to Assist Disadvantaged Youth, Garda Youth Diversion Projects, Neighbourhood Youth Projects and projects funded through the YPFSF.

Special Projects to Assist Disadvantaged Youth

Under the Special Projects to Assist Disadvantaged Youth (SPY) scheme, grants are made available to organisations and groups 'for specific projects which seek to address the needs of young people who are disadvantaged due to a combination of factors' including unemployment, social isolation, drug abuse, homelessness and inadequate take-up of educational opportunities (Department of Justice, Equality and Law Reform, 2006: 64). The scheme is operated by the Vocational Education Committees on behalf of the Youth Affairs Section of the Office of the Minister for Children and Youth Affairs (OMCYA). The projects themselves are run by youth work organisations including the regional youth services, Foróige, Ogra Chorcai, Catholic Youth Care and others.

According to the OMCYA, the projects 'aim to facilitate the personal and social development of participants to realise their potential and in particular to equip them with the knowledge, skills and attitudes necessary for their appropriate integration in society' (OMCYA, 2009a). This focus on the personal and social development of young people is a key aspect of youth work whether it be targeted or mainstream. However the two models differ significantly in relation to what the OMCYA refers to as 'appropriate integration in society', which assumes far greater significance in targeted interventions. As one of the main targeted youth schemes, SPY is comparatively well-funded: in 2004 special projects received €12.5 million (Department of Justice, Equality and Law Reform, 2006: 64), increasing to €21 million in 2008 (NYCI, 2009). However further expansion of the scheme has been curtailed due to the current financial crisis and widespread cutbacks in public spending. While the OMCYA continues to fund existing projects, new applications for admittance to this funding scheme are not being accepted (OMCYA, 2009a).

Garda Youth Diversion Projects
According to the *National Youth Justice Strategy 2008–2010* Garda Youth
Diversion Projects are:

> community-based initiatives intended to help divert young people away from
> crime and towards positive and socially responsible behaviour. The projects chal-
> lenge offending behaviour and develop children's skills so they are in a better
> position to avail of opportunities for education, employment, training, sport, art,
> music and other activities, as well as providing a structured environment to add
> stability to a young person's life. (Irish Youth Justice Service, 2008: 43)

The target group includes young offenders as well as those who have 'come to
the attention of the Garda' and are deemed to be 'at risk of entering the justice
system at a future date' (Department of Justice, Equality and Law Reform, 2003:
34). Young people are referred to the projects by various agencies, including the
Juvenile Liaison Officer, schools and social workers, though the project guidelines make clear that participation is voluntary (see Chapter 7).

The origins of this initiative can be traced to 1991, when the first two
projects were established on an ad hoc basis as a response to what was seen as
disorderly behaviour by young people in deprived areas of Dublin city. Over
the next two decades the number of projects increased steadily, reaching 100 in
2008. The total financial commitment for 2009 was in excess of €13 million (Irish
Youth Justice Service, 2009a: 7). Further projects are planned under the Youth
Justice Strategy 2008–2010, though the numbers are likely to be curtailed due to
recent cutbacks in public spending. The projects are funded by the Irish Youth
Justice Service and administered through the Community Relations Section of
An Garda Siochana. As we shall see in Chapter 7, the projects themselves are
implemented to a large extent by voluntary youth organisations, thereby creating an interesting interface between the youth justice system and the youth work
sector.

Neighbourhood Youth Projects
While the targeted initiatives described so far focus on young people,
Neighbourhood Youth Projects (NYPs) also work with parents and other family
members on the grounds that 'a young person's problems do not occur in isolation [and] they cannot be solved in isolation' (Dolan and Kane, 2005: 19).
Consequently the projects undertake group and individual work, home visits
and annual review meetings with families (Dolan and Kane, 2005). Young
people can be referred to NYPs for a variety of reasons, usually relating to
'personal, family or social problems' (Dolan, 2006: 5). Research carried out on
Foróige/HSE projects found that over half of the respondents were referred because of behavioural difficulties as identified by the referrer (Dolan, 2006). Such

behaviours included young people 'acting out' in school and/or community settings, truancy, risk taking behaviour or a 'propensity towards addiction' (*ibid.*: 6). Other young people were referred primarily because they exhibit low-self esteem and self-efficacy, or because they have estranged relationships at home and poor capacity to make and keep friends. Like other targeted interventions, NYPs are mentioned in policy reports on the prevention of juvenile crime and substance abuse. The *Report on the Youth Justice Review* (Department of Justice, Equality and Law Reform, 2006: 74), for example, lists Neighbourhood Youth Projects as one of the support services offered 'for the purpose of either preventing problems or addressing problems after they have emerged'.

Mentoring programmes: Big Brother Big Sister

Foróige's involvement in Neighbourhood Youth Projects led to the introduction of the international mentoring programme, Big Brother Big Sister (BBBS), to Ireland in the late 1990s (Brady *et al.*, 2005: 7). BBBS was initially funded by the then Western Health Board (now the HSE) and delivered through NYPs in Galway, Mayo and Roscommon. The essence of the scheme is that a young person who is considered 'at risk' or who is already experiencing adversity in their lives, is matched with an adult mentor with whom he/she meets on a regular basis (Brady and Dolan, 2007). According to BBBS Ireland, the programme aims:

> To make a positive difference in the lives of young people through a professionally supported one to one relationship with a caring adult volunteer. The volunteers, as Big Brothers or Big Sisters are friends, mentors and positive role models who assist these young people in achieving their unique potential. (cited in Brady *et al.*, 2005: 8)

In common with other targeted interventions, the BBBS programme claims to have a preventative function: 'a created relationship between an older and younger person will act to prevent future difficulties or be a support to a young person facing adversity in their lives' (*ibid.*). An evaluation of the BBBS programme was conducted in 2005, identifying the benefits of participation (e.g. gains in confidence, improved communication skills) as well as the challenges in implementing the programme, such as minimising the risk to children, involving and encouraging parents, appropriate targeting and so forth (see Brady and Dolan, 2007). While Foróige is currently the main provider of BBBS in Ireland, our research found that several other organisations are either planning or in the process of introducing the programme. The advantage of the BBBS scheme, according to one project worker involved in introducing the scheme, is that it attracts a younger 'at risk' age group (often as young as ten or eleven) and is therefore seen as more 'effective' in terms of early prevention.

Young People's Facilities and Services Fund (YPFSF)
Youth work interventions have also formed part of strategies designed to prevent alcohol and drug abuse. The Young People's Facilities and Services Fund (YPFSF) has been the main funding mechanism for providing activities for young people under the current National Drugs Strategy (Department of Community, Rural and Gaeltacht Affairs, 2009: 32–33). Established in 1998, the YPFSF sets out to:

> assist in the development of preventative strategies/initiatives in a targeted manner through the development of youth facilities (including sport and recreation facilities) and services in disadvantaged areas where a significant drug problem exists or has the potential to develop. The objective of the Fund is to attract 'at risk' young people in disadvantaged areas into these facilities and activities and divert them away from the dangers of substance abuse. The target group for the Fund are 10–21 year olds who are marginalised through a combination of risk factors relating to family background, environmental circumstances, educational disadvantage, involvement in crime and/or drugs etc. (OMCYA, 2009b)

In addition to providing activities to 'divert' young people away from drug use, YPFSF-funded projects provide counselling, drugs education and, where appropriate, referral on to more specialist services. School completion initiatives have been strongly supported by the scheme, on the grounds that there is a correlation between early school leaving and alcohol/drug use (Department of Community, Rural and Gaeltacht Affairs, 2009: 29). Indeed school completion programmes and 'second-chance' education schemes, such as Youthreach, have become significant strands of government policy more generally, both in Ireland and other European countries (McGrath, 2006). To date approximately €150 million has been allocated under the YPFSF to support in the region of 500 facility and services projects (OMCYA, 2009b). The majority of the funding has been allocated to the fourteen areas in which a Local Drugs Task Force has been established and four other designated urban centres – Limerick, Waterford, Carlow and Galway. Responsibility for the YPFSF transferred to the OMCYA from the Department of Community, Rural and Gaeltacht Affairs in 2009 (Department of Community, Rural and Gaeltacht Affairs, 2009: 29).

While each of the initiatives described above are distinct, they also have a number of common features. Firstly they target young people who are deemed to be 'at risk', a population who appear to have a broadly similar profile regardless of the particular intervention (i.e. early school leaver, living in a disadvantaged area and so on). The fact that targeted projects form a distinct group can be better appreciated by comparing their membership profile with that of mainstream clubs, cafés and uniformed groups. Our survey found that nearly three-quarters of targeted projects work with groups in which most or all young people are from financially disadvantaged backgrounds, compared to only 12% of mainstream youth work groups (Powell *et al.*, 2010). Similarly 48% of all targeted youth work interventions report that all or the majority of young people they are working with experience behavioural difficulties, compared to only 3% within mainstream youth work groups. Equally stark differences are observable in relation to alcohol and substance abuse, by young people themselves and within their families. This raises the issue of whether a focus on 'multiple deprivations' leads to a ghettoisation of disadvantaged young people in certain kind of interventions or whether it actually contributes to social inclusion.

A second distinguishing feature of targeted projects is that they claim to have a preventative function. They promise, for example, to 'divert' young people from juvenile crime or drug use by providing alternative activities, by raising their awareness of health risks, by addressing personal problems through counselling and so on. Recent reports on the Neighbourhood Youth Projects and the Big Brother Big Sister programme provide a more conceptually based analysis of how these interventions might have a preventative role, linking them to resilience theory, social capital theory and social control theory (Brady et al., 2005; Dolan, 2006). Young people are often referred to targeted projects – particularly the Garda Youth Diversion Projects – with referrals coming from a number of sources.

Thirdly, the budgets for targeted interventions are significantly higher than those for mainstream work and come from different departments and funding steams. As noted in Chapter 5, the vast majority of mainstream groups (85.6%) responding to our survey operated with modest budgets of less than €10,000 per year. On the other hand only 24% of targeted projects have budgets of less than €10,000 and 41% have budgets of over €80,000. While this represents a welcome injection of funding into the sector, working with various different funding partners (the HSE, Justice, Education) raises questions as to whether youth work is taking on a 'compensatory' function (discussed below). Moreover some of those interviewed as part of our research reported that there can be a 'clash of cultures' between the youth work sector and some of its partners; in addition to which there is a degree of professional snobbery with youth workers being seen as 'well-meaning amateurs'.

Finally there tends to be a greater emphasis on small-group or individual work within targeted programmes, though group activities remain a significant element. Our research also indicated that projects are more likely to offer 'issue-based' education programmes on general health, drug and alcohol education and sexual health (see Powell et al, 2010 for further details).

Ethos and objectives of youth work: commonalities and contradictions

At the beginning of this chapter we identified the key elements and objectives of youth work, based on a review of the relevant literature and policy documents. It was noted that while there is a certain consistency across the different definitions of youth work there are also a number of potential contradictions. This is perhaps most evident in relation to targeted interventions with some commentators arguing that initiatives such as the Garda Youth Diversion Projects undermine the ethos and objectives which the youth work sector has traditionally claimed for itself (Kiely, 2009). In the final section we will return to this theme outlining the objectives of youth work and the points of commonality and difference between targeted and mainstream provision. We will explore some of the tensions within the sector, particularly in relation to whether youth work is taking on a 'compensatory' rather than a complementary role; and whether targeted youth projects are instruments of inclusion or exacerbate existing divisions. The findings reported here are based on our survey of youth work provision and interviews with some of the main youth work organisations operating in Ireland. As such we hope to represent the views of those working on the ground, as well as policy-makers.

Personal development and social education
Youth work often lays claim to a range of objectives or issues including personal development, social education, empowering young people, fostering integration and so on. Uniformed groups, youth clubs, cafés and targeted projects were asked (in a closed-format question) to rate the importance of these different elements in their youth work provision. Personal development and social education emerged as key elements of their work with the vast majority (over 90%) of all groups rating these as important or very important. Given the centrality of these concepts in policy documents over the last few decades this was not surprising. What these terms mean in practice was explored through a series of interviews with youth workers, volunteers and heads of organisations.

There was a general consensus that personal development in the youth work setting is concerned with building the young person's sense of confidence and self-esteem. Youth work facilitates this development by involving young people in decision-making, providing leadership roles and training, and generally allowing young people to do things for themselves rather than, as one respondent noted, 'having their parents do everything for them'. Moreover youth work provides one of the few settings where young people and adults can meet as equals: 'it creates a space where the relationship is one of equal power ... instead of one where the young people feel that they are being instructed or ordered by the adult all the time'. While empowering young people is clearly an objective of youth work, the degree to which they are involved in decision-making and leadership roles varies, which is perhaps not surprising given the diversity of the sector. A local branch of one of the uniformed groups, for example, told us that the adults choose the youth leaders because if this decision was left to the young people themselves 'it would just become a popularity contest'. On the other hand, the ethos of youth participation appears to be particularly strong within the youth café model, with several respondents reporting that young people were involved in setting up the cafés, and played a central role in their management.

Youth work was seen to provide a social outlet for young people, and a means through which they can develop certain skills particularly in relation to communication, negotiation, compromise and group work. This was especially important in targeted interventions, according to one project worker, because participants often have 'poor social skills which can range from introversion to aggressive behaviour'. Similarly another youth worker noted that through group work young people learn 'how to relate to other young people and how to work with adults in a constructive way'. The relationship between adults and young people is regarded as central to the youth work process, indeed for one volunteer this was its defining feature:

> Youth work is about the relationship between adults that are there on a voluntary basis and young people that are there on a voluntary basis. They are coming together on common ground but everyone needs to be getting something out of it … That's what it's about, if you can sit down and have a cup of tea with someone and have a chat with them, and relate to them.

This relationship was seen to be especially important where young people are experiencing adversity in their lives, a common situation within targeted projects. Youth workers could provide support which is otherwise lacking: 'it's about having that one concerned adult that you know you can talk to, albeit very informally, and if there is something more serious that they might not be able to help with, they can certainly find out information on what to do next, arrange for them to see a counsellor or other professional if necessary'. Providing psychological support and counselling, while important across the youth work sector, is far more so in targeted interventions: 52% of targeted projects participating in the research rated these as important/very important aspects of their work compared with 32% for mainstream providers. The contrast is even greater if we consider uniformed groups as a separate category: only 12% of these groups rated psychological support and counselling as being part of their provision.

Social education

While the concept of social education has been deployed in many different ways, Kiely (2009: 22) argues, in the Irish youth work context it has been largely concerned with 'enabling young people to manage their lives as best they can in the society of which they are part', for example through life-skills programmes, peer education, teen pregnancy or crime prevention programmes. In contrast, a more radical social education approach might engage young people in consciousness-raising so that they develop an understanding of their 'oppressive life situations' and are prompted 'to collectively want to act on society in a way

intended to bring about structural or institutional change' (*ibid.* 23). Similarly
Hurley and Treacy (1993: 41) have made the case for 'critical social education'
which emphasises 'consciousness raising strategies that view the dominant value
system as an inherent part of young people's problems'. In our research on youth
work practice we found little evidence of the type of consciousness-raising social
education described by these authors. Instead social education tended to be seen
as an extension of personal development: as one respondent noted 'they were
on the same continuum'. Our findings are broadly in line with Kiely's (2009: 15) assertion that youth work in Ireland is concerned not with structural or institutional
change but with producing young people 'who are sufficiently informed and
skilled to live responsible lives'. For instance one youth worker, who was familiar
with Hurley and Treacy's critical social education model, rejected it as inappropriate to the immediate needs of the young people with whom he worked:

> What we have done very little of nationally, is looking at structures, society's
> structures and how these actually impact on young people. I don't think we've
> done much of that type of critical social education and maybe that goes back to
> targeting. And maybe if we look at the particular young people we are target-
> ing or engaging, they are not ready for that. Who cares about structures and all
> of that, when it's really the person, their own particular issues, you know, that
> they are much more interested in. There are some projects or organisations – like
> Amnesty International – that are involved in the political sphere, but that's rare.

This is not to suggest that the youth work sector does not engage in awareness-
raising or address difficult issues. The YMCA, for example, was involved in
anti-sectarian programmes in the North of Ireland and anti-racist programmes
in the South. However the programmes provided by some organisations tend
to be in areas which are relatively uncontroversial (e.g. environmentalism, citizenship education) or at a safe distance from Ireland (development education).
While not disputing that these are important issues, they are of a different type
to those described in Hurley and Treacy's model of critical social education. Of
course a lack of political engagement may not be entirely the fault of the adults,
as one volunteer pointed out: 'with my group, if you mention something like
NAMA (National Asset Management Agency) their eyes just glaze over, they
are not interested or they are completely cynical, like the rest of us'. She went on
to assert that the idea that youth work in Ireland had been more radical in the
1970s was probably an 'urban myth': 'That might have been the case in the cities,
maybe Dublin, but you must remember that rural Ireland was in those days a
very conservative society, and the volunteers were drawn from that society.'
     While there was general agreement across the sector that personal devel-
opment and social education were key aspects of youth work, there were also
concerns that the sector was taking on new roles and moving away from what
were seen to be the traditional values of youth work.

Complementary or compensatory?

The image of the youth work relationship (between adults and young people) as being unique and special has made the sector increasingly attractive to agencies and professionals who may have a less benign public image, including gardai, teachers, health professionals and social workers. As Kiely (2009: 15) has argued, youth work has come to be seen as 'a means of managing and socialising young people who move outside the radar of other agencies'. This view was shared by some of those interviewed, one of whom was particularly concerned at the way in which youth work was being 'used' by other sectors:

> If you look at some of the areas where the youth sector has created partnerships with other sectors – like education or the HSE – it's where the work demands the development of a trusting relationship with an adult, someone who can connect with young people etc. and they use youth work for that ... They view youth workers as well-meaning amateurs, but also as having some skills that they might not have.

Rather than being complementary to formal education (as set out in the Youth Work Act 2001) youth work appears to be taking on a compensatory role, making up for the failure of other sectors. By working with different partners the youth work sector may be adapting to their agendas and objectives and losing sight of its own, as a representative of Youth Work Ireland pointed out:

> One of my concerns has been because youth work is linked to many other areas of work – like justice, like health promotion, education, whatever – that we can be seen as compensating for the inadequacies of other systems or supporting them in tasks that they find difficult because our method is something that creates greater access to young people and influence with young people. But I think what we should be about is complementing rather than compensating for these systems through delivering our own distinctive programme for work. Which is that non formal education, education for citizenship, supporting young people in the transition from childhood to adulthood in a way that will ensure that they have the confidence, knowledge skills and experiences that will help them to fare well in their future lives... We need to have youth work positioned positively ... [Our role] is not to compensate or pick up on the work that other institutions fail to do.

The above comments are very much in line with the National Youth Work Development Plan which asserts that 'young people are not a 'problem' to be solved' nor is youth work 'a remedial service for those whose needs are not being met otherwise' (Department of Education and Science, 2003: 14). However our research suggests that these views are not universally shared within the sector. A senior representative from one youth work organisation had no qualms about seeing youth work in a compensatory role. Indeed his comments about targeted projects seem to suggest that they have an almost remedial purpose, helping to 'normalise' young people:

> ... there is a very specific role for youth work around compensatory ... that works with young people who have deficiencies or need additional help or support ... and that good youth work interventions can help almost normalise them or help to bring them on. So we would see that there is both generic and targeted youth work ... and both sit side by side and complement each other ... and one can't operate without the other.

Elsewhere in the interview he again ascribes a normative role to youth work, suggesting that mainstream clubs are something to which project members can aspire (or 'normalise') to: 'Youth work is about normalisation ... you can only normalise if you have something to normalise to ... if you have a mainstream ... and therefore you need to have a mainstream that is robust and well funded'. While none of the other interviewees or policy documents expressed themselves in such terms, the idea that young people need to conform to certain norms of behaviour was often implicit. Policy documents, as we have seen, make clear what is expected in terms of diverting young people from crime, preventing or addressing drug and alcohol use, encouraging school attendance and so on. The SPY projects, for example, emphasise the need for participants to be equipped with 'the knowledge, skills and attitudes necessary for their appropriate integration in society' (OMCYA, 2009a); while the Garda Youth Diversion Projects encourage 'positive and socially responsible behaviour' (Irish Youth Justice Service, 2008: 43). While not disputing that these might be worthwhile endeavours, some respondents expressed concern that they are beyond the remit of youth work and are increasingly casting the sector in a compensatory role. There was also frustration that youth work is seen as a 'panacea' or a solution to various social problems, though one interviewee acknowledged that this was at least in part because the sector has marketed itself as such.

Including or ghettoising young people?
Volunteers and project workers reported that mainstream youth work brings together people who might otherwise have little contact with each other. This was a factor not only in terms of ethnicity and socio-economic background but also gender: many primary and secondary schools in Ireland are still single-sex and so youth clubs and cafés provide an opportunity for all young people to mix socially. However, there were concerns that targeted interventions were undermining this inclusive aspect of youth work by segregating particular young people (often young men from the most disadvantaged backgrounds) in specialist projects. Indeed the work of these projects appears to be based on a paradox:

while claiming to integrate marginalised young people into mainstream society they run the risk of 'ghettoising' them (project worker). Moreover as the number of targeted interventions increases in response to government imperatives and funding there were concerns that the youth work sector *as a whole* may be stigmatised.

In defence of targeted projects, youth workers pointed out that some of the young people with whom they work would never have attended a mainstream youth club, less still a uniformed group, and that the only way of reaching them was through a targeted intervention. Indeed in some cases youth workers go out to where young people are (streets, parks, shopping precincts) to reach the most marginalised groups:

> And a lot of the best youth work we are doing at the moment is street youth work … where we recognise that for a whole lot of reasons a lot of young people are not able to work in groups. They are not going to be coming into a centre. And even if they would be coming into a centre, their behaviour might be so challenging for the youth worker that they end up not working with them anyways … so we will have developed and used a street work model and that is particularly used with the most marginalised young people.

While targeting might be the only way of getting some young people to participate in youth work, it may also provide them with a safe space to 'simply be themselves'. By way of example one youth worker recalled her experience with a youth group for people with Attention Deficit and Hyperactivity Disorder (ADHD). At one of their meetings a boy mentioned that he was taking medication, and this prompted the others to talk openly about their own medication. 'At that moment,' the youth worker recalled, 'you could feel the group bonding,' each youngster realising that they weren't alone, they hadn't really known that there were others in exactly the same situation as themselves'. Another point made by respondents was that targeted youth work is often the first stage in a young person's involvement with youth work. This may lead them to engage in more mainstream provision, which is in line with youth work's integrative role:

> It could work whereby we go out into a housing estate and we might set up a group and part of our plan there might be to integrate that group with the community. So we might work out in a housing estate with a group for six months. And then we might decide we'll stop that group for the summer and if everybody would come to the youth café for the summer. So we have everybody integrating together here [in the youth café] rather than ghettoising people in their little groups in their little housing estates. So it can work really well that way to integrate people into the community. But you start with them in their own place where they are comfortable. You work with them there for maybe six months and

then you encourage them to come down to the youth centre to the youth café
where they hang out with everybody.

The interviews (as well as literature produced by different youth organisations)
suggest that there is a considerable interchange of membership between different clubs and projects run by one organisation. A young person registered with
a targeted youth work intervention, for example, could also be attending another
facility (youth café, youthreach centre, etc.) offered by the same organisation.
Nonetheless respondents were keenly aware that certain projects risk stigmatising young people and confirming them in their status as 'outsiders'. In some
instances strategies were devised to counteract this possibility, for example by
broadening the membership base of targeted projects, though this is not always
popular with funding agencies. One regional director recalled, for example,
having 'heated discussions' with funders when he proposed 'a more inclusive'
membership policy.

Equality and inequality

One of the most powerful arguments in favour of targeted youth work is that it
represents a form of positive discrimination which is seen to benefit some of the
most disadvantaged groups in Ireland. The counter argument, of course, is that
by pooling resources into a relatively small number of projects the vast majority
of young people (particularly those living in rural areas) are not, to quote one
volunteer, 'getting their fair share'. A perceived lack of resources for some areas
or groups of young people can also give rise to resentment in the community.
One respondent noted that members of the public will complain if young people
are 'hanging-around and maybe getting into trouble', but when the youth service
provides facilities for them (for example through a targeted project) they are
accused of 'rewarding bad behaviour'. He noted wryly that parents will ask 'how
many windows does my son have to break before he gets to go on a day-trip?' In
these circumstances youth workers can find themselves between the proverbial
'rock and a hard place'. This of course relates back to the issue of youth work
being seen (and perhaps also representing itself) as the panacea to various social
problems.

While there was general support for targeted initiatives, project workers
were adamant that this should not come at the expense of mainstream provision. In some instance this was expressed in terms of the rights of young people
(that all had a right to access youth work) while others noted that mainstream
provision could have a preventative role, for example by addressing rural isolation which can lead to depression and other mental health problems. Moreover,
as noted above, young people attending targeted interventions could not remain
in these programmes indefinitely and would need something else to move on to,
such as a local youth club. If these mainstream services are not available, young

people leaving targeted programmes may simply 'drift back to their old ways' (project worker).

Conclusion

The origins of contemporary youth work in Ireland can be traced back to the late nineteenth century and while much has changed in the intervening period many of the basic principles and ideals have remained the same (O'hAodain, 2010). Concepts and trends that were established then continue to inform the development of the sector, including the predominance of voluntary organisations as the main service providers, the principle of voluntary participation by young people, and limited state involvement. At the same time the sector has evolved to reflect the changing needs and lifestyles of young people in Ireland. New forms of youth work have emerged (e.g. youth cafés, mentoring programmes) which co-exist with established models (youth clubs, uniformed groups). Continuity and change is also evident in relation to targeting. While youth organisations have always claimed to reach certain groups of young people, targeting has assumed far greater importance over the last few decades, largely in response to government priorities and funding. This injection of capital was welcomed by youth work organisations and was seen to represent a form of positive discrimination which would benefit some of the most underprivileged young people in Irish society. Critics, on the other hand, have suggested that targeted projects represent a form of social control and fail to address the structural problems which impact on young people's lives. Moreover the drift towards a two-tier youth service raises the question of whether certain young people are being ghettoised in targeted projects and thereby further marginalised. There are, therefore, a number of contradictions at the heart of contemporary youth work: while claiming to empower and integrate young people it could equally be seen to control and segregate them from their 'mainstream' peers. These are issues which we will explore in detail in the following chapter through an in-depth analysis of the history, rhetoric and practice of one particular targeted scheme, the Garda Youth Diversion Projects.

7

Negotiating tensions and contradictions in youth crime prevention initiatives in Ireland

The year 2001 constituted a watershed for Irish children and young people. In addition to the Children Act of 2001, which aimed to revamp the framework of dealing with children and young people in conflict with the law, the Youth Work Act of 2001 represented a significant milestone in trying to achieve improved delivery of youth services for young people. To different degrees, the youth justice system and the youth work sector have arguably always been concerned with balancing their dual functions of social control and welfare. As we have seen in Chapter 3, some of the early youth work organisations were particularly interested in shaping the behaviour of young boys into socially acceptable norms through the provision of regulated leisure-time activities. Some of them were also concerned with reforming the characters and minds of 'hooligans', who openly refused to conform to the expectations of the middle classes. The youth justice system of early twentieth-century Ireland was dominated by the reformatory and industrial schools which managed 'delinquent juveniles' and young people it considered at risk of corrupting influences, largely by removing them from the community and segregating them in a range of carceral institutions. Albeit, very few of the children incarcerated in these institutions were ever convicted by the courts of any offence. However, the public perception was that the inmates of Ireland's reformatory and industrial school system were 'delinquents', when in reality they were overwhelmingly the victims of poverty (see Chapter 8). However, since that period, social policy has progressed considerably. After decades of inertia, the Children Act 2001, amongst other things, raised the age of criminal responsibility from seven to twelve years for the majority of offences, introduced separate processes for dealing with juvenile offenders, enshrined the principle of detention as a last resort and provided a wider range of non-custodial sentencing options for young people in conflict with the law. The Act has been credited with redirecting the Irish youth justice system into a child-centred and welfare-oriented system that is predominantly concerned with the protection of the best interests of children in conflict with the law, while holding them accountable for their actions.

The Irish youth work sector has always maintained a certain degree of diversity in youth work provision, depending on the philosophies and practices of particular youth work organisations. However, its strong foundation in the voluntary sector and its focus – at least in policy terms – on empowering young people from the mid-1960s onwards (Jenkinson, 2000), meant that youth work has developed and retained distinct practices and characteristics. The Youth Work Act 2001 sought to reinforce these ideas by providing a definition of youth work that focuses on social education and personal development of the young person outside the formal schooling system; the importance of voluntary participation of young people in the youth work process; and the contribution of the voluntary sector as the main provider of youth work (see Chapter 6).

In official policy terms, the Irish youth justice system and youth work sector began to converge around certain issues from the late 1970s onwards. In 1980 the report *Development of Youth Work Services in Ireland* (colloquially known as the O' Sullivan report) for the first time explicitly acknowledged 'Young People In Trouble with the Law' and their particular needs for support from the youth work sector (Development of Youth Work Services, 1980). In the context of an ever-growing distinction between 'mainstream' youth work and 'targeted' youth work, a more programmatic collaboration between the two sectors emerged with the establishment of the first two Garda Youth Diversion Projects (then called Garda Special Projects) in 1991. Initially, these community-based youth crime prevention projects were set up on an ad hoc basis and in the localised context of public unrest in North/West Dublin city. Influenced by the conditions in these disadvantaged urban areas, the local Garda and officials in the Department of Justice were in agreement that an approach other than deterrence was needed to deal with young people depicted as troublemakers in these specific areas (Bowden and Higgins, 2000). Since these early beginnings, the scheme has expanded significantly. By 2009, there were 100 projects in operation nationwide with a total budget exceeding €9 million. The projects' official aim now is to divert young people from becoming involved or re-involved in criminal activity or anti-social behaviour and to simultaneously 'support and improve local Garda and community relations and enhance the quality of life in the area' (Irish Youth Justice Service, 2009a: 7). The diversion projects are financed by the Department of Justice, Equality and Law Reform (since 2006 by the Irish Youth Justice Service) and managed by the Garda Community Relations Office. However, the large majority of projects are run and managed by voluntary youth work organisations, thereby creating an interesting interface between the youth justice system and the youth work sector, whose potential for tensions and contradictions we will address in this chapter.

In the literature, diversion of young people from the criminal justice system is regarded as one of the least intrusive mechanisms of providing them with opportunities for changing their behaviour (Fionda, 2005). The Garda Youth

Diversion Projects have been studied three times since their inception with the aim to improve the effectiveness of the project interventions, but also to avoid probable shortcomings such as net-widening (i.e. the inclusion and potential labelling of non-offending young people in the projects). Overall, the establishment and expansion of the Garda Youth Diversion Projects is continuously perceived as one of the most progressive elements of Irish youth justice policy and practice (Bowden and Higgins 2000; Kilkelly 2006; O'Dwyer 2002) in recent years.

However, as is well known, the seemingly benign forms of crime prevention, diversion and community sanctions have been questioned and dissected by critical criminology. In *Visions of Social Control* (1985) Stanley Cohen famously argued that the new forms of punishment and prevention invented from the 1960s onwards in the Anglo-American context did not necessarily result in a decrease of the network of surveillance and social control. He warns of processes such as 'blurring', 'masking' and 'widening', which all contribute to the spread and deepening of the new crime agendas. Similarly, in *Culture of Social Control* (2001), David Garland describes the increased demand on 'the community' to participate in crime prevention and policing as 'responsibilization strategy', a process that in the Irish context has arguably resulted in an enhanced network of formal and informal crime control. Focused on new initiatives in this area in Ireland, Eoin O'Sullivan's (1998) study has commented on the concerns surrounding the politics and power relations embedded in seemingly benign forms of crime prevention. He argues that although 'we are far away from the days of the mass confinement of the children of the poor in a continuum of carceral sites' and engagement with young people in conflict with the law has shifted to 'community based projects, garda intervention schemes, programmes to educate the young by 'Copping On', partnerships and liaisons of various kinds between parents, social workers, community works and so on', fundamentally the 'ideology remains intact, as does the logic of where such sites are located and who are subjects of interventions. We have moved from the concept of dangerousness to the concept of risk, where the anticipation of future delinquency is ascertained by knowing the abstract factors deemed liable to produce risk populations' (O'Sullivan, 1998: 90).

In this chapter it will become evident that the participation of the Irish youth work sector in the youth justice system in the form of Garda Youth Diversion Projects does signify several fundamental shifts characteristic of the changed landscape of dealing with young people (potentially) in trouble with the law. But it also opens up questions regarding the changing context of youth work, illustrating the challenges of contemporary youth work provision. By looking in detail at the intersection of the Juvenile Justice and the Youth Work Sectors in the form of the Garda Youth Diversion Projects, the overall aim of this chapter will be to investigate how young people (potentially) in conflict with the law are being governed in twenty-first century Ireland.

The chapter will pursue this aim by firstly examining the wider context and development of youth justice reform in Ireland. By tracing the development of an increasing emphasis on youth crime prevention and diversion, this first section will identify to what extent it is possible to speak of advanced liberal governance patterns (Rose, 1996) in the Irish youth justice system. These are typically characterised by an increased emphasis on 'prescriptions of individual responsibility, an active citizenry and governing at a distance' (Muncie, 2004: 215). Secondly, the chapter will analyse the tensions and opportunities that emerge from the partnership of the youth justice and youth work sector, particularly from the youth work sector's perspective. By analysing survey data from the *Civil Society, Youth and Youth Policy* project as well as in-depth interviews with youth workers in Garda Youth Diversion projects, a better understanding will be gained of how the projects and the youth work sector take part in and reshape the new youth justice agenda.

Diversion and alternatives to custody: shifting ideologies in Irish youth justice

The criminal justice system is recognised as one of the 'mechanisms which shape the experiences and expectations of young people' (Smith, 2007: 161). In order to understand the micro-politics of the Garda Youth Diversion Projects, the broader changes in the Irish youth justice system have to be outlined. Historically, as already noted, the Irish youth justice system was characterised by a strongly punitive approach based on high levels of institutionalisation of young offenders. Shaped by the Irish interpretation of the Children Act 1908, children of the 'perishing classes' who were 'at risk' of getting in trouble with the law were placed in industrial schools (O'Sullivan, 1997). Outright 'non-conforming and delinquent children' of the 'dangerous classes' were locked away in Reformatory Schools (see Chapter 8). Albeit, they were very few in number, falling to fewer than 100 in the 1930s. It was only in 1979 that the Reformatory School system was fully abolished. Despite several piecemeal reforms of the Children Act 1908 and calls for fundamental change, it took until the Children Act 2001 for the introduction of a modern youth justice framework in Ireland. This slow pace of reform has been attributed to different factors by several commentators, including Ireland's cultural isolation and the strong influence of Catholic social teaching (Quinn, 2002; Seymour, 2006;). Above all, the slow process probably serves as a strong indicator of the almost endemically low level of importance accorded to children and young people by Irish policy-makers.

The first official initiative aimed at establishing an alternative non-custodial system to deal with young offenders was the Garda Juvenile Diversion Programme (previously entitled Juvenile Liaison Officer (JLO) Scheme) which was set up in 1963, initially only in Dublin. The programme, which in the literature is often not clearly differentiated from the Garda Youth Diversion Projects (Fionda, 2005), introduced a diversionary system of cautioning young people for offences rather than dealing with them through prosecutions in the courts. As a consequence, young people who had received a formal caution (usually after having received an informal caution previously) could be supervised in the community by specially trained Juvenile Liaison Officers, for a period of up to twelve months. The programme was expanded nationwide in 1981 and in 1991 the Garda National Juvenile Office was established with the task to monitor and coordinate the implementation of the scheme, as well as to train Juvenile Liaison Officers. The Children Act 2001 put the scheme on a statutory footing and introduced the additional element of a restorative conference, with the aim of mediating between offenders and victims and formulating tailor-made action programmes for offenders. The programme has been growing steadily. While in 1999, some 7,844 young people were included in the programme, this number had risen to 12,785 in 2004 and to 21,727 in 2007 (An Garda Siochana, Annual Reports 1999, 2007). By 2005, a total of 178,485 children had been included in the programme.

Although policy documents such as the 1970 *Reformatory and Industrial Schools Systems Report* (Kennedy Report) had acknowledged the connection between social and economic disadvantage and juvenile delinquency, this did not go far enough to stimulate fundamental youth justice reform (*Reformatory and Industrial Schools Systems Report*, 1970). It was the 1992 report, *Juvenile Crime – Its Causes and Remedies*, that delved deeper into explaining that juvenile crime was the result of a complex net of underlying factors often associated with social and economic disadvantage (Government Select Committee on Crime, 1992). This report was published in the same year as Ireland became a signatory to the Convention on the Rights of the Child and its proposals eventually led to the 1996 Children's Bill and later more importantly to the Children Act 2001. The Select Committee's report made a number of far-reaching suggestions. It recommended raising the minimum age of criminal responsibility from seven to twelve years, to put the Juvenile Diversion Programme on a statutory footing and to develop non-custodial and community-based sentencing alternatives for young offenders. These milestones were eventually implemented in the Children Act 2001. Other recommendations of the 1992 report, such as the establishment of coordination mechanisms in the youth justice system or the setting up of local Juvenile Crime Prevention Committees, were only implemented significantly later.

However, the Select Committee on Crime report did indicate a notable shift in policy dealing with young people in conflict with the law. In its recommendations the report outlined the importance of a 'multi-faceted response' at the level of prevention and intervention to the problem of juvenile crime', which needed to 'involve all relevant sectors whether at the level of the community, the State or society' (Government Select Committee on Crime, 1992: 38). More specifically it demanded that the relevant state actors would increasingly focus on preventative measures, by funding locally based programmes that would include elements of youth work and sport. It emphasised that this approach would be most successful by focusing these 'specifically tailored measures for individuals at risk in order to draw them out of any further trouble' (*ibid*.: 43).

To oversee these youth crime prevention activities, the Select Committee on Crime suggested the establishment of Juvenile Crime Prevention Committees for each Garda division, with the idea of bringing youth crime prevention matters to the level where it mattered most; the local community, where 'patterns of difficulty could be identified, solutions explored, and the overall performance of the different elements of the system reviewed' (*ibid*.: 44). The importance of the community and involvement of lay people was further emphasised by suggesting 'citizen volunteers' be included as part of local panels that would chair the Juvenile Crime Prevention Committees as well as by involving them in visiting committees for all residential/custodial units. Similar demands for reform were echoed in a report produced by the Interdepartmental Group on Urban Crime and Disorder (1992). This group was established in 1992 to investigate urban crime and disorder in the Ronanstown area of Dublin. The report underlined the complexity of juvenile crime and suggested an alternative 'treatment' of the problem of juvenile offending.

The emergence of a new consensus of how to deal with young offenders can be observed from the early 1990s. This consensus was arguably built around the ideas of the more systematic involvement of communities in preventing youth crime or dealing with young offenders; the importance of the involvement of the voluntary sector and the increased cooperation and coordination of multiple agencies at local level in contributing to dealing with young people in trouble or potentially in trouble with the law. The new consensus was formalised through the 2001 Children Act, which after almost a century of stalemate finally overhauled the Irish Youth Justice system. The implications of the 2001 Children Act have been widely discussed elsewhere and critiqued mainly for its slow implementation (over six years) and its 'lack of teeth' (Kilkelly 2004: 47). Many of its provisions such as the raising of the age of criminal responsibility from seven to twelve years, and the increased emphasis on diverting young people from the criminal justice system simply aligned Ireland's treatment of young offenders more with other Western European countries. Other elements, such as the introduction of three types of conferencing schemes and a wide range of community based sentencing options, have been described as more innovative (Kilkelly 2004: 37).

However, to the disappointment of many children's rights activists in Ireland, some of the significant advances made by the Children Act 2001 were reversed by the introduction of the 2006 Criminal Justice Bill. More specifically, it watered down, in clear contradiction with Ireland's obligations under the Convention on the Rights of the Child, the previously increased age of criminal responsibility, by allowing children of ten and eleven years to be tried for serious offences. As a consequence, the scope of the Juvenile Diversion Programme was also expanded, to allow ten and eleven year olds to be included in the programme. Most significantly, the 2006 Criminal Justice Bill introduced the widely disputed Anti Social Behaviour Orders (ASBOs). While the ASBO is a civil order, breaching it is a criminal offence with a possible custodial sanction as a consequence (Kilkelly, 2008). There are indications that the planned review of the ASBOs, announced by the Minister of Justice, Dermot Ahern, in June 2009, will lead to a further expansion of the ASBO regime, by amongst other things, expanding Garda powers to issue 'stay away orders' and 'restriction orders' and by creating new anti-social behaviour action teams in each local authority area (O'Brien, 2009). Needless to say, an expansion of the ASBOs simultaneously means a reduction of young people's liberties and increases the means by which they can be surveyed and regulated within the community.

Overall then, it seems that a certain contradictory position on young people in conflict with the law has come to light, as exemplified by the 2006 Criminal Justice Bill. Despite its otherwise progressive reforms, the government was seemingly never fully comfortable with categorically excluding young people under the age of twelve years from any form of criminal prosecution, as is usually the case in other countries. Furthermore, tools such as ASBOs and good behaviour contracts, including the responsibilisation of parents, do not recognise the complexity and underlying concerns associated with criminal or anti-social behaviour.

Youth justice and social partnership: the governance of youth

From the early 1990s the emergence of the youth crime prevention paradigm had already taken root in practice and a wide range of direct and indirect youth crime prevention programmes grew in number. As noted in Chapter 6, initiatives such as the Special Projects to Assist Disadvantaged Youth, Young People's Facilities and Services Fund (YPFSF) and Neighbourhood Youth Projects are seen as a means of preventing juvenile crime and drug abuse by providing leisure activities, support and counselling, and health education to those young people deemed to be 'at risk'.

The trend towards diffusing the responsibility for crime prevention involving young people amongst different statutory and voluntary agencies and communities was exemplified in 2002, when the National Crime Council published a Consultation Paper entitled *Tackling the Underlying Causes of Crime: A Partnership Approach*. The Council had been established by the government in 1999 as an independent research and policy formulation body, particularly tasked with focusing on crime prevention. The consultation paper set out provisional recommendations about how to systematically address crime prevention in Ireland. The largest part of the report focused on young people and youth crime prevention, linking it to the social inclusion agenda of the Irish government as outlined in the National Development Plan 2000–2006. The National Crime Council (2002) suggested that many of the social policy measures foreseen therein, such as investments in childcare, youth services, services to the unemployed, affordable housing, etc. 'whilst not having the stated aim of crime prevention, would be likely to have spin off effects in this regard' (National Crime Council, 2002: 11). While demonstrating the ways in which mainstream social policy was at least discursively re-located into the crime prevention framework, it further acknowledged the wide range of legislation and government agencies directly or indirectly involved with a variety of primary, secondary and tertiary crime prevention initiatives. This report also suggested that a national, multi-stakeholder crime prevention body be established for steering and overseeing crime prevention work in Ireland.

Reflecting the tone of local governance structures stimulated through the Irish Social Partnership agreements more generally, it proposed the establishment of local partnership structures, where the involvement of local communities would be coordinated by newly established local crime prevention committees, attached to existing structures of local governance (County/City Development Boards, Area Partnership Companies, Local Drugs Task Forces or RAPID/CLAR Committees). It specifically underlined the importance of involving communities in designing and implementing local crime prevention strategies in cooperation with statutory and voluntary agencies. In addition to youth crime prevention initiatives already ongoing, the Crime Council suggested a widening of the Probation and Welfare Service's remit to work with young people 'at risk' of offending. Although the Crime Council was careful to point out shortcomings of the risk-factor approach in trying to explain and predict human behaviour in statistical terms, it outlined four categories of risk factors, based on academic research in this field: Neighbourhood/Community Risk Factors; Socio-Economic Deprivation; Family Background/Parenting; Individual Factors; Academic and School Factors. The report also suggested the introduction of 'crime-proofing' of all policies and actions designed by government departments and statutory agencies. Furthermore, it suggested that the system of early intervention be intensified by proposing to establish a sort of feedback system, through which state or voluntary actors involved with families and young children could identify those deemed 'at risk' of problematic behavior and who needed additional intervention. As will be argued below, these trends towards discovering the likelihood of possible future offending in young people's private spheres, extends the framework of surveillance significantly. By demanding that social professions would perform duties not normally ascribed to them, the grip on disadvantaged communities would be significantly tightened. There is a worrying 'Big Brother' dimension to this Orwellian strategy.

The document was followed up by a consultation process which was consolidated into *A Crime Prevention Strategy for Ireland: Tackling the Concerns of Local Communities* (National Crime Council, 2003), which outlined the features of a National Crime Prevention model in more detail. This position paper suggested that the proposed local Crime Prevention Committees would include participants from statutory, voluntary and community sectors, business representatives and private individuals, who would embed themselves further into the community by operating as sub-committees to the existing City Development Board Social Inclusion Measures (SIM) Working Groups. The report maintained its emphasis on early prevention, particularly by highlighting the provision of parenting programmes in families. Interestingly, despite significant opposition expressed during the consultation process with regards to the suggested expansion of the Probation and Welfare Service's remit to young non-offenders, the Council's recommendation nevertheless maintained that this option should be '*at least kept under review*' (National Crime Council, 2003: 23). The report also strongly emphasised the important role of a wide range of youth services and facilities, particularly in rural areas. Interestingly, the report also advocated the need for a new vocabulary when talking about young people, particularly young offenders.

Many of the new approaches to governing youth raised by the Crime Council and their proposal to systematise the framework for crime prevention were echoed in the 2005 *Report on the Youth Justice Review*, prepared by a Working Group in the Department of Justice, Equality and Law Reform. In keeping with the reforming and efficiency seeking approaches common to many new public management techniques being experimented with by the Irish state, this group aimed at 'delivering a joined up approach across government bodies in the area of justice' (Department of Justice, Equality and Law Reform, 2006: 1). Based on what it described as 'best practices' from a variety of countries, it affirmed that the 'whole-government approach', which effectively 'links the provision of services to young offenders within the criminal justice framework into the wider framework of the delivery of care, education and social services' (Department of Justice, Equality and Law Reform, 2006: 25), was the path to choose when designing an Irish Youth Justice policy. Thus, the report particularly focused on the lack of coordination in the youth justice sector and proposed the establishment of a dedicated Irish Youth Justice Service. Not surprisingly it also emphasised the necessity to increasingly focus on preventative measures and early intervention for dealing with youth crime.

The Irish Youth Justice Service Strategy

As a consequence, the Irish Youth Justice Service was established in December 2005 as a unit within the Department of Justice, Equality and Law Reform. The Irish Youth Justice Service is responsible for the coordination and funding of all projects that provide services to young people who have been in trouble with the law and for guiding policy development towards enhanced cooperation in the youth justice system. The mission statement of the Irish Youth Justice Service itself is revealing, in terms of the ways it brings into focus potentially conflicting rights of communities to crime-free security and the rights of young people to be fully integrated into these communities. It states that the Service's mission is 'to create a safer society by working in partnership to reduce youth offending through appropriate interventions and linkages to services' (Irish Youth Justice Service, 2009b). While the Irish Youth Justice Service certainly has the best interest of young offenders in mind and has been designed with a strong child-centred focus, the emphasis on the creation of a 'safer society' as the end goal, rather than a means of contributing to improving young people's lives in terms of integration into their communities, would suggest that the ideology of the youth justice system prioritises the creation of overall community safety over the well-being of young people.

One of the first major initiatives of the Irish Youth Justice Service was the design of the Irish Youth Justice Service Strategy in March 2008. The strategy pursues five high-level goals, which amongst others, focus on diverting young people from offending behaviour and on the promotion of greater use of community sanctions to deal with young people who offend. The strategy has been criticised for lacking an independent monitoring strategy and for not putting a focus on improving compliance with Ireland's international obligations in the area of children's rights (Kilkelly, 2008: 560). Seemingly building on similar structures set up in Britain (Youth Offending Teams), the proposed Juvenile Crime Prevention Committees recommended by the 1992 Report on Juvenile Crime and resonating similar ideas with regards to administrative structures suggested in the Crime Prevention Strategy of 2003, the Irish Youth Justice Service sets out to create Youth Justice Teams at local level to coordinate the work of key agencies in the Youth Justice area. While as of 2009, they have not been established on the ground, these plans reflect the wider, more observable trend across the justice sector overall towards multi-agency cooperation and coordination in the community. Similarly, in setting out their goals, the National Youth Justice Strategy repeatedly emphasises the importance of developing 'effective programmes and representing value for money' (Irish Youth Justice Service, 2008: 11) and is designed on the basis of several performance indicators and targets to be achieved. Although this is obviously designed in order to 'target, focus and provide continuity when it comes to interventions and outcomes for young people involved in anti-social behaviour and crime' (Irish Youth Justice Service, 2008: 7), the explicit focus on efficiency and measurements of outcomes symbolises the new public management ethos which has also penetrated the youth justice system.

The Garda Youth Diversion Projects

The Garda Youth Diversion Projects represent an interesting case study to illustrate the changing nature of the Irish youth justice system. As community-based and multi-agency crime prevention initiatives, they unify many of the elements which stem from an advanced-liberal governance framework. Secondly, they allow for critical reflection regarding the dispersal of functions related to crime prevention to the youth work sector, which has traditionally been characterised by a welfare-oriented ethos, focusing on the personal development and social education of young people. In an ethnographic study that looked in-depth at a joined-up youth crime initiative in the UK, it was found that as comparable new modes of managing youth and crime were being rolled out, 'the social work ethic is a tough nut to crack' (Burnett and Appleton, 2004: 40). The study found that despite tensions between professionals from diverse backgrounds, the social workers' young person-centred welfare approach dominated within these multi-agency projects and positively influenced other professionals engaged in the project. With similar issues in mind, the following section, will investigate the implications of the collaboration between the youth work sector and the youth justice system and how it is negotiated in the Irish context.

As noted earlier, the origins of the Garda Youth Diversion Projects can be traced to 1991, when the first two projects were established on an ad hoc basis as a response to what was seen as disorderly behaviour by young people in de-prived, urban areas of North/West Dublin (Tallaght and North Clondalkin). Typical of poorly planned public housing estates, these areas were characterised by problematic developments around community building, a high demographic dependency ratio, high unemployment rates and low levels of Garda morale (Bowden and Higgins, 2000: 21). The Interdepartmental Group on Urban Crime and Disorder which was set up in 1992 as a response to clashes between the police, the fire brigade and a group of young people in Ronanstown, recommended the continuation of the two pilot projects.

Since their inception, the Garda Youth Diversion Projects have grown exponentially (see Table 7.1). From only two projects in 1991 which were funded from existing Garda funds (Bowden and Higgins, 2000) with a total of €55,000, the number of projects had risen to 100 with a yearly total budget expenditure of almost €8 million in 2008 and a total budget allocation of €13 million in 2009. The Youth Justice Strategy 2008–2010 aims to further increase the number of diversion projects to 130 projects by 2010 and further to 168 projects by 2012, though this expansion is likely to be cut back due to the financial crisis that became increasingly apparent during 2009. The projects are funded by the

Department of Justice, Equality and Law Reform (and since 2006 the Irish Youth Justice Service) who in turn accesses funds under the National Development Plan and the European Social Fund. As the diversion projects are usually staffed with at least one full-time project coordinator/youth worker, the project budgets are considerable. Thus, 60% of diversion projects responding to the 2008 Survey of Contemporary Youth Work Provision in Ireland (Powell *et. al.*, 2010) reported project budgets of between €70,000 to €90,000 and 36.3% reported budgets of €90–100,000. These relatively large amounts of funding per project are justified by the Irish Youth Justice Service in reference to the projects' main mission, which is to 'to directly impact youth crime which distinguishes them from other youth service interventions and underlies the logic for Irish Youth Justice Service investment' (Irish Youth Justice Service, 2009a: 9). This utilitarian rationale of 'effective youth crime prevention' for the project's intervention might indeed be understandable from the Youth Justice system's point of view, but arguably challenges the ethos and ideals traditionally associated with the youth work sector. Indeed, in its submission to the National Crime Council's Consultation Paper *Tackling the Underlying Causes of Crime* (2002), the National Youth Council of Ireland lamented that the expectation of the youth work sector to contribute to young people's social and personal development would not be supported by adequate funding for mainstream youth work.

While it is difficult to estimate the total number of project participants due to fluctuation in participation during the year and the diversity of projects, the survey results show that, on average, fifty-three young people participate per project. An evaluation report conducted in 2000 indicated that on average eighty-four young people participated per project in structured activities during 1998 (Bowden and Higgins, 2000: 45). Thus, the total estimated number of participants across all diversion projects lies somewhere between 5–8,000, which is a considerable reach in terms of numbers of young people involved in the projects on a yearly basis. While this expansion in numbers of projects and participants is not indicator enough to suggest that the 'net of social control' through the diversion projects is widening, they are a strong indicator of the shift to youth crime prevention in more alternative community settings.

Referrals to the Garda Youth Diversion Projects come from a wide range of sources and are then considered by the Referral Assessment Committee, which usually consists of the Juvenile Liaison Officer of the respective area, the project coordinator and 'where possible and appropriate', the Probation and Welfare Officer (Department of Justice, Equality and Law Reform, 2002: 30). Members of the committee can make referrals to the project, but also review requests for referrals from social workers, schools, residents and the project committee. In practice, project coordinators also attract many young people to the projects through 'taster' activities during the summer and outreach work, visiting young people's homes or inviting friends of referred young people to participate in the projects. The analysis of the survey data shows that the largest number of referrals is received from the JLO, followed by schools, social workers and, interestingly, also parents.

Table 7.1 Garda Youth Diversion Project funding 1991–August 2009

Year	Number of projects	Amount of funding
1991	2	€55,000
1992	2	€55,000
1993	2	€55,000
1994	4	€155,000
1995	6	€256,995
1996	10	€517,996
1997	12	€557,997
1998	14	€675,000
1999	29	€1,296,500
2000	51	€1,743,192
2001	64	€3,215,080
2002	64	€4,490,151
2003	64	€5,066,936
2004	64	€4,904,656
2005	64	€5,182,798
2006	74	€6,423,747
2007	100	€7,270,141
2008	100	€7,996,223
2009 (August)	100	€4,948,307

Source: Irish Youth Justice Service, 2009a

An interesting trend is observable when looking at the composition of participants in the projects. The Garda Youth Diversion Projects are officially defined as 'community-based, multi-agency crime prevention initiatives which seek to divert young people from becoming involved (or further involved) in anti-social and/or criminal behaviour by providing suitable activities to facilitate personal development and promote civic responsibility' (Department of Justice, Equality and Law Reform, 2002: 1). They envisage a dual role, namely of preventing young people from getting involved in criminal behaviour in the first place and from getting re-involved, usually after having been cautioned under the Juvenile Diversion Programme. The *Garda Youth Diversion Project Guidelines* of 2002 elaborate in further detail on this dual nature of the Diversion Projects, by outlining the primary and secondary target group of participants. The project guidelines define primary participants as 'young people who have entered the Garda Juvenile Diversion Programme and are considered at risk of remaining within the justice system', whereas the secondary target group is defined as 'young people who, although they have not been referred directly by the JLO, have come to the attention of the Gardai, the community or local agencies as a result of their behaviour and are considered at risk of entering the justice system at a future date' (Department of Justice, Equality and Law Reform, 2002: 41). The guidelines go further to elaborate that this secondary target group might be young people who the community see as 'trouble makers'. Indeed, the analysis of the survey data shows that only half of all male project participants and only one-third of all female project participants belong to the primary target group. This is also corroborated by the findings of the 2000 Evaluation Report on participants of the Garda Diversion Projects, in which only 59.1% of the project participants indicated that they had previously been in trouble with the Gardai. This means that effectively, a significant majority of young people have officially not been involved in criminal offences or deviant behaviour, but are only considered 'at risk' of becoming involved. This issue of net-widening has been recognised as a potential problem of the diversion projects in the 2000 Evaluation Report which noted that in the case of non-offending participants 'it is unclear what criteria are used' (Bowden and Higgins, 2000: 150). Consequently the report recommended that the referral process be tightened by increasing the focus on young offenders and by introducing a clear referral process through Juvenile Liaison Officers for non-offenders.

The response to this proposal was to integrate participation criteria in the project guidelines, to ensure that the projects work with those young people who are in most need. Arguing that a list of 'at risk' indicators would not be used due to lack of international agreement of what 'risk' constitutes, the following participation criteria were highlighted: poor school attendance/early school leaving, offending behaviour/offending peer group, known to the JLO/local Gardai, alcohol, drug use, family involvement in crime and difficult relationships with parents/authority figures. The guidelines furthermore highlighted that priority would be 'given to those who, due to their life circumstances and behaviour in the community, are considered less likely to be diverted from crime by means of a caution and may benefit from further interventions' (Department of Justice, Equality and Law Reform, 2002: 40). However, as we have seen from the survey data above, this has not had any effect in practice and the proportion of secondary participants seems very large. In practice, project coordinators, youth workers and Juvenile Liaison Officers justify this by arguing that 'non-offending' peers, who are often family members or close friends of the 'primary target group' could have a positive influence on individuals and the group dynamic.

Secondly, many situations arise, where young people are arguably entering into problematic behaviour, for which they might be cautioned if no projects were available otherwise:

> A young fellow is kicking windows and cars in town ... he hasn't been cautioned yet, but the JLO asks me 'could you work with him'. (Garda Youth Diversion Project Coordinator)

Equally, the flexibility of inviting non-offenders to participate in the projects is seen as 'normal' and 'positive' by youth workers:

> In my opinion, the 'at risk' definition is basically open to interpretation. And that is kind of good. For example, we had a case where we had one young guy and he hadn't come into trouble with the law now, but all his friends had been; so we involved him in a project – it wouldn't have made sense to leave him out. (Garda Youth Diversion Project Coordinator)

This focus on secondary participants potentially also represents what Cohen (1979) calls a blurring of boundaries between offenders and non-offenders. This outcome has been criticised by Cohen in the context of thinking about community sanctions: 'the fact that many of these multi-purpose centres are directed not just at convicted offenders, but are preventive, diagnostic or screening enterprises aimed at potential, pre-delinquents, or high risk populations, should alert us to the more important forms of blurring behind this administrative surrealism. The ideology of community treatment, allows for a facile evasion of the delinquent/non-delinquent distinction' (Cohen, 1979: 346).

However, it ultimately seems to remain open to interpretation whether the large proportion of non-offenders in the Garda Youth Diversion Projects should be described as net-widening or whether it represents an organic development which could also contribute to reducing the stigmatising effect of young offenders to participate in the projects. A similar concern about net-widening arises when looking at the age-range of participants. As per the project guidelines, the 'optimum age' of participation in projects is indicated as twelve to seventeen years, whereas it leaves the option for the Referral Assessment Committees to make decisions on a case-by-case basis. The survey results showed that roughly 57% of the participants are between the ages of eleven to fifteen, whereas 40% were between the ages of sixteen to eighteen. Interestingly, there is a very small percentage (2%) of young people under the age of ten years participating in the projects.

The geographic locations, as well as the socio-economic backgrounds of project participants, reflect the typical profile of young people who are being processed into the criminal justice system in Ireland. Geographically, the majority of projects are located in urban areas (twenty-nine in Dublin; eleven in Cork, six in Limerick). Only one of the twenty-seven projects responding to the survey had participants from rural areas. As the projects are designed and financed on a needs basis, they have to provide evidence of indicators such as high levels of juvenile delinquency, early school leaving and single-parent families. Not surprisingly, the large majority of the projects are located in disadvantaged areas. As is evident from Table 7.2, the contrast between participants of Youth Diversion Projects compared to all youth work groups in the survey is quite stark. Almost all (93%) diversion projects that responded to the 2008 Survey of Contemporary Youth Work Provision in Ireland (Powell *et al.*, 2010), indicated that the most significant issue affecting the project participants was their financially disadvantaged position. This is in stark contrast to the 34.7 % of all groups who reported financial disadvantage.

Table 7.2 Challenges facing young people

Most significant issues	Youth Diversion Projects	All youth work groups
Financially disadvantaged backgrounds	93	34.7
Behavioural difficulties	80	19
Alcohol misuse	70	16
Alcohol misuse in family	62	17.7
Substance misuse	55.5	13.6
Substance abuse in family	48.1	12.8
Violence in the home	25	7.1
Mental health issues	13.6	4.3
Survivors of abuse	5.5	3

Source: Working With Young People (Powell *et al.*, 2010)

Problematising youth work: the dilemmas of social control

At a national level, the Garda Youth Diversion Projects are administered through the Community Relations Section of An Garda Siochana, who are also responsible for Community Policing, Neighbourhood Watch, Joint Policing and Racial and Intercultural Affairs. On the ground, the Garda Youth Diversion Projects are implemented to a large extent by voluntary youth organisations (see Table 7. 3). For all of these organisations, youth diversion projects only represent a small part of their portfolio of youth services.

Table 7.3 Organisations implementing Garda Youth Diversion Projects

Implementing organisations	Number of projects
Foróige	29
Independently managed projects	25
Catholic Youth Care	10
Waterford Regional Youth Service	7
Kerry Diocesan Youth Service	6
Midlands Regional Youth Service	4
Limerick Youth Service	3
Ogra Chorcai	3
Youth Work Ireland	3
North Connaught Regional Youth Service	3
Cloyne Diocesan Youth Service	2
Kildare Youth Service	2
Clare Youth Service	2
City of Dublin Youth Service Board	1
Total	100

Source: Irish Youth Justice Service, 2009a: 9

On a local level, the projects are overseen by a Project Committee, which usually consists of representatives of the employing agency (usually the Project Coordinator), the Project Treasurer (usually the JLO, who through the Gardai represents the Department of Justice, Equality and Law Reform), various agencies and community organisations/individuals. The Project Committee acts as a consultative body, which is 'responsible for determining the direction of the project and the programme of the project' (Department of Justice, Equality and Law Reform, 2002: 28) and monitors and evaluates the project actions and outcomes. In addition to the representation of several agencies and community members on the Project Committee, the projects are also, informally and to different degrees, involved in a network with other agencies in the health, community, education, training sector, drug treatment and local employment services, for the purpose of networking, support and referral of young people if necessary (Bowden and Higgins, 2000). The projects' set-up does therefore not go as far as to characterise the diversion projects as genuinely 'joined-up' project work, in the sense that a variety of different agencies collaborate on a daily basis with the same group of young people. However, on a case-to-case basis, this seems to take place, particularly where projects are located in community facilities, usually housing a wide range of projects in areas related to health and drug use.

Undeniably, the Garda Youth Diversion Projects follow a 'social control' agenda as an explicit rationale exists to divert young people from causing disruption to public order. Debates about whether youth workers should be involved in these types of initiatives have been conducted since the 1970s onwards, both in Ireland and the UK. As we saw in Chapter 6, there are concerns that the shift in emphasis towards targeted forms of youth work may undermine some of the values which the sector has traditionally claimed for itself. Because young people are referred to the Garda Diversion Projects by various agencies, it could be argued that they undermine one of the most fundamental principles of youth work, that of voluntary participation. Officially, the Diversion projects are based on voluntary participation: 'Young people who participate in the project do so voluntarily. A young person cannot be directed by the courts to participate in the project nor should participation be a condition of supervision' (Department of Justice, Equality and Law Reform, 2002: 45). This practice is confirmed by the finding that some young people chose to opt out or not join projects, even if referred to them by the JLO. However, to assume that this automatically implies genuinely voluntary participation in all cases would deny the subtle power inequalities which are at play between authority figures and young people. Equally, one youth worker admitted that some young people had to be 'convinced' to participate in the projects:

> It's very strict in the Garda Youth Diversion Projects – that it is voluntary. However, that is not the case in practice. Because the JLO refers them … it's up to me to follow up … if they [the young person] say no the first time … I leave it for a while … I try another thing … Let them come to the Youth Café … I pull them into the building that way … (Garda Youth Diversion Project Coordinator)

The dual and sometimes contradictory roles demanded of youth workers in diversion projects was also highlighted by some of those interviewed in the course of our research:

> You see, you have to sell it twofold: we have to say it's about empowering young people and reaching young people, so we have to say what [our youth work organisation] is about; young people developing themselves naturally in their own communities; but we also have to sell the Garda Youth Diversion guidelines, where young people have to..you know take civic responsibility for their actions; understand their behaviour in a way that they might move away from getting into trouble with the Gardai or with the law … It took me a while to get around it. (Youth Diversion Project Coordinator)

Other youth workers on Garda Diversion Projects have seemingly not consciously reflected on the different nature of diversion projects and mainstream youth work or consider targeted youth work as merely another form of youth work:

> I never thought about it to be honest. Diversion is certainly about changing behaviour ... Mainstream ones are more relaxed. No need to talk to young people about what they did on the weekend; did they drink; did they take drugs in the mainstream projects. Diversion is hoping more to get them away from certain behaviours.
>   It depends on the worker and how they can focus – it's just another aspect of it ... it's just another element ... it's a slant, I call it ... it's for us at the bottom level, there has to be a prevention element in it ... I don't know if it would be too different ... or off the scale from 'ordinary youth work' – but it also depends on the youth worker I guess.

Ultimately, the interpretation of the youth worker's role in the diversion projects is likely to remain somewhat contested. From a critical perspective, it could be said that youth workers of the twenty-first century have not been instilled with the ideological idealism of the youth workers trained in the 1960s and 1970s, when more radical ideas about youth work were popular. An alternative interpretation might be that in practice youth work is not fundamentally different in the diversion projects than in general youth work projects. In fact, the 2000 Evaluation Report claimed that many of the projects were not focusing sufficiently on explicit crime diversion and were almost indistinguishable from mainstream youth projects. Some of the youth workers mentioned during the interviews that in addition to unstructured activities, they planned highly organised sessions with young people, discussing their behaviour and other crime-related issues. However, others claimed that many young people often would not realise the specific difference between the diversion project and mainstream youth work.

Conclusion

Within certain limitations, the shifts in the youth justice system described above, mirror international trends that have emerged with regards to treatment of children and young people in conflict with the law in 'advanced-liberal' government regimes (Rose, 1996). The consensus that has emerged with regard to the treatment of young people in conflict with the law in Ireland includes the following features: firstly, prevention is to be preferred over non-intervention. The new system of regulation aims to govern young people through mechanisms of risk factor analysis and other actuarial practices emphasising effectiveness and rationality. This prevention is to start from an early age onwards and to be provided by a variety of statutory and voluntary providers to children and young people who seem to be at risk of getting involved with deviant behaviour. As we have seen, crime reduction policy has shifted towards new forms of social prevention practices. This focus on prevention is then implemented through the 'risk-factor' paradigm which is used widely by both voluntary and statutory agencies providing targeted services to young people. While there is always a certain caution expressed regarding the blunt use of a risk factor paradigms, its positive aspects of being able to explain correlations between certain risk factors (individual, family, neigbhourhood, etc.), seems to convince policy-makers and practitioners of its usefulness. In a political landscape which understandably focuses its limited financial resources on young people most in need, the adoption of the 'at-risk' paradigm wants to provide a coherent approach to selecting a certain set of interventions for young people. However, this 'at-risk' approach also does indicate that it is ultimately the individual and the individual's failings that are seen as a major cause of social problems, despite the fact that environmental factors are also taken into consideration. From a critical perspective, these new politics of risk rationalities and risk management signify a qualitative shift in how deficit assumptions of young people are attempted to be formalised and quantified. From an idealistic viewpoint, such an approach should be particularly problematic for youth work organisations, which have subscribed to an ethos of social education and empowerment of young people.

The second feature of the emerging consensus then has been that, since detention is the last resort for young people in conflict with the law, diversion from the criminal justice system or correction in the community have become the standard. Arguably, they represent the least intrusive solutions for young people in trouble with the law. However, as Cohen (1985) has outlined, diversion is only an indicator of a softer approach to youth justice, if it deals with the hard end of offenders. So far, the rapid expansion of the Garda Juvenile Diversion Programme since the mid-1980s and the over-reliance on detention for children indicates an overall widening of social control over young people's lives in Ireland (Carroll and Meehan, 2007). However, this will hopefully constitute only a transitory phase, particularly since the full range of community sanctions have become available for use by the courts since late 2008. Paradoxically, one of the reasons cited in the literature for slow reform of the youth justice system in Ireland was the strong belief of communities that the challenge of youthful offending could be solved within and by local communities (Mulcahy, 2007). This informalism of community involvement is gradually being replaced by a more centrally designed, strategic and formalised system of involving community representatives on referral committees for targeted youth projects and on local youth justice teams.

A similar rationale underpins the third factor that underlies the emerging consensus, namely that a wide range of statutory and voluntary sector agencies

need to get involved in dealing with the prevention or correction of youth offending. Since it is widely accepted that crime always represents a multi-faceted
and complex social phenomenon, a similarly wide range of actors have to get involved in dealing with this variety of circumstances. The shifts towards increased
inter-agency cooperation and multi-stakeholder initiatives arguably represent a
two-track development: on the one hand, public services are concentrated at the
centre (e.g. through the creation of the Irish Youth Justice service), looking for
enhanced coordination and ultimately greater efficiencies, while on the other
hand distributing responsibilities for managing risk to the youth work sector
and associated agencies, working with youth and their families in the community. Consequently young people who are in conflict (or potentially in conflict)
with the law are regulated quite differently than before.

Whether these developments signify a 'waning' of the culture of control, as has been argued with regard to the general criminal justice system for
adults, for example (O'Sullivan and O'Donnell, 2007: 45), probably depends on
whether one adopts a 'benevolent' or a 'conspirational' interpretation of these
shifts. Cohen (1985), for example, argues that strategies of community sanctions
should be exposed to the same kind of rigour that original forms of punishment
like imprisonment were earlier. He particularly points out that seemingly benign
forms of community control contribute to a 'blurring' of boundaries between
those outside and inside the correctional 'institution'. As we have seen earlier,
the Youth Diversion Projects do represent such a case where both young people
who have committed offences and those who are only 'at risk' of offending participate in the same programmes of intervention. Cohen (1979: 15) warns that
this might result in a future where 'it will be impossible to determine who is
enmeshed in the social control machine at any one time'. He also argues that
the ideological shift towards such measures as community control and diversion from the criminal justice system would lead to more intervention by the
State, rather than less. This will widen the net of social control, if also through
the operation of 'softer' systems. Certain indications such as the relatively steady
and at certain points even increasing detention rates of juvenile offenders, in
correspondence with a simultaneous increase in alternative sanctions and diversion, support this 'more intervention' hypothesis, rather than less. Similarly, the
creation and possible future expansion of the ASBOs signify such a widening
of the system of controlling young people. Cohen also points out a process of
'masking', which 'concerns the way in which the benevolently intentioned move
to the community may sometimes disguise the intrusiveness of the new programmes' (Cohen, 1979: 611). Indeed, it has been recognised that a potential
risk of the Diversion Programmes would be that the young person loses their
legal protection in various stages of the process (Kilkelly, 2008; Walsh, 2005).
Similarly, the power to regulate young people's lives has gradually been diffused to a wider network of actors who practice supposedly more 'benign' and

less harmful activities with young people (potentially) in trouble with the law (Cohen, 1979). As we have seen, the Garda Youth Diversion Projects offer such an example where crime prevention and control functions have been diffused to seemingly unrelated sectors.

As a consequence of the analysis presented in this chapter, a mixed picture seems to emerge as to what extent the youth work sector participates in the explicit social control agenda of the youth justice system. While we have seen that the projects do to a certain extent contribute to the widening, blurring and masking of the boundaries and processes characterising the youth justice system, there were also strong indications that the youth workers, who are working on the ground with young people, are more attached to the ways of working with young people typical in their youth work organisations. Although lack of structure from the side of the Irish Youth Justice Service was also commented upon as a challenge by some youth workers, it would be important from the youth work perspective to maintain this relative distance, so as to be able to maintain their integrity as youth workers.

PART III

DISADVANTAGED YOUNG PEOPLE, INSTITUTIONALISM AND HUMAN RIGHTS: THE RYAN REPORT IN PERSPECTIVE

8

Outcast youth and public policy: institutionalism, social genetics and charity

Such children were socially constructed as a grotesque 'other', seen as a polluting presence and in need of retraining and reforming. Focused as it was on a particular (lower) class of family, these children were the 'moral dirt' of a social order determined to prove its 'purity', and other children and good citizens needed to be protected from their 'contaminating' influences. In its deep connections to class and notions of nation-hood, in its own way this was nothing less than a persecutory form of ethnic cleansing. (Ferguson, 2007: 133)

In the modern Western model of humanity, charity moved into the sphere of secular morality, which had little concern for religious sentiment – being primarily preoccupied by the preservation of public order, the health of the population and the promotion of the work ethic (Piven and Cloward, 1971). While the process of secularisation was much less dramatic in Ireland than England, where the Elizabethan social reforms in 1601 represented a major social policy development, it, nonetheless, was significant. The new consciousness within Irish civil society involved a much broader concept of charity. Public charity emerged as a public-private partnership, in which the Catholic Church, after the Charitable Bequests Act 1844, became the dominant partner. Its new social role represented tacit recognition by the Catholic Church that charity had largely lost its religious meaning in modern society. As far as the Catholic Church was concerned, charity had became an instrument of social power that supported its mission for the remoralisation of Irish society, forged during the heat of the Devotional Revolution in the mid-nineteenth century. The Catholic Church sought to impose a rigid form of civility influenced by French Jansenism, that focused on the control of sexuality, particularly amongst the youth population (Inglis, 1987: 135). Catholic charitable activity was primarily focused upon the socialisation of youth, through the control of education and social care. The latter was to take the form of a vast system of institutional care for unwanted children that severed the links between youth and their families in a project that Barnes (1989: 88) has termed 'social genetics'. While the science of genetics in its modern form is associated with Gregor Mendel (1822–1884), the term is traceable back to the Ancient Greeks, who used the word *genetikos* to describe the fact that living things inherit traits from their parents, including unhealthy traits. It provides a fitting metaphor for the system of institutional care that first emerged under state-civil society patronage during the eighteenth century, was handed over to the Catholic Church in the mid-nineteenth century and reluctantly closed by the State in the late twentieth century, after a scandalous history of abuse (see Chapter 10). Within the Western model of humanity, Levene (2005: 3) has described genocide as 'modernity's potential for lethally tidying up human material perceived as surplus to requirements and/or, more pointedly as extraneous *other*'. The core emphasis is on cleansing the population of unwanted social groups (Mann, 2005: 16–18). Burleigh (2000: 244) observes 'totalitarian regimes are sometimes described as 'gardening states' which sought to transform society by eradicating those they regarded as 'alien', or 'unfit' so that the 'fit' may flourish'.

As Mann (2005) demonstrates, genocide (a term invented in 1944 by the Polish lawyer Rapheal Lemkin) is the extreme end of a continuum of human behaviours with the aim of cultural, social and political suppression of minorities. Eugenics is a less extreme form of biologically based cleansing of the population that purports to protect and improve it, through discouraging breeding by social groups perceived to have inheritable undesirable traits. It was particularly influential on policy formation in the first half of the twentieth century in America, Sweden, Britain and notoriously Nazi Germany (Burleigh, 2000: 345–404). Our study adopts Barnes's (1989) concept of 'social genetics' to describe behaviours within Irish society aimed at cleansing itself of an outcast youth population, variously described as foundling, orphan, destitute, syphilitic, delinquent, etc. The legacy of this eugenic policy continues to be felt right down to the present day. Ferguson's (2007) association of Irish industrial schools with a policy of 'ethnic cleansing' clearly makes this connection. Both Barnes (1989) and Ferguson (2007) construct the policy of institutionalisation in eugenic terms.

In this chapter we seek to chart the history of institutional care of children and young people in Ireland. We search for explanations as to why this oppressive system was allowed to flourish for so long. The motivation of both state and civil society is interrogated. We explore the Catholic Church's remoralisation of Irish society project in terms of the imposition of a rigid form of religious civility upon Irish society, in pursuit of social power in a secular age. We deconstruct Irish collective consciousness in an attempt to understand this dark historical narrative and what it tells us about the nature of charity and the treatment of an outcast youth population. Drawing on the work of Barnes (1989) and Ferguson (2007), we suggest that the underpinning logic shaping institutionalisation was not charity but eugenics that targeted vulnerable children from socially disadvantaged backgrounds as 'moral lepers' (Smart, 1999).

Sex, death and confinement

Chronologically, the first group to be segregated and confined on a large scale in early modern Irish society were syphilitic orphan children or 'foundling children' as they were more discreetly referred to by contemporaries. These children were one of the most overt examples of the 'problem population' of social outcasts, since they were by definition unwanted. They were normally the product of illegitimate birth and were associated with the growth of the urban problem of prostitution. According to McDowell (1979: 26) prostitution was widespread in eighteenth-century Irish society. Apart from being a threat to the social fabric, prostitution spawned a series of other risks, which equally challenged the maintenance of public order. To the eighteenth-century Irish mind probably the most serious of these risks was venereal disease. Syphilis was the principal venereal infection. Endemic syphilis and 'button scurvy' (caused by malnutrition) became prevalent in seventeenth and eighteenth-century Ireland. Both diseases were believed to be spread by social and sexual contact and were thought to be especially common amongst children living in poor and unhygienic conditions (Morton, 1972: 26–27).

The decision to outlaw infanticide in 1707 (a common means of disposing of unwanted children) led to the establishment of three foundling hospitals in Ireland – located in Dublin, Cork and Galway. European society dealt with the problem of the unwanted child through the institutional solution of the foundling hospital. The latent purpose of the foundling hospital was bluntly characterised by Malthus (1878: 157) as follows:

> Considering the extraordinary mortality which occurs in these institutions ... if a person wished to check population and were not solicitous about the means he could not propose a more effectual measure than the establishment of a sufficient number of foundling hospitals unlimited as to their reception of children.

Malthus's revealing remark encapsulated the outcast status of the foundling children and draws attention to their high mortality rates in the order of 80% (or even 90%) across Europe. For the foundling child, segregation and confinement usually involved death, which provided a permanent solution to the problem which contemporaries believed these children posed to the health of the population. Foundling children in eighteenth-century Ireland were viewed as the syphilitic products of prostitution. They were popularly referred to as 'whore's brats' or 'whores gets' (Robins, 1980: 50).

The mortality figures for the Dublin Foundling Hospital, which opened in 1730 as a national facility, were remarkably high even by the standards of the time. Ireland had a relatively high infant-mortality rate, which Mokyr (1983: 37) has calculated to have been approximately 12% in 1838. In the first seven years following the opening of the Dublin Foundling Hospital 3,235 children died out of 4,025 admitted, representing a mortality rate of 80%. This level of mortality was to remain broadly consistent throughout the history of the Dublin Foundling Hospital with minor fluctuations. During 1737–1743 the mortality rate fell slightly to 75% (Robins, 1980: 17). Between 1750–1759 the mortality rate rose to 89% (*ibid.*: 22). Figures for the period 1756–1771 indicate that the mortality rate fell again to 70% (*ibid.*: 25) During the period 1781–1790 out of 19,368 children admitted to the Dublin Foundling Hospital some 10,428 died. However, 6,526 were 'struck off', leaving only 2,414 definitely alive (*Journal of the Irish House of Commons*, 1791 XIV: ccci). Between 1796 and 1826, 41,524 children perished representing a mortality rate of approximately 80% (see Table 8.1).

How can these consistently high mortality rates be explained? Several contemporary observers pointed to the presence of venereal disease. A physician employed at the Foundling Hospital remarked to a committee of inquiry into its conduct in 1758 'that the children were in a bad state of health when they came into the house: disorders mostly venereal' (*Journal of the Irish House of Commons*, 1758, VI: xcvi). The English social reformer John Howard reported to the Irish Parliament in 1788 on his visit to the Dublin Hospital, declaring that there was 'too little attention to cleanliness' and that 'most of the children (were) bad with a cutaneous [skin] disorder' (*Journal of the Irish House of Commons*, 1788, XII: dcccxlv). Official reports produced by the officers of the Dublin Foundling Hospital tend to cite venereal disease as the major cause of death within the institution. For example, James Shaughenissy, the apothecary, declared that of the 4,204 children who died within the nursery at the Foundling Hospital between 1781 and 1789, 3,470 were suffering from venereal disease (*Journal of Irish House of Commons*, 1791, XIV: ccci).

Venereal disease was not the only cause of death. Those children who survived long enough to be fostered out (prior to being returned to the hospital at the age of six to train and work) were often neglected and frequently died. The Blaquiere Committee in 1792, reckoned that the number of deaths of children fostered in the country during the previous year was 1,838 (*Journal of the Irish House of Commons*, 1792, XV, p.ccvii). Out of the 41,524 child mortalities associated with the Dublin Foundling Hospital between 1796–1826, some 26,181 died while they were being fostered in the country compared with 15,343 in the institution (see Table 8.1). The overall mortality rate is exceptional. The distinguished social anthropologist Margaret Mead has offered an explanation, suggesting that institutions for foundling children were 'only a prolonged, ritualized method of disposing of the infant for whom nobody wished to care' (cited in Kadushin, 1980: 36). The Foundling Hospital was merged into the Poor Law after 1838 and was ultimately replaced by the reformatory and industrial school system.

Table 8.1 Disposals of children admitted to the Dublin Foundling Hospital, 1796–1826

Died in the hospital whilst infants	14,613	
Returned as dead whilst at nurse in the country	25,859	
Died in the Infirmary, after returning from nurse	730	
Died in the country, grown children sent there for health	322	41,524
Eloped from the hospital		413
Delivered up to parents whilst infants		1,093
Ditto from the grown department		34
Apprenticed to trades		5,466
Ditto to schoolmasters		204
Transferred to charter schools		526
		49,260
Remaining in the hospital and at nurse 5th January 1826		6,339
		55,599
Deduct the number of children in the hospital and at nurse 25th June 1796		3,410
		52,189

Source: Third Report of the Commissioners of Irish Education Enquiry, 1826–1827, xiii: 5.

Reformatory schools and the culture of violence

The imprisonment of youth had been a major source of controversy for many years. Social reformers including John Howard (1729–1790), Elizabeth Fry (1780–1845) and Mary Carpenter (1807–1877) campaigned against imprisoning young offenders in gaols. The *Report of the Reformatory and Industrial Schools Commission* 1884 noted 'during the four years ending 1852, 63,332 young offenders, vagrants and criminals (5,141 being under 10 years of age) were arrested in the City of Dublin and committed to gaol' (para. 83). In relation to girls, the 1884 Commission further noted that 'larceny, as well as vagrancy, these so enormously prevailed among the female population that during the years 1850, 1851, 1852, 5,189 young girls were committed to the Dublin female prison at Grangegorman' (*ibid.*). Mary Carpenter was one of the most distinguished social reformers of the Victorian era. Her interests spanned the anti-slavery movement, education, women's rights and penal reform. In 1851 Mary Carpenter published an influential book entitled *Reformatory Schools for the Children of the Perishing and Dangerous Classes, and for Juvenile Offenders*. In this work, which made her a national figure, she advocated a system of schooling for the poor including good free day schools; feeding industrial schools and reformatory schools. She observed in the introduction to her book that 'it is not needed at the present day, to demonstrate the immense importance of the juvenile portion of the community to the future and even the present welfare of the state – or to the need of education to prepare the young to be good citizens and useful members of the community' (Carpenter, 1851: 10). Mary Carpenter (*ibid.*: 84) argued that imprisoning juveniles must be replaced by a more humane system of reformatory schools based upon love: 'The principle already laid down will make it evident that love must be the ruling feature of the treatment of their children; this must not be weak sentimental feeling; but wise love which shall evidently have as its object the true welfare of the child'.

In order to prove her principle Mary Carpenter established a reformatory school in Bristol during 1852 and a second reformatory for girls in 1854. Her concept of 'wise love' involved discipline. Carpenter posed the question to society 'we usually regard the juvenile thieves as a distinct class … could they be submitted more readily to stringent reformatory discipline?' (*ibid.*: 84). However, she made it clear that discipline did not mean the use of corporal punishment in reformatory schools: 'in a school where such views are adopted no punishment of a degrading or revengeful nature will ever be employed' (*ibid.*: 87). Mary Carpenter (*ibid.*) pointed out the negative consequences of the use of corporal punishment: 'nor less injurious is the practice of employing corporal punishment, which not only inflicts a disgrace most sensitively felt by all high-spirited children, but usually excites a vindictive spirit, which must utterly neutralise the influence of the master for the good'.

The reformatory school model, championed by Mary Carpenter emerged as an alternative to prison. Arnold (2009: 24) comments 'the theory behind the reformatory system was good. Their aim was to treat, not to punish. The reality was rather different'. The government was willing to establish a system of reformatories in Ireland for young people. However, when a bill was introduced in 1856, the Catholic Church condemned it on the grounds that it did not provide sufficient safeguards for the protection of the religion of the young offender population. By 1858 legislation acceptable to Catholic opinion was enacted, which empowered the Chief Secretary to certify appropriate institutions for the reception of young offenders. Essentially, reformatories were to be denominational in character and subvented from the public purse. The emphasis was purportedly on training in the crafts and trades, with the prospect of apprenticeships for those inmates who proved amenable to reform (Robins, 1980: 297). There were never more than ten reformatories in Ireland – five for girls and five for boys. By 1944, there were only two, St Joseph's in Limerick for girls and Daingean, County Offaly, for boys. In addition, St Anne's School in County Dublin was registered as both a reformatory and industrial school from 1949. Letterfrack

industrial School became a junior reformatory in 1954, with up to 76% of its inmates coming from Dublin, despite its remote location in Connemara, County
Galway. In reality, reformatories and industrial schools 'merged' into one punitive system and 'the lines of distinction between them became blurred' (Barnes,
1989: 42).

Within a quarter of a century of their establishment searching questions
were being asked about the suitability of reformatory schools in Irish social conditions. The Reformatory and Industrial Schools Commission 1884 noted that
no new reformatories were built after 1870 (probably due to the introduction of
industrial schools in 1868) and the fact that numbers were low (see Table 8.2).

Table 8.2 Children in Irish reformatories in 1881

Boys	Girls	Total	
Roman Catholic	808	191	999
Protestant	128	22	150
Total	936	213	1,149

Source: Report of the Reformatory and Industrial Schools Commissioners 1884.

Ferguson (2007: 132) observes that there was a sharp division between
gender groups, with boys predominating in reformatories, while girls were the
majority in industrial schools.

Numbers continued to decline in Irish reformatories. The Inspector of
Reformatory and Industrial Schools, Sir Rowland Blennerhassett, noted in 1896
that numbers within reformatories fell between 1880 and 1895 by 50% – from
1,169 to 589 and that this decline resulted in four reformatories being closed,
including the only female Protestant reformatory (*Thirty Fourth Report of the
Inspector of Reformatory and Industrial Schools of Ireland*, 1896: 3–7). A further reduction took place in 1927, when the new Irish government reduced the
number of reformatories to two, as noted above. The paucity of numbers resulted in young children being inappropriately placed in reformatory schools.
The *Report of the Reformatory and Industrial Schools Commission* (1884: para.
91) observed: 'One of the most striking features of the reformatory schools in
Ireland is the scarcity of older and more criminal inmates, whose place is to a
great extent filled by children committed at an early age for trifling offences'.
The 1884 Commission concluded that 'it seems clear, however, that considering
the unfitness of the reformatory system for young children, and the prejudi-
cial effects of conviction, imprisonment and detention in a reformatory upon
a child's career, the present system should in some way be modified. If genuine reformatory cases are scarce in Ireland, some of the present reformatories
might be certified as industrial schools' (*ibid.*). While numbers were small the

'symbolic power' of institutionalisation served as a disciplinary strategy that utilised social fear amongst the poor and marginalised, discouraging those who
might be tempted into a life of crime (Ferguson, 2007: 132–133).

Numbers in reformatories continued to decline after independence as is illustrated in Table 8.3. The reasons are various. As already noted the system was
not suited to Irish social conditions. The population was in decline. Courts were
reluctant to incarcerate young offenders for the minimum sentence of three
years. But undoubtedly the most significant factor in explaining reformatories'
low level of usage was that industrial schools offered a more flexible alternative
(in terms of admission criteria), while providing a similarly punitive environment – if not quite so harsh.

Table 8.3 Children in reformatories

Year	Number under detention	Admission	Discharges
1930	116	33	43
1931	106	17	30
1932	93	36	57
1933	72	19	14
1934	77	27	18

*Source: Report of the Commission of Inquiry into the Reformatory and Industrial School
System*(Cussen Report), 1936: 67.

In the century from 1858 to 1969, a total of 15,899 children and young people
were committed to the reformatory school system. They were overwhelmingly
male: boys accounted for 13,428 of the total reformatory school population,
compared with 2,471 girls. Under the Irish Free State an average of 150 children
per annum were sentenced for periods of several years in reformatories. Often
there was not evidence of criminal behaviour but simply social prejudice, such as
a thirteen year old boy in Dublin being 'a regular street arab' or the child whose
father drank a little and whose mother was 'good, but Protestant' (Raftery and
O' Sullivan, 1999: 27). In the case of girls, they were frequently sent to reformatories because they were perceived as being sexually precocious or exposed to
immoral influences (*ibid.*: 27–28). In common with industrial schools (which
were almost indistinguishable) reformatories sought to cleanse their inmates of
undesirable character traits through ruthless discipline.

Reformatory schools' relative failure to institutionally thrive compared with
industrial schools was due to the fact that both were part of an integrated child
penal system – in Bruce Arnold's (2009) description – *The Irish Gulag*. However,

the failure of reformatories to thrive was more than compensated for by their excesses in the violent repression of the unfortunate children (aged twelve to seventeen years) that populated them. At Daingean Reformatory School there were three riots by inmates during 1956 and 1958. They were suppressed following the intervention of the Gardai. At least forty inmates were involved in the 1956 riot. The ringleaders were imprisoned in St Patrick's Institution (a children's prison) (Ryan Report, 2009, Volume 1: para. 15.228–15.236). No attempt seems to have been made to establish the cause of the riots other than 'a shortage of reasonable food' (*ibid.*: para. 15.233). One of the survivors of the riots told the Ryan Committee that he received 140 blows for his part in these events (*ibid.*: para 15.248). In 1968 a number of residents attempted to burn down Daingean but were foiled in their plans (*ibid.*: paras 15.250–15.251). Daingean Reformatory School was described by the Ryan Report (*ibid.*: para. 15.252) as 'a frightening and threatening environment'. It further noted that there were 'no recorded instances of riots in Daingean after the abolition of corporal punishment in 1970' (*ibid.*). It is notable that the Kennedy Report had recommended its closure in 1970, which occurred in 1973. Similarly, the regime in Letterfrack has been analysed by the Ryan Report (*ibid.*: Chapter 8) as revealing a regime of endemic violence towards children. But, arguably the most telling indictment came from a survivor, Peter Tyrrell, who later was a prisoner of war in Nazi Germany, imprisoned at Stalag IIB Fallingbostel, which he describes as 'a Heaven on earth in comparison to my life at [Letterfrack] school' (Tyrrell, 2006: 156). While the violence in reformatory schools was extreme by any standards, it was paralleled in many industrial schools, where a predominantly female population was exposed to a regime similarly based upon the discipline of fear and corporal punishment.

Industrial schools, social genetics and remoralisation

In 1867, the O' Conor Don, MP for County Roscommon, claimed that the number of homeless street children in Ireland was double the number for England and Wales. He simultaneously introduced a bill for the establishment of an industrial schools system. The bill lacked government support and was strongly opposed by Irish Protestant MPs on the grounds that this was a sectarian measure designed to place the control of disadvantaged Irish youth in the hands of Catholic charities. The O' Conor Don withdrew the proposal but reintroduced it the following year. This time he was successful (Robins, 1980: 301–302). The stated purpose of the industrial school was officially defined as 'to bring up destitute or criminal children in habits of religion and virtue' (Heywood, 1978: 48). The latent purpose was very different. The physical contagion (syphilis and scurvy) associated with children in the foundling hospital had been replaced by public concerns with moral contagion, albeit physical contagion of syphillis through sex outside marriage remained a major concern. Child abuse was not conceptualised as such but as incest, sexual assault or other 'immoral acts' (Ferriter, 2009).

The Industrial Schools (Ireland) Act 1868 provided for the institutionalisation of homeless youths, street children, orphans, children exposed to immoral influences (e.g. incest, prostitution and child abuse) or whose parents were in prison. Burke (1987: 227) argues that the industrial school system, which developed under religious management, was part of 'the movement to make provision for specialised groups of people outside the workhouse, or, to put it another way, the movement to secure people from the workhouse'. This benign construction locates industrial schools within the child-saving movement. It would seem to be at odds with the facts. There was a community-based alternative available for destitute and homeless children in the form of the poor law system of boarding-out to foster families. The name industrial school clearly echoes the workhouse – the emphasis was on punishment rather than welfare. In reality, it is hard to escape the conclusion that the establishment of the industrial school system in Ireland was motivated by a remoralisation agenda aimed at the control of Catholic youths from the lower classes and was based upon a philosophy of social control. Sir Rowland Blennerhassett's clarification of the role and function of industrial schools that they were reformatories at the lighter end of the disciplinary scale, also questions Burke's analysis (*Thirty-fourth Report of the Inspector of Reformatory and Industrial Schools of Ireland*, 1896: 8–9). The system of orphanages developed by the Catholic Church provided the prototype for the industrial schools that grew to seventy-one in number by 1899, containing 8,422 children (Robins, 1980: 305). Ferriter (2009: 48) notes 'in 1901 for every 1000 children under 14, 6 were in industrial schools in Ireland; the corresponding figures for Scotland and England were 3 and just over 1'. Between 1868 and 1969 more than 105,000 children were committed to industrial schools, with an average annual population of 6,000 children up to the 1950s. By 1969 the total population of the 31 remaining industrial schools had declined to 2,000 (Raftery and O' Sullivan, 1999: 20).

There were five main legal grounds empowering the State to send children to industrial schools: 'needy or destitute', 'non-attendance at school', and 'criminal offences', plus being sent by a local health authority or voluntary committal (Ryan Report, 2009, Volume 5: 11). In reality, destitution arising from poverty was the key factor in decisions to institutionalise children. The presenting reason for sending most children to industrial schools (over 80% of all children and 90% of girls) was social need (Raftery and O' Sullivan, 1999: 22). This term could mean anything and was largely employed to cloak the State's failure to provide adequately for needy children in the community by supporting their families in times of want. The use of the legal fiction 'lack of proper guardianship' was a catch-all term for needy and destitute children. Raftery and O' Sullivan (*ibid.*) concluded 'however, in all these cases, the language and procedure of the courts was to place the onus of guilt on the child'. The Ryan Report (2009, Volume

1: para. 2.09) noted that 'in 1882, over 70% of committal entries to industrial schools were made under the category of begging'. The State, rather than attempting to address the poverty that existed amongst deprived families 'chose instead to fund religious orders to effectively incarcerate these children' (*ibid.*). Very few of the children were guilty of any offence – just 1% of girls and 11% of boys! From the 1950s onwards, St Joseph's Industrial School at Lettertrack, County Galway became the centre for receiving young boys who had committed minor offences (*ibid.*). Up to that point there had been no differentiation, underscoring the link between child poverty and the policy of criminalising this outcast youth population.

From the inception of the industrial school system there was a significant gender imbalance. Out of seventy-one industrial schools (at their maximum number in 1898), forty-two catered for girls. Table 8.4 gives a breakdown of numbers by gender in industrial schools in 1895. Ferguson (2007: 125) observes what 'a significant factor this was that girls tended to be committed earlier than boys and spent longer periods of time in the schools'. Girls were often the victims of child sexual abuse for which the victim was frequently blamed. Fear of syphilis continued to be associated with sex outside marriage (Ferriter, 2009). Contagion was a major public concern often resulting in child abuse victims being institutionalised or threatened with institutionalisation (*ibid.*). Both the Inter-departmental Committee of Inquiry Regarding Venereal Disease (1926) and the Carrigan Committee (1931), which inquired into sexual offences and juvenile prostitution, underlined the public interest in the control and regulation of sexuality.

Table 8.4 Children detained in Industrial Schools in 1895

	Males	Females	Total
In school (number paid for under the school rules)	3,289	4,179	7,468
In school (in excess of number paid for)	47	265	312
On licence	337	321	658
Absconded	5	—	5
Sentence complete, remaining in school	3	77	80
Total	3,681	4,842	8,473

Source: Thirty-fourth Report of the Inspector of Reformatory and Industrial Schools of Ireland, 1896: 9.

Jane Barnes's (1989) study, entitled *Irish Industrial Schools 1868–1908*, examines the origins and development of the system as a form of social genetics. She notes 'in order to carry out the central work of character formation and moral training, remaining links between the child and the home were ruthlessly cut ... conversion to a new set of values was to be the objective; purging the children of their parents' views and habits the method. The whole process amounted to social genetics' (Barnes, 1989: 88). Ferguson (2007), as already noted, constructs institutionalisation as a strategy of 'ethnic cleansing'. The idea of social genetics is also taken up by Raftery and O' Sullivan (1999: 312): 'there was one constant theme that continuously informed the way in which industrial school children were treated. That was the clear perception from the religious that they were in some way less valuable and less worthy than other children.' While some of these children were illegitimate they were almost certainly in the minority. A smaller group were from ethnic minority backgrounds (e.g. African-Irish, Travellers, etc.) (*ibid.*: 312–313). All of the children in the Irish industrial schools were stigmatised by their social backgrounds and institutionalisation. They were treated as social outcasts. Irish civil society colluded in this policy of social genetics, which has some parallels with other European countries influenced by Social Darwinism (i.e. survival of the fittest). Raftery and O' Sullivan (*ibid.*: 317–318) in reference to the collusion of civil society, make a direct comparison with Nazi Germany.

Maguire (2009: 48) notes 'a remarkable degree of ambivalence towards illegitimate children amongst Irish clerics, lawmakers and judges'. This ambivalence reflected the view of civil society. In Ireland, illegitimacy was viewed as a threat to the blood lines or genes within families upon which property inheritance was based in a land-owning economy. During the adoption debate between 1948 and 1952 the issues of blood and property arose. Adoption had been introduced in the wake of the First World War to England (1926), Northern Ireland (1929) and Scotland (1930). A belated campaign, following the Second World War, by the Adoption Society (founded in 1948) to introduce similar legislation to Ireland met with powerful resistance. One officer of the Adoption Society recalled a rural TD telling him that to interfere with the line of succession to property was 'like interfering with a stud-book' (cited in Whyte, 1980: 187). Manifestly genes and property were fundamentally linked in Irish society. Illegitimacy (real or imagined) or membership of a minority ethnic group was viewed as a threat to the gene pool. Like the foundling children of the eighteenth century, who were viewed as carriers of syphilis, youths in industrial schools were regarded as the carriers of bad genes. Public anxiety about bad genes continued to be associated with the problem of syphilis, which was very often the product of sexual exploitation. Young girls were frequently targeted in cities by paedophiles offering sweets or money (Ferriter, 2009: 52). They were, instead of receiving care and protection, subjected to social exclusion in the form of a confinement and isolation from Irish society as a population of social outcasts. The Catholic

Church made their remoralisation the centre of its agenda in an effort to 'cleanse' them of any links with their biological origins in a patriarchal society where the female victim in many cases was held responsible for the crime. All of the children in institutions were the victims of poverty – this is a core theme under-pinning the findings of the Ryan Report in 2009 (see Chapter 10).

In order to facilitate remoralisation, young people were usually detained in industrial schools until they reached the age of sixteen years, regardless of legality. Family ties were viewed as polluting. Mail was censored. Family visits were discretionary and rare. Parents (especially single parents) were made to feel uncomfortable. They were treated with distain by the clerical managers, often involving physical exclusion from the buildings, however inclement the weather. This policy of discouraging contact between children and their natural parents was carried out despite monetary payments from the parents (Raftery and O' Sullivan, 1999: 314–315). In a traditionalist society that professed to value the family, this would appear to be fundamentally contradictory policy. Yet as Raftery and O' Sullivan (*ibid.*: 315–316) assert both Church and State cooper-ated in this policy:

> It is clear that families of a particular class of people, those who lived in poverty, were of less value and less importance in this context … While the bulk of this hostile attitude to family came from the religious orders, there is no doubt that the state colluded in it. Many children were deliberately committed by the courts to industrial schools hundreds of miles from their homes. This was a highly effec-tive means of cutting off all contact with their families as the expense of traveling to visit was an effective barrier for very many of their parents … It was one of an arsenal of tactics used – particularly by nuns – to break the children's spirit and to shape them for life – mainly as docile servants …

Barnes (1989: 89) concludes, 'moral regeneration – which implied incisive di-vorce from home and family – was the goal'. Raftery and O' Sullivan (1999: 338) assert that there is a contradiction in our perception of Irish social policy, which has been widely viewed as non-interventionist and pro-family but in reality it was highly directive towards these children's incarceration in church-run in-dustrial schools: 'this standard view may now need to be re-examined in the context of the sheer scale of the state's direct intervention in the lives of such vast numbers of families, through committal of their children to industrial schools'. However, this robust policy of state interventionism did not extend to protecting children from punishment and abuse once they were incarcerated in industrial schools. The children were undergoing a process of remoralisation intended to change their attitudes and identity. This was the project of the industrial school system. Remoralisation had replaced the foundling hospitals policy of liquida-tion. Ferguson (2007: 134) has aptly described the remoralisation process:

In the Irish Industrial school regime, however, 'forgetting' the past extended into systematic abuses which involved annihilation of identity itself, such as being given and only known by a number, and being sent as far away as possible from one's family and community of origin. As religious conversion was seen as central to saving the souls of these impure children, they were systematically regarded as second class citizens, as undeserving of the kinds of love and care afforded the 'uncontaminated' non-abused children. Re-moralising children meant returning them to 'innocence' by knocking the devil out of them. Thus, what children were supposed to be helped to forget created a rationale for their systematic abuse.

Discipline in industrial schools was ruthlessly enforced. As Barnes (1989: 101) puts it, 'although corporal punishment was cast in as favourable light as possible, strong evidence exists that some schools featured frequent and severe beatings'. She based this conclusion on an analysis of inspectors' reports, which 'while inspectors reported on the one hand a low incidence of corporal punishment, on the other they felt obliged to censure some managers for excessive use of the cane' (*ibid.*). Once again we are confronted by contradictory behaviour by the State, raising fundamental issues about the social construction of the industrial school child's identity as victim, criminal and outcast. Sir Rowland Blennerhassett, Inspector of Industrial and Reformatory Schools, reported on the problematic issue of corporal punishment in 1896:

> I am glad to be able to state that corporal punishment is steadily diminishing and the punishment books are better kept than formerly. I notice, too, that the decrease is most marked in the schools which are best managed. I should be glad to see it, if possible, abolished altogether. I do not think the cane should ever be used; it is always more or less dangerous to the class of children who are sent to industrial schools ... I must draw the attention of managers seriously to this matter, and they must understand that they will be held responsible for any excessive punishment inflicted by any master or official under them. (*Thirty-fourth Report of the Inspector of Reformatory and Industrial Schools of Ireland,* 1896: 20)

While Sir Rowland's attitude is reassuring, it reveals an underlying concern that the use of corporal punishment was being abused in industrial schools. Barnes (1989: 102) discusses the challenges the inspectors faced in addressing the issue of corporal punishment in industrial schools between 1868 and 1908:

> [Inspector] Blennerhassett's unease about corporal punishment was taken up by his successor, John Fagan. Fagan made several attempts to investigate allegations of brutality in schools run by Christian Brothers. His enquiries were invariably frustrated, as the following revealing incident indicates. On one occasion at Artane during an interview with the school director, Fagan asked to see two boys who had made complaints to him about one of the school officers. The manager

of the school, who discovered what was afoot, sent a warning to the director. The director then 'opened Mr. Fagan's eyes – told him to beware – that he was on dangerous ground, etc. ... Fagan seemed to feel that he was in an awkward position ...' The inspector had effectively been intimidated and when the boys arrived for the interview he dismissed them immediately, telling them to make their grievances known to the manager or sub-manager. 'Thus' reported the school manager 'ended most satisfactorily what seemed to be a serious matter.' It proved difficult to establish the full truth about the extent of corporal punishment in industrial schools at the time, it is even more so a century later. However, it is possible to draw some conclusions from the available evidence. Corporal punishment featured in most boys' schools. Whipping with leather straps or canes occurred regularly, and there can be little doubt that boys were treated brutally in some institutions. Girls' schools appear to have a better record than boys' schools. The sisters made more use of alternative punishments such as the withdrawal of privileges and treats, withdrawal of food, and solitary confinement. Cutting off hair and whipping were reserved for the most serious offences.[1]

Apart from his failure to address corporal punishment, Dr John Fagan appears to have carried out his duties with considerable independence. He commented critically on the poor physical environment including diet, heating, clothing, hygiene and the unsuitability of the buildings. Dr Fagan also drew attention to the unacceptably high death rates amongst the children placed in industrial schools. He condemned the industrial school system as being 'managed and disciplined on cast iron lines' (Barnes, 1989: 115). Dr Fagan's reports resulted in public outrage, causing the industrial school system a considerable level of negative publicity and criticism (Raftery and O' Sullivan, 1999: 124). But it was of little consequence. As the Ryan Report (2009, Volume 1: para. 8.36) noted over a hundred years later:

> What this scenario also demonstrated was that, while the Department of Education funded the industrial and reformatory schools and carried out periodic inspections of schools, these schools were in reality controlled by the congregations that ran them, and it mattered little the level of opposition, or indeed who might be opposing any changes the Congregation proposed – their decision in the matter was final.

In essence, the Irish Catholic Church regarded itself as above the law, reflecting its view of Church–State relations. This hubristic belief was supported by Irish civil society. Ferguson (2007: 134) concludes: 'the assumed deviancy of the children was used to justify them not being treated as victims of child abuse or childhood adversity in the schools ... it helped create a context where for those children who were sexually as well as physically abused within the schools, their true victimisation was never understood or responded to and remained hidden behind a veil of secrecy, repression and social fear'. This public silence on the part of Irish civil society created the context that allowed these abusive regimes to flourish. Raftery and O' Sullivan (1999: 19) note:

> The sheer scale of the system has in part resulted in the strange public silence on these institutions for most of this [the twentieth] century. While there were some courageous expressions of concern and dissent, the general absence of questioning was profound. Yet the majority of these institutions were not hidden away in remote areas. They were situated in prominent locations in towns and cities all over Ireland.

It is difficult not to conclude that Irish civil society knowingly colluded with this policy of institutionalised victimisation because it supported the religious in their project of remoralising 'moral dirt' in the perceived genetic interests of the population as a whole. This is the unpalatable truth. The abuse of children in Irish industrial and reformatory schools was a 'known-unknown'.

The Cussen Report and the failure of state regulation

The establishment of the Irish Free State appears to have led to an absence of state regulation over industrial schools. In Britain the system was reformed to constrain the use of corporal punishment. In Ireland, the Derrig Rules in 1933 had the opposite effect. Arnold (2009: 32) comments, 'in Ireland there seemed under Tomás Derrig [Minister for Education] to be a deliberate attempt to turn the country away from these reforms, to give broader license to the [Religious] orders running the [industrial and reformatory] institutions and to ignore lapses when these came to public attention'. Public concern did, however, lead to the establishment of a Commission of Inquiry. The subsequent *Report of the Commission of Inquiry into the Reformatory and Industrial School System Report* (1936) (better known as the Cussen Report) was essentially a reaffirmation of the system that served to dampen public criticism. All records of the Cussen Committee have disappeared (Raftery and O' Sullivan, 1999: 78). The Cussen Report was published on 17 August 1936 and received both a muted public and political reaction. Perhaps that was inevitable, given its endorsement of the status quo. But at a deeper level one senses that it was the product of a cover-up. While the Cussen Report envisaged changes in nomenclature (which were officially ignored) and more informality (i.e. less legalism) in a judicial structure that was oblivious to children's human rights, as well as better education and training (in a system which relentlessly exploited child labour and neglected educational development), it offered no convincing critique of the system of industrial and reformatory schools. Ireland was about to adopt a new constitution in 1937 that was both in theory and practice as theocratic as it was democratic.

The social power of the Catholic Church was, in 1936, at its apogee, its authority unchallengeable. The Cussen Report bore testament to the dominance of the Church over State but also to collusion by the State in a violently oppressive system that mirrored labour and concentration camps across the European continent during the 1930s and 1940s. What was unique in Ireland was that the inmates were children.

Yet the Cussen Report (1936: 10) was remarkably revelatory about why children were placed in industrial schools, observing 'in the main the problem is one not of criminal tendencies, but poverty'. Approximately, 90% of children admitted to industrial schools during the first five years of the 1930s were for reasons of poverty and neglect (see Table 8.5). Furthermore, the Cussen Report (1936: 11) comes to similar conclusions regarding reformatories:

> These observations apply also in large measure to Reformatories. Although the young people committed to the Reformatories have been found guilty of offences it is the case that the percentage of those who subsequently make a further appearance in the Courts is negligible. It follows, we suggest, that such young persons cannot in any sense fairly be looked upon as criminals.

Table 8.5 Reasons why children were committed to Industrial Schools 1930–1934

Year	Serious offences %	Failure to attend school %	Poverty and neglect %	Other causes %
1930	3.8	7	89.1	0.1
1931	5.2	5.1	89.4	0.3
1932	3.4	6.2	90.3	0.1
1933	4.5	5	89.9	0.6
1934	6.2	6.1	87.7	–

Source: Cussen Report, 1936: 10

In reality, most of the children in institutional care were sent to industrial schools, with only a small fraction attending reformatories (see Table 8.6). The direct cause of most children being in institutional care in Ireland during the 1930s was consequently poverty.[2]

It is very difficult to avoid the conclusion that reformatories were in terminable decline and 90% of children placed in industrial schools were misplaced. Yet the Cussen Report (1936: 49) in its primary recommendation fulsomely endorsed the system of reformatory and industrial schools declaring 'The present system of reformatory and industrial schools should be continued subject to modifications suggested in the Report. The Schools should remain under the management of the Religious Orders who have undertaken the work.' Despite the overwhelming evidence regarding the unsuitability of the industrial school system the Cussen Report fully endorsed the system and the clergy, which effectively owned and administered it. However, the Cussen Report (*ibid*.: 49–57) did make detailed recommendations for the better management of the system in terms of diet, education, inspection, management, aftercare and health. It also, as noted above, recommended a name change, to no avail (*ibid*.: 50). All of these recommendations were disregarded.

Table 8.6 Children in Reformatory and Industrial Schools 1930–1934

Year	Reformatory Schools	Industrial Schools
1930	116	6,682
1931	106	6,701
1932	93	6,697
1933	72	6,653
1934	77	6,481

Source: Cussen Report, 1936: 67.

However, in 1939 two inspectors were appointed, Dr Anne McCabe and P.O. Muircheartaigh who were very vocal in their criticisms of the industrial school system as 'Dickensian'. Dr McCabe described the industrial school children as 'cowed and frightened, shrinking, when spoken to like little savages' (cited in Raftery and O' Sullivan, 1999: 126). P.O. Muircheartaigh remarked that one industrial school manager deserved to be put in prison (cited in Raftery and O' Sullivan, 1999: 127). Towards the end of his tenure in 1945, Inspector Muircheartaigh reported that:

> Dr. McCabe and myself have conducted a strenuous campaign against this semi-starvation. On her inspections, she has attacked it in every school in which she found it and indicated the improvements to be made in the diet etc.. I followed up the reports in all such cases with official letters, generally in strong terms.
>
> We have before us the task of uprooting the old idea that industrial schools children are a class apart and have not the same human needs and rights as other children and that they should be thankful for anything they get because it comes to them from charity. There may have been something to this idea in the last century, but the present position is that from a material point of view running an industrial school on an aggregate grant of about 18s/ 3d per head per week is a business proposition and the community should get value for its money. If the present deplorable conditions are to be abolished we must deal firmly with the flagrant cases. (Cited in Raftery and O' Sullivan, 1999: 131)

Despite the inspectors' criticisms of the industrial school system the government remained largely unmoved. Little was done for this outcast youth population. Ferguson (2007: 135) has offered an explanation for the Irish government's inertia 'in the context after 1922 of post-independence Ireland, child care practice drew on racial imagery in the sense that the regime was deliberately instructed to assert the difference of the Irish from the former British coloniser'. It was not until the Kennedy Report in 1970 that the scandalous conditions of endemic exploitation, neglect and abuse of institutionalised young people resulted in the closure of the industrial school system in Ireland, albeit without exposing the reality of institutional violence, which was once again covered up (see Chapters 9 and 10). It took another four decades before the Commission of Inquiry into Child Abuse (Ryan Report) in 2009 finally challenged the censorship of public discussion of the human rights violations in industrial and reformatory schools system, albeit while continuing to ensure the anonymity of perpetrators.

Conclusion

Irish youth were socially constructed as a problem population during the eighteenth century, as Ireland began to be shaped by the forces of modernity. Urbanisation changed Ireland in socio-economic terms. The growth of the city brought new risks, including urban poverty, prostitution and venereal disease. Illegitimate children were often the unwanted consequences of changing social life in this new urban landscape. Foundling children, as they were called, epitomised the dark side of early modern Irish social life. Unwanted and treated as social outcasts, they were allowed to die. Successive public enquiries resulted in no change. Why? Because civil society viewed these children as the carriers of a contagious disease (syphilis) their deaths provided a convenient solution to an endemic social problem. Social genetics underpinned the logic of cleansing the population of children perceived as being unhealthy. Ultimately, Ireland's three foundling hospitals in Dublin, Cork and Galway were closed and the children subsumed into the poor law system after 1838. By the 1850s a new system of industrial schools and reformatories, under the control of the Catholic Church, became the main form of institutionalisation for young people. This system of institutionalisation of youth was to dominate the Irish social landscape until 1970, albeit largely shrouded from the public gaze. It was a harsh regime, where abuse and cruelty were normalised into everyday life. The hidden history of these industrial schools, reformatories and workhouses raises searching questions about the ethical basis of Irish charity and its treatment of youth. The answers are complex. Charity in modern Irish society lacked an ethical basis. It was an expression of social power in which the Catholic Church embedded itself at the core of Irish social policy. Both state and civil society colluded in this system of public charity, where the State paid and the Church controlled the lives of destitute youth. The reason for confining and secluding the destitute youth population of the Irish institutional care system away from their families and communities is explicable in terms of their outcast status. They were viewed as a threat to the gene pool, leading to the suggestion that the institutional care system was based upon the principles of social genetics, informed by a desire to cleanse the population. In Ireland social genetics were closely linked to the protection of property in a society where land-ownership was a core element of the economic system. Illegitimacy (or more accurately the perception of illegitimacy) raised questions about the integrity of the gene pool and threatened property and succession rights within families. Chastity was therefore, highly valued in Irish society. The Catholic Church established itself as the moral agency in this system of Darwinian social control. The lives of many Irish youths were to be deeply damaged by this social policy that remained in place until 1970. It represents a dark and hidden history of Irish social life with youth as its victims that has blighted Ireland's record as a democratic community based upon human rights and the rule of law. If Ireland had followed the rest of Europe and established a welfare state based upon social justice this tragic saga might not have occurred. Charity, administered by the Irish Catholic Church, proved to be a system (as we shall see in Chapter 9) that condemned many Irish youths to unparalleled abuse with effectively no recognition of their human rights.

Notes

1   The Ryan Report (2009) provides detailed evidence which suggests that both girls and boys were subjected to a regime of endemic violence with little or no respect for gender difference.
2   Professor Harry Ferguson (2007) argues that poverty was only one factor in admissions to industrial schools. He suggests that many of the children admitted at the request of the ISPCC were victims of family failure, including child abuse. The Ryan Report (2009, Volume 5: 9) endorses Ferguson's analysis regarding the significance of the role of the ISPCC but concludes that committals were due to family poverty rather than child abuse.

9

Child abuse, youth policy and human rights: contextualising the Ryan Report

The *Report of the Commission to Inquire into Child Abuse* is the map of an Irish hell. It defines the contours of a dark hinterland of the State, a parallel country whose existence we have long known but never fully acknowledged. It is a land of pain and shame, of savage cruelty and callous indifference. The instinct to turn away from it, repelled by its profoundly unsettling ugliness, is almost irresistible. We owe it, though, to those who have suffered there to acknowledge from now on that it is an inescapable part of Irish reality. We have to deal with the now-established fact that, alongside the warmth and intimacy, the kindness and generosity of Irish life, there was, for most the history of the State, a deliberately maintained structure of vile and vicious abuse. *(Irish Times, 21 May 2009: 19)*

The publication of the Ryan Report during 2009 was a seminal event in the vindication of the human rights of survivors of child abuse in Irish reformatory and industrial schools and truth-telling. The Ryan Report was 2,600 pages in length and composed of five volumes. It contains the testimony of over 1,500 witnesses. It is a powerfully revelatory document that stands as a unique testament to child suffering in the modern world. However, in terms of truth-telling it is arguably a flawed document because the alleged perpetrators of abuse (living and dead) have been given anonymity following legal action, but on the other hand the danger of a witch-hunt has been avoided. Furthermore, the original Chair of the Commission to Inquire into Child Abuse, Justice Mary Laffoy, resigned in 2003 because of an alleged lack of official cooperation, notably on the part of the Department of Education (Arnold, 2009: 98–109). She was replaced by Justice Sean Ryan. The Ryan Report reveals the child abuse was endemic in the industrial and reformatory school system in Ireland. Its shocking revelations have been reported around the world, exposing the failure of Ireland's human rights record in relation to children, to critical international scrutiny. The alleged crimes against children described in the Ryan Report are on a systemic scale and involve a degree of sadistic cruelty that is difficult to comprehend in a developed society (see Chapter 10). Public reaction has been one of shock and horror. But perhaps inevitably media interest is transient and sensational. There is an unwillingness to confront the deep underlying human rights issues that reveal Ireland as a cold climate and heartless society, if you are young, weak or poor. There is also the challenge of developing a moral literacy that informs and guides the rhetoric of children's rights. Ireland has been slow to develop a moral literacy of human rights. This chapter seeks to explain the background, context and political response to the Ryan Report, published in May 2009. It is argued that there were two phases – in the form of distinctive campaigns for children's rights – leading to the investigatory process into industrial and reformatory schools that produced the Ryan Report in 2009.

The background

The system of reformatory and industrial schools dates from the middle of the nineteenth century. Between 1858–1969, some 15,899 (mainly male) children were committed to reformatory schools. The regime, typified by Daingean Reformatory School in County Offaly, was based upon physical and mental terror, administered with extraordinary cruelty in the country's ten reforma-tory schools. Many of these reformatory schools had closed by the end of the nineteenth century. All five female reformatories were closed. There simply was a lack of demand. But the small number of remaining reformatory schools pro-vided a symbolic warning to the children of the poor that justice could be brutal and severe (see Chapter 8).

There were over 105,000 children (predominantly female) committed by the courts to Ireland's seventy-one industrial schools between 1868 and 1969. Artane in Dublin with 800 male children was the largest and according to Arnold (2009: 13) the most famous, probably because of the Artane Boy's Band. The administration of these institutions was largely in the hands of the clergy. Most of the children were placed in institutions because they were poor and treated as 'moral lepers' (Smart, 1999: 404). They were widely regarded with contempt by Irish civil society because of their perceived moral contagion and placed in care by child protection services – usually the Irish Society for the Prevention of Cruelty to Children (ISPCC), the main child protection agency. The care of these needy children was placed in the hands of the Catholic clergy, ostensibly in the name of Christian charity. The 'charity myth' provided a con-venient moral shroud behind which acts of child abuse (unparalleled in the civilised world) were allegedly carried out without restraint or accountability (Raftery and O'Sullivan, 1999). Other countries, notably Australia, Canada and Germany, have also experienced child abuse in institutional care but not on the Irish scale. The common link is the Catholic Church. In the case of Austrialia and Canada, Irish religious orders have been closely linked to these public scandals (*ibid.*: 265–267). Bruce Arnold (2009) has described this system of reformatory and industrial schools as *The Irish Gulag*, borrowing the title from Alexander Solzhenitsyn's famous exposé of Soviet Labour Camps in *The Gulag Archipelago*. Arnold (*ibid.*: 2) asserts 'during the greater part of the twentieth century the Irish State owned and managed a prison system for children across the whole Republic ... They were places of shame in the communities where they were located and they were shameful places'. Arnold's angry words of condemnation capture the moral revulsion experienced by readers of the Ryan Report. How could this have happened and been kept secret for so long?

The chronology of events that led to the exposure of child abuse in industrial and reformatory schools dates from the 1950s and 1960s, when a social movement began with the aim of achieving a thoroughgoing reform of the Irish social care system, based upon the twin principles of deinstitutionalisation and human rights. Its impact over the ensuing half century was to fundamentally alter the direction of social care in Ireland away from institutionalisation. It represented the voice of liberal civil society in Ireland – made up of minority counter-publics that questioned the human rights record of the Irish state in relation to the institutionalisation of children. Mainstream civil society showed little or no interest in the fate of institutionalised children, other than to cooperate in returning absconders or to participate in the benefits of the local economy. Raftery and O' Sullivan (1999: 318) have drawn parallels between public attitudes towards victims in Nazi Germany with Ireland: 'both Irish and German society shared a similar pattern of denial'.

O'Sullivan and O'Donnell (2007: 33) have analysed a paradigm shift in the use of coercive confinement (i.e. institutionalisation) in Ireland during the half century between 1951 and 2002:

1   the massive downsizing of the population in coercive confinement: from over 31,000 (1,069 per 100,000) to just under 5,000 (126 per 100,000);
2   the narrowing of the range of sites: the number of institutions, which coercively held unmarried mothers and their children, has been reduced to zero;
3   the changing gender balance of those held in coercive confinement: from a majority of women to a minority;
4   the increasingly dominant role of the State: voluntary religious or non-profit agencies have virtually disappeared as providers of coercive confinement.

As a result of this transition, community care has replaced institutionalisation and the State has replaced the Church as the custodian of care. This fundamental change in youth policy did not happen in a vacuum. It was the produce of a protracted human rights campaign that was relentlessly resisted by Church and State in the interests of what Inglis (1987) has called 'moral monopoly'.

The first campaign

The first impetus towards social reform came from liberal civil society during
the 1950s and 1960s, inspired by the Joint Committee of Women's Societies and
Social Workers (JCWSSW), founded in 1935 (Ferriter, 2009: 146). It was officially
regarded as a 'prejudiced organisation that was engaging in unwarranted criticism of the reformatory and industrial schools system' (Raftery and O'Sullivan,
1999: 356–357). However, when the OECD Committee *Investment in Education*
(OECD, 1966) highlighted the issue, it was clear that something needed to be
done, if Ireland was to pass the necessary tests on democratic citizenship and
human rights for entry into the European Union (then EEC). Ireland's dark
secret of institutional child abuse could have stopped its application on human
rights grounds. Michael Viney wrote a series of insightful articles on young
offenders in the *Irish Times* during 1966, which exposed the system's shortcomings. Outside the country, away from the pressures of censorship, the London
branch of Tuairim (Opinion), an organisation of young intellectuals, produced
a report entitled *Some of Our Children: A Report on the Residential Care of the
Deprived Child in Ireland* (1966). This influential report included participation
by survivors of the Irish industrial schools system. Peter Tyrrell (2006), who had
survived the controversial Letterfrack institutional regime in Connemara, had
an input into the production of the report. However, the report was guarded in
its criticism of the punitive regime in Irish industrial and reformatory schools
(particularly the use of corporal punishment), which it suggested had been 'excessive' in the 'past' stressing the 'hypothetical' nature of the criticism (Tuairim,
1966: 39). An exasperated Peter Tyrrell, despairing of the possibility of truth
and justice in Irish public discourse, committed suicide. It is remarkable that
an organisation of Tuairim's standing, which included some of the most liberal
intellectuals in mid-twentieth century Ireland, should have been so restrained in
its criticism of what were clearly very serious human rights violations. However,
both the Tuairim report and the OECD report in 1966 were to prove highly
influential. In the following year, the government reluctantly established an official inquiry into the industrial and reformatory school system, known as the
Kennedy Committee.

The State already knew about the conditions in industrial schools and reformatories. An unpublished Inter-Departmental Committee Report on Crime
Prevention and Treatment of Offenders (*Report of Committee on Prevention
of Crime and Treatment of Offenders*, 1963) had highlighted some of the core
problems including: inadequate finance; ineffective inspection; poor clothing
and dilapidated facilities seriously in need of repair; inappropriate location far
away from populous urban centres; the need for matrons and nurses to care
for the children's health and hygiene and the deficient system of education
and training. All of its recommendations were rejected by the Department of
Education, the agency responsible for the oversight of the system of industrial

and reformatories (Raftery and O'Sullivan, 1999: 356–360). The Department of Education, according to Raftery and O'Sullivan (*ibid.*: 363), was primarily concerned about supporting the financial position of the religious orders, who were losing funding due to falling numbers. Their emphasis was on attempting to find ways in which more children could be detained in the schools, rather than proposing an alternative method of care in the community. Proposals from the Irish Association of Civil Liberty advocating deinstitutionalisation were rejected out of hand by the Department of Education (*ibid.*: 364). But it was clear that the liberal tide of social reform was beginning to engulf both the power of the Irish state and the moral authority of the Catholic Church in maintaining a system of institutional care that had begun to be investigated by the media on the grounds that there was evidence of endemic abuse. This included allegations of repressive institutional regimes that not only used corporal punishment but shaming practices, such as shaving children's heads. There were also concerns about sexuality, which at this point were not specified (*ibid.*: 365–367). The Commission to Inquire into Child Abuse (Ryan Report, 2009, Volume 4: para. 3.107) refers to the iron curtain, which stifled media reporting on industrial and reformatory schools. Censorship repressed discussion of public issues in Ireland at this time. The hegemony of the Church over the State was all pervasive during most of the twentieth century (Blanshard, 1954; Whyte, 1980).

Liberal civil society responded to the challenge of child care reform. The formation of CARE – Campaign for the Care of Deprived Children, in 1970, put human rights at the centre of its agenda. During 1972 the campaign published *Children Deprived: CARE Memorandum on Deprived Children and Children's Services in Ireland*. The first chapter of the CARE Memorandum (1972: 8) sets out the human rights case for reforming services for children and young people:

> In claiming from the public special attention for deprived children and a will to do better for them, CARE can make a case based on many principles. We would especially emphasise the principle of the rights of these children. We can distinguish between (a) children's rights as persons and as young citizens of the state and (b) children's special rights as children.

The CARE Memorandum (*ibid.*: 9) asserted that the Irish state had failed to vindicate the rights of the child:

> In Ireland too we have recognised the special rights of children, in word if not in deed. The first Dáil (Parliament) stated that the *first duty* of the Republic was to children. In the Constitution the State's special role in relation to children and other weak groups is spelled out.

While it is true that the Proclamation of 1916 promised 'to pursue ... happiness and prosperity ... cherishing all the children of the nation equally', this political and social goal had not been achieved. The highly respected writer and political commentator, Bruce Arnold, in his book *The Irish Gulag* (2009: 39) has commented:

> The claim made in the 1916 Proclamation, about cherishing the nation's children equally, and repeated in the 1919 Dáil, was sacred in Irish political texts. It was offered up as a verbal sacrifice on the altar of independence whenever the public vindications of such social charges and obligations were being aired. It meant nothing at all. It was just 'air'. No constructive purpose was served by the repetitious hypocrisy of the child-cherishing mantra. Those who fought for Irish freedom knew that such rhetoric would attract public support for their campaign of violence. Their true intentions were revealed when they came to power. As soon as the last British administrator departed from Dublin, the notion of children's rights – when children were seen as wrong doers, rather than criminals was comprehensively dismissed.

Arnold's reference to 1919 is to the Democratic Programme, a socialist statement of the children's rights as paramount, which was quickly dropped on the basis it was Marxist (Powell, 1992: 158–159). Furthermore the social justice philosophy of the Children Act 1908 (Ireland's principal child care and juvenile justice statute for most of the twentieth century) was completely ignored. It was called the Children's Charter and was the product of the UK's Liberal reforms at the beginning of the twentieth century. No group of children could have been more in need of a charter of rights than the vast population of disadvantaged children across Ireland, incarcerated in industrial and reformatory schools. The Irish state ignored their human rights. Instead, as Arnold (2009) persuasively argues, the political violence that created an independent state, based upon a crude appeal to populist nationalist sentiment, visited a regime of social violence on the unfortunate inmates of industrial and reformatory schools in a brutal project that denied children's most basic human rights. Arnold (2009: 2) asserts 'together with certain other establishments for children who were euphemistically described as being "in care", these institutions in reality constituted an "Irish Gulag"'. A regime of political conservatism (state) and social conservatism (church) had created conditions totally hostile to children's rights. This was to have catastrophic consequences for the most vulnerable section of Irish society – the legacy of which continues to be felt right down to the present day by its victims. Arnold is correct in his assertion that political independence was a disaster for children's rights. In a state controlled by the Catholic Church, deprived children were reconstructed as a problem population and subject to a moral regime of coercive institutionalisation at a point where this form of care had been condemned in the UK (*Report of the Inter-departmental Committee on Child Care*, 1896). Smart (1999) presciently observes that innocent children went through the process of institutionalisation in which they were reconstructed as 'moral lepers' and treated as child criminals.

The CARE Memorandum (1972: 29–30) vigorously put the arguments for reform of the child care system:

> Are we prepared to tolerate this state of affairs? Must we accept that the present standard of provisions for deprived children is the best we can achieve? Do we content ourselves with praising the efforts of those working with various children's difficulties while ignoring our responsibilities as individuals and as a community? CARE strongly urges the case that we should not and cannot be complacent about the present situation, that for a number of reasons we must improve it. Firstly, for reasons of justice ... secondly, deprived children deserve a better deal for reasons of charity ... But if we are not moved by considerations of justice and charity there is a third argument which can be stated thus: the deprived children of today are the dependent adults of tomorrow, if we do not provide for them adequately today we will have to support them and their families tomorrow.

A second platform for children's rights was established in 1975, called Children First. Its campaign was carried out through a newsletter, correspondence in the press and the production by its chairman, Charles Mollan, of a book, entitled *Children First* in 1979. Mollan (1979: 6) took the 1937 Constitution to task: 'of course it is right that the state should seek to support the family: but the Constitution does not seem to take sufficiently into consideration the rights of the child'. The reality has been that, since the inception of the Irish state in 1922, children have been denied basic human rights and still are within a welfare state that has been unable to articulate a secular value system based upon social justice principles. The 1937 Constitution vindicates the rights to the family at the expense of the rights of the child. Children (apart from the unborn) are constitutionally invisible.

The campaign for child care reform was supported by the other liberal civil society organisations such as the Irish Association of Social Workers and the Irish Council for Civil Liberties (ICCL). The ICCL published a report in 1977, called *Children's Rights Under the Constitution*, which called for a more equitable balance between the claims of parents and the rights of children. In the previous year, to mark National Children's Day, a protest march took place to Dail Eireann and a Proclamation on Children's Rights, fifty years after the Easter Rising (Irish Revolution), was read to the assembled protestors including representatives of CARE, Children First, the Irish Society for the Prevention of Cruelty to Children, the Irish Association of Social Workers and many other organisations. The Proclamation of Children's Rights declared:

> We, the undersigned, representatives of organizations, concerned about the welfare of children, on this National Children's Day June 13, 1976, demand that the Government take necessary action to ensure maximum protection, security, and happiness for the children of the state. We demand that legislation be introduced

to provide that in any case in which the care and custody of a child is at issue, the welfare of the child shall be the first consideration. In the event that the enactment of such legislation is thought to be repugnant to the Constitution, the Government should take steps to have the Constitutional issue decided, and, if repugnant, to make the appropriate Constitutional amendment. (cited in Mollan, 1979: 17–19)

The advocacy of a Constitutional referendum on children's rights was a farsighted proposal that has yet to be acted upon. It is clear that equality of rights for children is impossible without a constitutional referendum. While there have been two referendums in Ireland on the rights of the unborn child, advocated by the traditionalist pro-life movement, a referendum on children's rights has been resisted by both the State and conservative civil society, often opaque in its influence over social policy (O'Reilly, 1992).

Apart from its advocacy of a constitutional amendment on children rights, the Proclamation of Children Rights made several specific recommendations:

1   The interests of a child require that he receives continuous loving care in a family. He should remain with this caring family, and it should get support where necessary. Particular attention should be paid to helping single parent families.
2   The state must protect the interests of the child where family cannot or will not provide the care he needs. To this end, a comprehensive child care system incorporating adoption, fostering, and residential care must be provided. Each child should receive the care that is appropriate to his own particular needs.
3   In order to support family care, the state should ensure that its policies, with regard to income maintenance, housing and education should take account of the special needs of children, particularly deprived and handicapped children.
4   Children should not be accountable under the criminal law. Any system for dealing with young offenders should protect their interests and take account of their needs as children.
5   In addition in which a decision is taken about the welfare of a child, he should have appropriate representation in his own right. (Mollan, 1979: 17–19)

These were very progressive recommendations that amounted to a manifesto for child care reform in Ireland. The Proclamation of Children's Rights sought to challenge the Irish state to take action to vindicate children's rights. Both CARE and Children First represented a vibrant social movement committed to child care reform.

The State's response

The initial response from the Irish state to the growing campaign for children's rights following the publication of the Tuairim and OECD reports in 1966 was the establishment of a committee to examine the role of the reformatory and industrial school system. The 1970 *Reformatory and Industrial Schools Systems Report* (known as the Kennedy Report) recommended the closure of the reformatory and industrial school system but failed to reveal the scale and extent of child abuse within these institutions, leading to accusations of 'cover up' by recent commentators (Arnold, 2009). However, the Kennedy Report was generally welcomed at the time of its publication in 1970. Given the pervasive climate of censorship and the hostility of conservative civil society to reforming youth policy, it must be evaluated within the context of the time, while recognising that Bruce Arnold's criticism is absolutely correct and the consequences of the Kennedy Committee's failure to disclose the truth has seriously impacted on survivors.

Valerie Richardson (1999: 175) has described the Kennedy Report as 'a watershed in terms of child care policy' in Ireland. In essence, the Victorian system of institutional child care was to be replaced by community care. As Raftery and O'Sullivan (1999: 379) put it: 'The Kennedy Report sounded the death knell for the institutional model of child care which had remained remarkable resilient in this country for almost exactly 100 years'. That constituted a major proposal for social reform, upon which subsequent policy was built. The Kennedy Report (1970: 6–7) made thirteen recommendations, which included the immediate closure of the boys' reformatory at Daingean and Marlborough House Remand Home and the replacement of the system of reformatories by 'modern special schools'. It also recommended that 'all children in residential care or otherwise in care, should be educated to the ultimate of their capacities' (*ibid.*). Educational neglect was part of the abusive system of care. A system of aftercare was recommended, which was largely absent despite long periods of institutionalisation. At a policy level the Kennedy Committee recommended a new child care statute, the ending of capitation payments (which encouraged institutions to play a numbers game) by block grants and the vesting of responsibility for children's services within the Department of Health (Kennedy Report, 1970: 6–7).

Recent commentators have taken a much more critical view of the Kennedy Report. In Arnold's view there were three core policy issues that were not tackled by the Kennedy Committee. First, Arnold (2009: 71) states that 'the exercise of discipline was a physical tyranny' within the industrial and reformatory school system and the Kennedy Committee's decision not to address this issue was very serious: 'to ignore punishment was to bypass the most fundamental problem of all'. Second, Arnold (*ibid.*: 71–72) is concerned about the committal procedure used to send children to industrial and reformatory schools: 'central to the dreadful nature of the system, and not examined at all in the Kennedy Report, was the committal procedure by the Courts ... She (Justice Eileen Kennedy) knew that the system used was not only dreaded by the victims of it and by their parents, but it was also more widely feared by the public. She also knew that it was being administered illegally'. Third, Arnold (*ibid.*: 72) asserts 'District Justice Eileen Kennedy and her committee failed to examine the character, training and psychological capacities of those who did work within the industrial school system: these were the nuns, brothers and priests involved in the supervision and control of inmates'. Arnold's analysis of the Kennedy Report amounts to a very serious indictment of Justice Eileen Kennedy and her colleagues. Given the composition of the Kennedy Committee, it is not possible to assume that they were naive or ill-informed. It would seem with hindsight that the Kennedy Committee, despite the many plaudits it received from contemporaries in the 1970s, opted for closure over disclosure. While its recommendation to close this system was good, its failure to disclose the human rights abuses (e.g. corporal punishment) was bad. Presumably, the social power of the Catholic Church was too great an obstacle to permit the Kennedy Committee to open up the issue of child abuse within the industrial and reformatory school system to public discussion. Its silence was to keep the issue of child abuse in industrial and reformatory schools repressed for another four decades. This silence was very damaging for the survivors of the system, who deserved justice and reparation long before they achieved it.

The entry of the Labour Party (with an agenda of social reform) into government in 1974 led to the allocation of responsibility for deprived children to the Labour Party leader, Mr Brendan Corish, as Tanaiste (Deputy Prime Minister) and Minister for Health. CARE (1974: 1) reacted enthusiastically, observing 'from the very beginning we have said, and we still believe, that making one Minister and one Department, responsible for planning in respect of deprived children and children's services was the first step towards the sensible and humane reforms demanded in this whole area'. Action followed swiftly in the form of a Task Force on Child Care Services, established in 1974 and mandated to make recommendations on (i) the extension and improvement of services for deprived children and children at risk; (ii) to prepare a new Children's Bill to modernise the law; and (iii) provide a basis for administrative reforms of the child care system (Task Force on Child Care Services, 1980: 26).

When the *Task Force on Child Care Services: Final Report* was eventually published in 1980, it proved to be a disappointment to those who supported fundamental child care reform. It was divided into a majority report (reflecting the dominant view of five civil servants) and a minority report (authored by the two surviving independent representatives – an academic and a social worker). While the final report offered a comprehensive analysis of the child care system, there were major divisions, notably in relation to juvenile justice, where the majority view was against fundamental reform. However, there was broad agreement amongst the membership of the Task Force on Child Care Services (1980: 265–275) in their principal recommendations that children should be cared for in the community rather than residential care and that a new statute was needed to replace the Children Act 1908. The main reason for public disappointment was that the Task Force's report had not produced the blueprint for childcare reform that had been expected. But it was to prove highly influential in terms of accelerating the process of deinstitutionalisation. In 1968–1969 of the 4,834 children in care, three-quarters were placed in residential institutions. In marked contrast, of the 2,641 children in care in 1988, only one-quarter were in residential facilities, which had undergone substantial reform (Gilligan, 1991: 185). Manifestly, a step-change had occurred in Irish social policy in relation to the deinstitutionalisation of deprived children and young people in need of care and protection. There was a basis for a new child care statute, even if there was not agreement in relation to juvenile justice reform. But the official inertia towards social reform remained as a powerful obstacle towards change. The 1980s was a period when the liberal agenda of social reform stalled and Catholic social teaching was once again in the ascendant (Considine and Dukelow, 2009: 63). It took another decade to enact a new principal child care statute to replace the Children Act 1908. While the Irish state had systematically ignored the welfarist orientation of the Children Act 1908, it had been historically unwilling to provide an alternative. Finally, reform had become inevitable. In 1991 the Child Care Act was passed, which finally updated Irish child care law after a century of inertia. But the Irish child care system continues to fail children. In response to growing public concern about the deaths of children in care the *Irish Times* (5 March 2010) in an editorial comment on the death of Tracey Fay declared:

> The State's obligations towards children who cannot be cared for by their families are clear. Health authorities have a positive duty under the Child Care Act, 1991, to 'identify children who are not receiving adequate care and protection' and to provide them with suitable protection. The crushing reality, however, is that social services are operating against a backdrop of scarce resources, staff shortages and heavy caseloads.
>
> This crisis in child protection services is not helped by a culture of excessive secrecy on the part of the Health Service Executive (HSE) management. The HSE has consistently failed to publish any of the reports into the deaths of children in its care. It only became apparent that there was a report in existence on Ms Fay's death when details were leaked to this newspaper last year.
>
> Even the most basic statistics regarding social work services are far too often hidden behind a veil of confidentiality. For example, an annual report into the adequacy of child and family services is heavily censored and omits virtually all criticism of child protection services.

While the location of care has moved from institutional settings into the community, the child care service in Ireland remains a minimalist response to the needs of deprived children. HSE figures indicate up to 188 children in care or contact with Irish social services have died over the past decade (O' Brien, 2010a). Carl O'Brien (2010b) reported on a 'potential dereliction' of duty over the safety of foster children in parts of Dublin. These accumulated reports suggest that while children are being cared for in the community the quality of service offered by the Irish state continues to be a poor service for poor children. It is difficult to avoid the conclusion that there is a problem of moral literacy in Ireland. Public morality continues to be predominantly defined within the medieval value system of the Catholic Church. Human rights in general and children's rights in particular have no place in this world view. But there are real signs of change in public attitudes in the wake of the publication of the Ryan Report in May 2009.

The second campaign

By the end of the twentieth century attention turned to exposing the abuses that had taken place in the industrial and reformatory school system in a campaign led by the media and the survivors' movement. The year 1999 proved to be a watershed. Mary Raftery produced her television documentary series *States of Fear*, which was accompanied by her revelatory book, co-authored with Eoin O'Sullivan entitled *Suffer the Little Children: The Inside Story of Ireland's Industrial Schools*. These two important events changed the public consciousness. There followed an apology from the then Taoiseach, Bertie Ahern, and the establishment of the Commission to Inquire into Child Abuse which, in 2009, produced its final report (commonly known as the Ryan Report). It was the culmination of a half century of campaigning for children's rights by social reformers, rights activists, liberal intellectuals, social workers and survivors of child abuse. A key element in changing public opinion in relation to children's rights has been the role of the campaign group One in Four. Arnold (2009: 227) notes 'the One in Four group became quite outspoken on behalf of the abused generally at this time and countered what it called an attempt to rewrite the history of sexual abuse'. Under the dynamic leadership of Colm O'Gorman, One in Four began to transform Irish public consciousness regarding the significance of child abuse in Irish society. There were many other survivor groups who also became instrumental in unlocking their own narratives including: Irish SOCA (Survivors of Child Abuse), SOCA (UK), The Irish Deaf Society, Right to Peace, Right to Place, Alliance Victim Support, Irish Survivors of Institutional Abuse International, the Aislinn Centre and the London Irish Women's Group (Ryan Report, 2009, Volume 1: para. 1.149). All of these organisations began to provide a survivors' perspective on the growing public scandal of institutional child abuse that challenged both the Church to account for its actions and the State for a serious failure of regulation in human rights terms. Survivors' groups became a moral voice which could not be ignored. Truth was beginning to assert itself. Colm O'Gorman (2009: 119) in his autobiographical book *Beyond Belief* asserts:

> Abuse is only possible in a silent world. And just like the rest of society, my family was silent; there were certain words that were never spoken for fear of what consequences they might bring. Instead, we demanded the silencing of truths that would inevitably tear apart our idealistic view of ourselves. The truth demands action while secrets and lies allow us to avoid taking action, they allow us to continue to pretend that everything is fine, even when it is most definitely not.

The survivors' voice became the evidential basis of the Ryan Report, which was modelled on the post-apartheid Truth and Reconciliation Commission (TRC) in South Africa between 1995–1998. It is the survivors' truth told with a compelling authenticity that cannot be denied, which makes the Ryan Report the most important event in the social history of Irish children, since the inception of the State. It put children's rights at the centre of public discourse and shamed both Church and State. Child abuse has become a metaphor for the failure of the Irish public sphere to modernise.

The testimony courageously provided by the survivors enables us to revisit their experience. Through their intense social suffering, we begin to gain access into a secretive world where a policy of relentless dehumanisation shaped their lives – a world of unrelenting medieval style terror. This process has began to confront Irish civil society with the task of shaping a moral vocabulary that goes beyond outrage and results in policy responses that acknowledges the rights of children in public discourse and legal action. The Ryan Commission saw the value of a process of opening up the truth and democratising survivors' memories as a means to symbolically heal the wounds of the victims and hold the victimisers to public account. In this way it followed the South African TRC model (Keane, 2009: 693–695) (see Chapter 10).

Volume 3 of the Ryan Report (2009) provides statistical and verbatim analysis of survivors' evidence given by witnesses to the Confidential Committee, regarding the nature and scale of child abuse in Irish institutional care up to 1989. There were 857 reports of child abuse, involving 474 males and 383 female survivors, given to the Confidential Committee. This evidence is corroborated by testimony from 493 survivors given to the Investigation Committee, summarised in Volume 4 of the Ryan Report (2009): paras 5.01–5.142. The mandate of the Confidential Committee was to hear evidence 'of those survivors of childhood institutional abuse who wished to report their experiences in a confidential setting … to be conducted in an atmosphere that was informal and as sympathetic to, and understanding of the witnesses as was possible in the circumstances' (Ryan Report, Volume 1, 2009: para. 1.09). It exposes a catalogue of alleged physical, emotional and sexual abuse, in tandem with neglect that cannot be explained by unique historical or cultural circumstances. While most of the reported abuse occurred prior to the Kennedy Report (1970), which as already noted recommended the closure of the system, complaints continued up to 1989, the end date for the statistical evidence. The clergy emerge as the primary agents of child abuse in both statistical and verbatim evidence, which would seem to be introvertible and could not be considered normal in any culture at any time. While the forms of child abuse within the reformatory and industrial school system encompassed physical, emotional, sexual abuse and neglect, the over-arching form of abuse was physical. It permeated the entire 'care regime', turning the reformatory and industrial schools into a vast system of terror in which 'these children were the moral dirt of a social order' (Ferguson, 2007: 13).

Contextually, the use of physical abuse might appear to mean the exploitation of the body as a site of punishment and domination. What we constantly need to bear in mind is that the survivors' narrative of institutional child abuse is experientially and morally on a par with survivors of penal regimes in totalitarian societies – there is a common thread of an absence of a human right to bodily integrity associated with democratic societies (Arnold, 2009; Raftery and O' Sullivan, 1999). Power was total and exercised without restraint. This disadvantaged child population had no protection and no rights. They were allegedly systematically dehumanised by their clerical custodians, which sought to deny their humanity. The publication of the Ryan Report (2009) unlocks this world of uncontrolled violence, where children were systematically dehumanised on a mass scale in an atmosphere of terror and humiliation, ironically in the name of charity. Violence became the moral language of control of these children, which Ferguson (2007: 13) argues were 'socially constructed as a grotesque other'. The State somehow remained morally blind to this macabre reality, supporting a youth policy that was driven by the banality of evil, in which human rights were simply dispensed with as irrelevant. The value of the Ryan Report is that it has provided a public forum in which these human rights violations could be ventilated and a moral vocabulary constructed to give context and meaning to child abuse within the context of institutional care.

The British Broadcasting Company (BBC) News website on 20 May 20 2009 summarised the main findings of the Ryan Report:

- Physical and emotional abuse and neglect were features of the institutions.
- Sexual abuse occurred in many of them, particularly boys' institutions.
- Schools were run in a severe, regimented manner that imposed unreasonable and oppressive discipline on children and even on staff.
- Children were frequently hungry and food was inadequate, inedible and badly prepared in many schools

- Many witnesses spoke of being constantly fearful or terrified, which impeded their emotional development and impacted on every aspect of their life in the institution.
- Prolonged, excessive beating with implements intended to cause maximum pain occurred with the knowledge of senior staff.
- There was constant criticism and verbal abuse and children were told they were worthless.
- Some children lost their sense of identity and kinship, which was never recovered.
- Absconders were severely beaten, at times publicly. Some had their heads shaved and were humiliated.
- Inspectors, on their occasional visits, rarely spoke to children in the institutions.

These facts confirmed Raftery and O'Sullivan's (1999: 11) conclusion that the industrial and reformatory schools had been based upon a myth of religious charity: 'the first and most pervasive myth was that the children within the system were objects of charity, cared for by the religious of Ireland when no one else would do so'. The Ryan Report (2009) exposed the charity myth by revealing a Kafkaesque world of abuse, neglect, enforced labour and sexual exploitation. Why was it allowed to exist for over 100 years?

The distinguished Irish writer and commentator Fintan O'Toole has sought to provide an answer to explain why the system of industrial and reformatory schools was not reformed. He argues that it continued for three reasons: 'power, sex and class'. According to O'Toole (2009: W1), The first force enabling the abuse of children was power: 'The perpetrators abused children because they could. They drew that power from the immense stature of the church, its ability to command deference and intimidate dissenters'. The second force, identified by O'Toole (2009: W2) is sex: 'There was a religious hatred of the body, expressed in an infinite variety of ways the Brothers found to hurt and violate the bodies of their charges. There was also a perverted sexuality that swung between an obsession with purity and the rooting out of *badness* on the one hand and obsessive sexual predation on the other'. In O'Toole's analysis (*ibid.*) the third force behind the saga of institutional child abuse is class: 'this was a society in which the middle classes expressed their insecurity about their own status in a hysterical contempt for the poor. The function of industrial schools was to punish poverty'. In addition to these three factors, O'Toole (*ibid.*) suggests a fourth force, which evokes the Darwinistic side of the Irish social mind:

That violence was fuelled, by a psychotic hatred of everything that did not conform to the model of the good, respectable Christian family. 'What are they' one Brother remembered being told by a superior, 'but illegitimate and pure dirt'. In Goldenbridge [Industrial School], girls were told they were 'filthy', 'dirty', and 'worse then the soldiers who crucified Christ'. Boys who were the sons of single mothers were told their mothers were 'slags' and 'old whores'. Children from working-class backgrounds were told their families were 'scum', 'tramps', and 'from the gutter'.

The connection with the foundling hospitals of the eighteenth century in terms of social attitudes was direct. The children in industrial schools, in the eyes of their fellow citizens, were also lesser beings. As one unnamed educational journalist from a national newspaper put it during the 1960s, the children in industrial and reformatory schools constituted 'the lesser breeds within the law' (cited in the Ryan Report, 2009, Volume 4: para. 3.109). The State's unwillingness to intervene and defend the human rights of the inmates of the Irish industrial and reformatory school system can ultimately only be explicable in these Darwinistic terms. Irish democracy was a dark democracy that rejected the weak and poor, visiting its contempt and moral Puritamism upon defenceless children. Fintan O'Toole (2009: W2) concludes: 'These warped relationships to power, sex and class were played out with nightmarish clarity in the institutions, but were woven into the broader society. They were the dark shadows of a Republic that had never really come into existence'. Mary Raftery (2009a) asserts that the Ryan Report was 'devastating' in its critique: 'it is a monument to the shameful nature of Irish society throughout the most of the decades of the twentieth century, and arguably even today'. While the Catholic clergy were the perpetrators of these human rights violations, at the very least they had the tacit support of both the Irish state and civil society. The abuse of children in Irish institutions, as already suggested in Chapter 8, was a 'known unknown'. There is certainly evidence that coming to grips with the truth about children in care continues to be constrained by systematic resistance. The issue of vaccine trials which are alleged to have been carried out on children in care, is illustrative of this resistance.

Vaccine trials on children in care: an unresolved issue

The *Irish Independent* raised the issue of vaccine trials on children in care (McDonagh, 2010). This issue had been addressed by Justice Mary Laffoy, the first Chair of the Commission to Inquire into Child Abuse, without success. It is not covered in the final report of the Commission to Inquire into Child Abuse (Ryan Report, 2009) and remains an unresolved issue. The inference behind the *Irish Independent* report is that there has been a political cover-up. In fact the investigation was not completed due to legal proceedings, which ruled the issue was *ultra vires*, i.e. beyond the competence of the Commission to Inquire into Child Abuse.

At the beginning of the 1990s former residents of children's institutions began to publicly report that they had been subjected to clinical vaccination trials while in care. The then Minister of Health and Children, Michael Martin, in response to questions in Dail Eireann reported that an investigation was carried out by the Chief Medical Officer (CMO) on clinical trials involving babies and children in institutional settings over the periods 1960/61, 1970 and 1973. The main findings in the CMO's report were summarised in the *Third Interim Report of the Commission to Inquire into Child Abuse* (2003: 414) as follows:

> *Trial 1:* This was a trial in which 58 infants resident in five children's homes in the State took part which sought to compare the poliomyelitis antibody response after vaccination with a quadruple vaccine (diptheria, pertussis – that is whooping cough – and tetanus (DTP) and polio combined) with standard vaccines in use at the time which consisted of DTP and polio administered separately and at different sites. This trial was conducted between December 1960 and November 1961. The results of the trial were published in the British Medical Journal in 1962.
>
> *Trial 2:* In one strand of this trial, 69 children resident in an orphanage in Dublin had blood taken. 12 were subsequently administered intranasal rubella – that is German measles – vaccine. In another strand of this trial, 23 children living at home in a rural area in the midlands were administered the same vaccine. The purpose of the trial was to investigate whether there was a propensity for intranasally administered vaccine to spread to susceptible contacts, for example pregnant women, and to estimate antibody levels and acceptability of the intranasal technique of 6. vaccination. The trial was conducted during 1970. The results of the trial were published in the Cambridge Journal of Hygiene in 1971.
>
> *Trial 3:* In this trial 53 children, in 'Mother and Baby' homes and children's homes in Dublin and 65 children living at home in Dublin were administered vaccine to compare the reactogenicity of the commercially available batches of Trivax vaccine (that is proprietary name for Diptheria Tetanus and Pertussis vaccine) and Trivax AD vaccine with a vaccine of equivalent efficacy but in relation to the pertussis or whooping cough component of lesser potency. This trial was apparently conducted in 1973. The outcome of this trial was not published.

In an ensuing Dail Debate (Dail Eireann, 2000) the Minister for Health and Children stated:

> The chief medical officer's report is a good one but it is incomplete. It raises as many questions as it answers and some of those questions go to the heart of our attitudes to children and their rights. The report is incomplete because in some areas the most rigorous interrogation of the system failed to produce documentary records of the trials. In some cases the consultant who conducted the trials believed they took place in particular homes, but the homes do not have files that substantiate this.
>
> While we must remember that the trials were not recent, this lack of documentation is, at best, puzzling. It is certainly unsatisfactory. It is my hope that

publication of this report, with the action I will propose to the House, will perhaps help us fill in the missing bits of the jigsaw by stimulating memories or helping to locate lost files. I have read and re-read this report and I have discussed it with the chief medical officer in detail. In spite of the information gaps and the indications that no child was medically harmed, each reading made me more sure that his work must be regarded as the beginning, not the end, of the matter. When a child comes into the care of the State, the State must fight fiercely for all that child's rights, including bodily integrity. The State does not have the right to view children in care as lesser citizens. Their bodily integrity is a basic human right which can never be watered down or infringed.

Clearly, when we look at vaccination trials, the issue of informed consent is immediately involved. I am not satisfied that the chief medical officer has been able to find solid, informed consent, on the record, given by the people who were entitled to give it. Let me put this in context. The history of drug trials includes some ghastly case studies where the rights of individuals were grievously ignored. There have been cases in other countries where prisoners and members of the armed forces were involved in the trials of substances without their knowledge or informed consent. There have even been cases – again, in other countries – where prisoners suffering a lethal illness were used as a 'control group'. In other words, they were not given a medicine which the authorities knew would save their lives. Instead, they were left untreated to suffer and die in the interests of providing a point of comparison.

The Chief Medical Officer's report had recorded that there were no statutory controls in force in Ireland regulating clinical trials. However, ethical standards were set by the Nuremberg Code (1947), the Helsinki Declaration and the medical profession, as well as the Medical Research Council.

At the request of the Minister for Health and Children, the Commission to Inquire into Child Abuse, established in 1999 to investigate allegations of child abuse in institutional care, was asked to investigate the vaccination trials issue. The Minister identified several core questions that needed to be answered:

- Why children in care received the experimental vaccines?
- Why were some of the recipients outside the normal age for the administration of the vaccines?
- Was the end result for commercial gain or public good?
- Why were the records of the trials so inadequate?

(*Third Interim Report of the Commission to Inquire into Child Abuse*, 2003: 212)

The Commission advertised in the media in Ireland and the United Kingdom seeking responses from former survivors of the institutional care system who believed they were involved in vaccine trials. The scope of the enquiry was enlarged to cover the period 1940–1987. The Commission provided a questionnaire for survivors who wished to respond. It received a total of 877 replies from survivors who believed that they had been subjected to clinical vaccination trials while in institutional care.

The evidence from the 877 survivors of the Irish institutional care system that responded was as follows:

- One hundred and fifty-eight (158) correspondents positively alleged that they had been involved in a vaccine trial.
- Two hundred and nineteen (219) correspondents suspected that they may have been involved in a trial.
- One hundred and forty-three (143) correspondents both alleged and suspected that they were participants in a vaccine trial.
- One hundred and thirty-six (136) correspondents indicated that they were not part of a vaccine trial.
- One hundred and eighty-four (184) correspondents indicated that they did not know whether they were involved in a vaccine trial or not, and
- Thirty-seven (37) correspondents failed to complete the relevant portion of the questionnaire.

(*Third Interim Report of the Commission to Inquire into Child Abuse*, 2003: 214–215).

The Commission to Inquire into Child Abuse under its then Chair, Justice Mary Laffoy, set about establishing public hearings in relation to the vaccination trials. These hearings were called the Vaccination Trial Inquiry. It prepared a book of documents, held six days of public hearings in relation to procedural issues between March and July 2003, received applications for legal representation, appointed its own legal teams and established the vaccination trials as a division of the commission's investigation committee. However, as already noted, the Vaccination Trials Inquiry was deemed *ultra vires* (beyond the power) of the Child Abuse Act 2000, which was the legal basis of the commission. On 25 November 2003, the Commission to Inquire into Child Abuse gave the High Court an undertaking that it would not proceed with the hearings until the matter was legally settled, which given the *ultra vires* of the Child Abuse Act 2000 judgment meant, in effect, that the Vaccination Trials Inquiry was terminated before its substantive hearings had started. The vaccination trial issue had been successfully prevented from coming into the public domain through an open inquiry.

The issue was, therefore, not due to a political cover-up but rather a judicial decision that prevented the Commission to Inquire into Child Abuse from pursuing its investigation. Clearly, there is an unresolved issue here that is likely to become the subject of a future investigation. The evidence that was revealed by the Commission's preliminary investigation gives serious cause for disquiet and manifestly needs to be fully investigated.

Church, State and child abuse: the issue of 'cover-up'

The official response to the public scandal of institutional child abuse has been slow and, at times, controversial. Arnold (2009:89) critically observes 'from the Taoiseach down, the public picture that was presented was a meretricious one: that this was on behalf of the abused. It would take many years for truth to emerge , and even now the detail continues to be hotly argued.' A state historically dominated by the Catholic Church has had difficulty in facing its past. While the model officially adopted in 2000 was based on the post-apartheid South African Truth and Reconciliation Commission, in the form of the Commission to Inquire into Child Abuse (The Laffoy/Ryan Commission), there has arguably been a lack of good faith by both State and Church. These are essential ingredients in the process of disclosure.

But the scale of revelations of clerical child abuse eventually engulfed the Church. There was no denying that it had betrayed the exalted trust that Irish civil society had placed in it. The revelations had begun in 1994 with the Fr. Brendan Smyth affair in which a monk from Kilnacrott Abbey in County Cavan had systematically abused young children from both sides of the Irish border over many years, as well as molesting children in the USA. Evidence of complicity by his clerical superiors, including sending Fr. Smyth to the USA without revealing his record of abuse, caused major public concern. The failure of the Irish state, to extradite Fr. Brendan Smyth to Northern Ireland to answer charges of child sexual abuse led to the collapse of the Fianna Fáil/Labour government on 17 November 1997 (Moore, 1995). In a comment on the Fr. Brendan Smyth affair, Kevin Hegarty, a Catholic curate and former editor of the Catholic Church journal *Intercom*, observed:

> The Brendan Smyth case and allied scandals raise fundamental questions that are germane to the revelations but also wider ranging: on the culture of secrecy in the Church, on seminary formation, on the need to develop a theology and practice which stresses the rights and dignity of children. Should the Church address these questions I am convinced that the present crisis would be a period of purification for it. (Hegarty, 1995: 10)

Fr. Hegarty was sacked by the Catholic bishops as editor of *Intercom* after raising issues about child sexual abuse, celibacy and the ordination of women. Fr. Hegarty was accused by the Catholic bishops of publishing articles that were 'bad for morale' amongst the clergy (Cusack, J., 2009). The problems that the Catholic Church has experienced in coming to terms with its responsibilities were further highlighted in the Ferns Report (2005), which catalogued a litany of complaints of clerical child abuse in County Wexford. Once again the clerical authorities failed to adequately address their responsibilities to report these complaints to the State, according to the Ferns Report (2005: 259), which stated:

'The Inquiry wishes to record its revulsion at the extent, severity and duration of the child sexual abuse allegedly perpetrated on children by priests acting under the aegis of the Diocese of Ferns.' The Ferns Inquiry had identified over 100 allegations of child sexual abuse which involved twenty-one priests. There was according to the Ferns Report, a general lack of communication between the agencies involved:

> A particular difficulty for all of the authorities is the manner in which rumours or suspicions of sexual abuse should be dealt with. It has not been the practice of the Diocese of Ferns to communicate to either the Gardai [police] or the SEHB [social services] suspicions or rumours of child sexual abuse concerning a member of the clergy unless the Bishop is satisfied that the suspicion is a reasonable one. (*ibid.*)

In essence, the power of the Bishop of Ferns was decisive in determining the response to allegations of child sexual abuse within the Diocese of Ferns. This created a situation where the Church was above the law with severe consequences for the youth of the diocese, who were abused by some of its clergy over many years. One of the Ferns survivors, Colm O'Gorman, in his autobiographical book *Beyond Belief* (2009) has described his experiences at the hands of Fr. Sean Fortune. Much of the abuse carried out by Fr. Fortune against children and young people was perpetrated under the guise of youth work. From Fr. Fortune's days as a seminarian his exploitation of children became evident. Ironically, while he was banned from being a Scout leader, he was considered worthy of ordination as a priest.

The publication of the Murphy Report (Commission of Investigation into Catholic Archdiocese of Dublin, 2009) into child abuse within the Archdiocese of Dublin proved to be another watershed in the exposure of the scale and nature of clerical abuse of children in Ireland. The Murphy Report demonstrated that the Archdiocese of Dublin largely acted outside the law in an investigation into the handling of allegations against a sample of 45 priests out of 102 accused during the period 1975–2004. Over 320 children were abused by priests, mainly boys. Four archbishops are accused of suppressing evidence of child abuse. The Gardai are accused of colluding in this cover-up of clerical child sexual abuse in the Archdiocese of Dublin. The Murphy Report (2009, Part I: para 1.55) concludes: 'The Church is not only a religious organisation but also a human/civil instrument of power and control'. This goes to the core of clerical child abuse in Ireland. The Catholic Church was allowed to behave as a 'state within a state' where clerical criminality went unpunished, with grave consequences for the welfare of children, who became the objects of their abuse of power.

Many other cases of clerical child sexual abuse are in the process of emerging, notably in the diocese of Cloyne, but potentially in all dioceses. There is still a strong sense that full disclosure remains an elusive goal because of the shameful nature of the truth. Truth is a form of reconciliation that the Catholic Church finds difficult to accept. Mary Raftery (2009b) in a comment on the Murphy Report has likened the Catholic Church's concern with secrecy to the Cosa Nostra. She was echoing the ex-Governor of Oklahoma, Frank Keating, who in 2003 resigned as head of the US Catholic Church's panel on child abuse, which he likened to the Mafia because of his frustration with its obsessive secrecy. This culture of secrecy is not compatible with a modern democratic society, where the importance of human rights has come to be increasingly valued. In this context the disclosure of child abuse incidents has become obligatory in the public interest.

The verdicts of Ryan: scapegoating the Catholic Church?

The revelations of the Ryan Report about human rights abuses in Irish industrial schools and reformatories are so damning that some commentators have sought to question the validity of the report and others its public reception and the balance of media reportage. Fr. Tony Flannery, a Redemptionist priest, has edited a book which critically interrogates the Ryan Report. In the introduction to the book, called *Responding to the Ryan Report,* Flannery (2009: 9–10) asserts:

> What was most needed was something that would broaden the debate and introduce the sorts of voices that I felt were largely absent. I believed that the issue was of such crucial importance to the future of our society that all attempts at scapegoating had to be contested, and the focus brought back to the extent, the nature and possible solutions to the problem. So I decided that the best way to respond was to try to get a wide range of people, from different backgrounds and expertise, to address it for me.

The view that the Catholic clergy have been made 'scapegoats' for the failures of the industrial and reformatory school system is the core argument in *Responding to the Ryan Report,* initially in the introduction and then by several subsequent contributors. Fr. Donal Dorr (Flannery, 2009: 112) asserts that he wishes 'to challenge the kind of scapegoating which has taken place, where the blame for the radical failures in the system has been loaded unfairly on just one segment of those who were responsible'. Another contributor, Dr Fainche Ryan (*ibid.*: 155), a theologian, similarly argues 'it is too easy to condemn and judge the past. To scapegoat or blame, comes easily to many of us. The religious are easy scapegoats. In Ireland by and large they are elderly, and somewhat lost'. The 'scapegoating' argument put forward by these contributors to *Responding to the Ryan Report* seeks to highlight the failures of state regulation. While there is considerable truth in this argument, the unpalatable reality is that most of the alleged abuse was carried out by members of the clergy, which is clear from the statistical analysis of the Ryan Report. But it is clear that the Irish state also bears culpability. Some commentators argue that it was the agent of abuse through its failure to regulate. For example, Arnold (2009: 11) argues that the State was ultimately responsible: 'The state did know of them [abuses] and it did not act'. His argument is that the State provided a legal system and prison system for destitute Irish children, which it failed to regulate. He also notes the key role of voluntary organisations in sustaining the system of industrial and reformatory schools, notably the Irish Society for the Prevention of Cruelty to Children, which was heavily criticised in the Ryan Report (Arnold, 2009: 4). Clearly, the Irish state and some voluntary organisations were morally blind and share culpability with the Church. Furthermore the State almost completely failed to regulate the industrial and reformatory school system. This cannot be denied and contextualises the concerns of the clergy about scapegoating. The allocation of responsibility is clearly a very complex task involving Church, State and civil society.

However, the fact that the Irish state lamentably failed in its duty of regulation does not absolve the Catholic Church from being the primary actor in the narrative of child abuse. The public perception of the Catholic Church is that it is morally ambivalent about child abuse. Public antipathy towards the Catholic Church has been fuelled by its apparent unwillingness to fully grapple with the two underlying principles that informed the approach of the Ryan Report – truth-telling and reparation.

The Church's insistence of anonymity for the perpetrators of abuse (both living and dead) suggests to a sceptical public that it is still in denial about the enormity of the human rights violations for which it was directly responsible. Recent news reports that the Vatican regards the ordination of women priests as one of the greatest crimes in Church law, morally equivalent to clerical child abuse, suggests a moral incapacity to understand the gravity of child abuse (Hooper and Siddique, 2010). This legacy of moral ambivalence has made it very difficult for the Catholic Church to address the issue of clerical child abuse. It consequently continues to fail to confront its past and the need for public atonement.

Furthermore, intense public anger has been caused by the alleged unwillingness of the Catholic Church to fully pay compensation to the victims. This is an essential step in the process of reconciliation and atonement for clerical child abuse. The Church's view is that financial responsibility should be shared with the State. This is not an unreasonable position, given the State's clear culpability. But the critic's perception is that the Church does not want to pay its fair share and is in league with the State against the interests of the abused. Arnold (2009: 147) asserts: 'it was the Church that was protected, and in company with the State, is committed to the protection of the State as well. Meanwhile the abused will remain abused'.

Conclusion

There is both a sense of circularity and progress in analysing the evolution of children's rights in Irish youth policy. It is circular in the sense that social conservatives constantly seek to deny the past and frustrate change and social reform. On the other hand, there is a human rights strand in this narrative that has gradually gained momentum over the past half century, as social reformers in civil society have pressed for change and disclosure. Ireland has not only modernised during this period, it has also internationalised, by joining the United Nations (1955) and European Union (1973). Both of these developments have put pressure upon the State and civil society to adopt higher standards in the treatment of children and young people. Modernisation and internationalisation have also turned Ireland into a more secular society in which a growing moral literacy has gradually undermined the social power of the Catholic Church. We have noted the influence of pressure groups in civil society (e.g. JCWSSW, Tuairim, CARE, Children First, ICCL and the Irish Association of Social Workers) in promoting the agenda of social reform and moral responsibility. Such liberalising campaigns were effective in their determination to vindicate children's rights. But much remains to be achieved. Media reports of further delays in promised constitutional referendum on children's rights underscores the point. The *Irish Times* (28 July 2010) reported:

> There are fears bolstering children's rights could prevent the deportation of parents unlawfully in the State and entitle children faced with expulsion from schools to legal representation. (Smyth, 2010)

The implications for children from ethnic minorities are serious, raising the question 'are we constructing a new generation of outcast children?' However, in 1992 Ireland ratified the UN Convention on the Rights of the Child (UNCRC). It was followed by the establishment of the Children's Rights Alliance in Ireland between 1993 and 1995, with an agenda to promote the UNCRC agenda in Ireland and specifically to campaign for the establishment of an Office of Ombudsman for Children, which has been successfully achieved. Composed of an alliance of over eighty children's organisations, the Children's Rights Alliance is a potent influence on policy formation, underlining the continuing vitality of liberal civil society in pressing for youth policy reform in Ireland. All of these developments are building moral literacy within Irish society. Sadly, conservative civil society and the Irish state continue to exhibit real deficiencies about what children's rights really mean – callous neglect is still an issue for children in care, as is witnessed by the large number of children dying in care due to public neglect.

Perhaps the most impressive development within Irish civil society in relation to children's rights has been the emergence of survivors' groups. The power and authenticity of their narrative voice confronts Irish civil society with the reality of its moral ambivalence and human rights record in relation to children. Organisations like SOCA, One in Four, the Aislinn Centre and many others speak a truth based upon survivor experience. Their courageous attempts to confront both Church and State with their failures takes civil society into new and unexplored levels of consciousness in relation to the rights of the child. All the signs indicate that this is a difficult process of truth, revelation and reparation in reference to many damaged lives. In relation to social reform and children's rights much remains to be done but moral literacy is growing against a conservative grain of denial and resistance. The Ryan Report has not only exposed the culpability of the Church but the moral blindness of the Irish state over most of the twentieth century and the moral blindness of most of Irish civil society.

Irish industrial and reformatory schools were based upon a philosophy of dehumanisation that subjected the bodies and minds of their inmates to regimes of medieval violence, involving cruelty and in many instances torture. The Ryan Report (2009) is not simply a narrative of child abuse. Its revelations of human rights violations against children in institutional care belong to the same realm of violence and oppression as Soviet Gulags and Nazi concentration camps. In some respects the issues are even more morally challenging. These human rights crimes were not committed by a totalitarian state but by Church organisations in a state that purported to be democratic. All of the alleged victims were children. Most of the alleged perpetrators were clergy. How do we make sense of these events? How do we deal with the social and moral issues? We have discussed the Catholic Church's difficulties with engaging with a process of atonement and reconciliation. The value of the Ryan Report (2009) is that it is an exercise in truth-telling, even if it is flawed by the anonymity of the accused. This was the compromise the Commission to Inquire into Child Abuse was prepared to make in order to provide the survivors with a forum to tell their truths and Irish society with the opportunity to bear witness to that truth. The challenge for Irish society is to engage with the moral and social legacy of the Ryan Report. This legacy demonstrates a lack of moral literacy amongst the clergy, who were responsible for the administration of the reformatory and industrial school system. But their moral ambivalence towards these victims of child poverty was shared by both the post-independence Irish state and civil society. There was a fear of what Smart (1999) has called 'moral contagion' in which the child victim is reconstructed as the 'evil or wicked' other. The consequences of this moral ambiguity was that the children placed within the reformatory and industrial school system were dehumanised and without the most basic rights to bodily integrity, food, education, health care and love. The failure to fully investigate the vaccine trials issue suggests that there continues to be resistance to fully grappling with the truth about children in care.

10

In search of truth and reconciliation: the Ryan Report from the survivors' perspective

The key to understanding these attitudes is surely to realise that abuse was not a failure of the system. It was the system. Terror was both the point of these institutions and their standard operating procedure. Their function in Irish society was to impose social control, particularly on the poor, by acting as a threat. Without the horror of an institution like Letterfrack, it could not fulfil that function. Within the institutions, terror was systematic and deliberate. It was a methodology handed down through 'successive generations of Brothers, priests and nuns'. (*Irish Times*, 21 May 2009)

Abuse is only possible in a silent world. (O' Gorman, 2009: 119)

The Commission to Inquire into Child Abuse, established in 2000, was a landmark in terms of exposing the dark secrets of institutional care in Ireland for over a century. It consisted of two committees: the Investigation Committee and the Confidential Committee. The Commission to Inquire into Child Abuse was chaired by Justice Mary Laffoy until 2004 and from 2004–2009 by Chief Justice Ryan. It heard evidence from eighteen religious orders and congregations. It quickly became evident that its ability to operate as a truth and reconciliation commission was highly constrained, due to an unwillingness on the part of most religious orders to accept responsibility for their alleged deeds. Judge Sean Ryan, who succeeded Justice Mary Laffoy as Chair of the Commission in 2004, worked out a compromise that granted anonymity to the accused both living and dead. While this compromise can be criticised for perpetuating the culture of secrecy, it did allow the Commission to carry out its investigation. A key element in the campaign of truth-telling has been the role of the campaign group One in Four. Arnold (2009: 227) notes 'the *One in Four* group became quite outspoken on behalf of the abused generally at this time and countered what it called an attempt to rewrite the history of sexual abuse'. Under the dynamic leadership of Colm O'Gorman, One in Four began to transform Irish public consciousness regarding the significance of child abuse in Irish society. There were many other survivor groups who became instrumental in unlocking their own narratives including: Irish SOCA, SOCA (UK), The Irish Deaf Society, Right to Peace, Right to Place, Alliance Victim Support, Irish Survivors of Institutional Abuse International, the Aislinn Centre and the London Irish Women's Group (Ryan Report, 2009, Volume 2: para. 1.149). All of these organisations began to provide the survivors' perspective on the growing public scandal of institutional child abuse that challenged both the Church to account for its actions and the State for a serious failure of regulation in human rights terms. Survivors' groups became a moral voice, which could not be ignored. Truth was beginning to assert itself. But reparation remained a contested reality, because of the serious institutional financial implications.

The Residential Institutional Redress Act 2002 established the Residential Institutions Redress Board. Its purpose is to provide compensation for survivors of 123 institutions, who have experienced abuse. Its establishment was accompanied by what has been called 'The Secret Deal' which indemnified the Catholic Church for its involvement and cooperation in the redress scheme (Arnold, 2009: 206). The terms of the agreement between Church and State limited the liability of the Church to approximately €128 million. This has generated considerable controversy since critics argue that the Church should bear equal responsibility with the State for compensating survivors of institutional abuse, which is estimated to cost the Irish State at least €1 billion in compensation payments. Further criticism has arisen in relation to the willingness of the religious orders to fully apologise for the violations of human rights in the institutions which they managed. The publication of the *Report of the Commission to Inquire into Child Abuse* (Ryan Report), in May 2009 was to intensify pressure on the Church to address these issues. A review audit of the assets of the religious orders and congregations was initiated by the State during 2009, in response to growing public anger regarding the Church's position on compensation to the survivors. The Church continues to have difficulties in relation to atonement because it believes that it is being unfairly scapegoated by the media (Flannery, 2009).

The publication of the Ryan Report during 2009 was a seminal event in the process of disclosure and truth-telling. Its revelations are thorough and deeply shocking, identifying over 200 institutions. Most of the alleged abusers were members of the clergy. These are the stark facts that underpin the powerful testimony of the survivors of these abuse regimes during most of the twentieth century. The Ryan Report reveals that over a thirty-five year period child abuse was endemic in the industrial and reformatory school system in Ireland. Its revelations have been reported around the world, exposing the failure of Ireland's human rights record in relation to children to critical international scrutiny. The crimes against children described in the Ryan Report are on a systemic scale and involve a degree of sadistic cruelty that is difficult to comprehend. Public reaction has been one of shock and horror. This chapter is about examining the evidence of survivors of child abuse in the Irish reformatory and industrial school system. The argument is that the evidence tells its own truth in all its stark brutality. Reconciliation will only follow when this truth is fully acknowledged.

The evidence

The scale of child abuse in Irish industrial schools has already been discussed in Chapter 9. The issue of responsibility is contested, with the clergy claiming that they are being scapegoated. The burden of evidence is complex in the sense that the clergy administered the industrial and reformatory schools. However the State was responsible for their regulation.

With regard to the 'scapegoating' of the clergy argument put forward by contributors to *Responding to the Ryan Report* (Flannery, 2009) and other critics of the Ryan Reports, the burden of evidence contained in the Confidential Committee's report, both statistical and oral, clearly indicates that the Catholic Clergy were the main perpetrators of child abuse within the Irish institutional care system. The Ryan Report (2009, Volume 3: paras. 7.90–7.91 and 9.55–9.58) demonstrates that, in relation to male industrial and reformatory schools, 71% of the 556 reported as physically abusive were male religious staff within the schools, and a further 7% were religious sisters. In the case of female industrial and reformatory schools, 68% of the 354 reported as physically abusive were female religious staff. With reference to sexual abuse in male industrial and re-formatory schools 65% (151) – the majority of those named – were religious staff (139 Brothers and 12 priests) (Ryan Report, 2009, Volume 3: para. 7. 139). However, in female industrial and reformatory schools the majority – 144 (77%) of those identified as sexual abusers – were non-staff members (*ibid.*: paras 9.94–9.95). Apart from sexual abuse in female industrial and reformatory schools, members of the Catholic clergy were clearly and overwhelmingly the alleged perpetrators of child abuse. Detailed content analysis below strongly supports this conclusion, in relation to the overall context of child abuse. Furthermore, the sexualised nature of child physical abuse (as will be demonstrated in this chapter) makes differentiation between established categories of child abuse problematic and artificial. These were care regimes where child abuse was multi-dimensional and pervasive. Child abuse became an expression of the abuse of total institutional power – a phenomenon described in Erving Goffman's celebrated sociological study, *Asylums* (1961). While our analysis is based upon the survivor evidence given to the Confidential Committee (Volume 3 of the Ryan Report), it is notable that the Investigation Committee interviewed 250 male survivors and concluded 'the principal complaints of male interviewees was physical abuse' (Ryan Report, Volume 4, 2009: para. 5.04). Contextually, the use of physical abuse might appear to mean the exploitation of the body as a site of punishment and domination. What we constantly need to bear in mind is that the survivors' narrative of institutional child abuse is experientially and morally on a par with survivors of penal regimes in totalitarian societies – there is a common thread of an absence of a human right to bodily integrity associated with democratic societies. Power was total and exercised without restraint. This disadvantaged child population had no protection and no rights. They were systematically dehumanised by their clerical custodians, which sought to deny their basic humanity. The Irish state failed to regulate these institutions and remained morally blind to the human rights violations perpetrated within them for most of the twentieth century.

Physical abuse

The Ryan Report (2009: para. 7.06) defines physical abuse as: 'The wilful, reckless or negligent infliction of physical injury on, or a failure to prevent such injury to, the child'. There were 474 reports of physical abuse involving twenty-six reformatory and industrial schools given in evidence to the Confidential Committee by 403 male witnesses, some of whom had been admitted to more than one school (Ryan Report, 2009, Volume 3: para. 7.08). Similarly, the Confidential Committee received 383 reports of physical abuse from 374 female witnesses in thirty-nine schools (Ryan Report, 2009, Volume 3: para. 9.06). In total, calculating all reports from male and female witnesses there were 857 reports (see Tables 10.1 and 10.2).[1]

Table 10.1 Physical abuse combined with other abuse types – male industrial and reformatory schools

Abuse types	Number of reports	%
Physical, emotional, neglect and sexual	166	35
Physical, emotional and neglect	120	25
Physical and neglect	66	14
Physical, neglect and sexual	49	10
Physical	24	5
Physical, emotional and sexual	20	4
Physical and emotional	15	3
Physical and sexual	14	3
Total reports	474	(100)

Source: Report of Commission to Inquire into Child Abuse (Ryan Report), Volume 3, 2009: para. 7.11.

Table 10.2 Physical abuse combined with other abuse types – female industrial and reformatory schools

Abuse types	Number of reports	%
Physical, emotional and neglect	226	59
Physical, emotional, neglect and sexual	123	32
Physical and neglect	20	5
Physical and emotional	8	2
Physical	3	1
Physical, emotional and sexual	2	1
Physical and sexual	1	—
Total reports	383	100

Source: Report of Commission to Inquire into Child Abuse (Ryan Report), 2009, Volume 3: 9.07

The Ryan Report (2009, Volume 3: para. 7.16) records a wide variety of forms of physical punishment from the male witness statements, including: 'punching, flogging, assault and bodily attacks, hitting with the hand, kicking, ear pulling, hair pulling, head shaving, beating on the soles of the feet, burning, scalding, stabbing, severe beatings with or without clothes, being made to kneel and stand in fixed positions for lengthy periods, made to sleep outside overnight, being forced into cold or excessively hot baths and showers, hosed down with cold water before being beaten, beaten while hanging from hooks on the wall, being set upon by dogs, being restrained in order to be beaten, physical assaults by more than one person, and having objects thrown at them'.

The locations, according to the witnesses' statements encompassed classrooms, offices, cloakrooms, dormitories, showers, infirmaries, refectories, the bedrooms of staff members, churches, work areas and trade shops, fields, farm yards, play/sports areas and outdoor sheds (Ryan Report, 2009, Volume 3: para. 7.17). Male survivors in their witness statements gave chilling examples of the diversity of locations, the use of corporal punishment as public theatre and for initiation rights in a macabre atmosphere of *manqué* religiosity: 'I had a hiding in the boot room, you had to take your shirt off, you were completely naked and he … [Br. X] … beat me with a strap and a hurley stick on the behind and the legs and that.'

A culture of fear was created within the industrial and reformatory school system through the policy of dehumanisation based upon corporal punishment. Several survivors gave examples of this atmosphere of unconstrained physical abuse and its tyrannical application:

> One fella ... [co-resident] ... called my mother a bastard. I hit him a box ... They ... [Brothers] ... told me to get into my togs and go up to the shower. After the cold shower the 2 of them ... [Brothers] ... got 2 sally rods and they beat me, God did they beat me. You would feel the welts on your legs, I mean real dents on your skin.

> [Named School] ... ruined my life. Night-times were the worst; if you weren't taken out of bed and beaten you were listening to it happening to someone else. You could hear the screams all over the whole building at night it was so quiet. Up to 4 Brothers would come and take a boy out of bed on some pretext and give him a hammering, make you take off your nightshirt, they would do what they wanted. They were like a pack of hunting animals.

> At night-time you'd be in your nightshirt, 2 of them would hold you down, you could be asleep or on the mark of going asleep, it was always at night time. Three of them would come in. Two of them and the third one would do the beating. The strap ... [standing up demonstrating hitting] ... it was done in frenzy, like they did not want to be caught ... (Ryan Report, 2009, Volume 3: para. 7.79)

The Ryan Report (2009, Volume 3: paras 7.80–7.81) records that sometimes beatings were administered by several staff:

> There were five accounts of boys being tied down before being beaten; in one circumstance a witness described being tied to a bench and beaten. Another witness reported that a Brother sent him to the office, where he was told to take his clothes off, two Brothers took turns beating him on his body and hands until '*I thought I was going to be killed*'. The witness further reported his legs were swollen with open lacerations.

A witness, who reported he was wrongly accused of stealing from another resident, described being told by the Resident Manager 'to take your punishment like a man'. He was then taken to the office and beaten by two Brothers, on the face, buttocks, hands, wrist and arm until the witness confessed to something he had not done. In a number of schools the Resident Manager was reported by witnesses to be involved directly in the physical punishment of residents along with other religious staff and in other schools there were reports of the Resident Manager being called on to agree a punishment.

The Ryan Report (2009, Volume 3: para. 7.20–7.27) recorded evidence from male witnesses in relation to the implements used in physical abuse that the 'leather' (strap) was most commonly used instrument (381 witnesses) but that there were a further 232 witness accounts of being hit by sticks (including canes, ash plants, blackthorn sticks, hurleys, broom handles, hand brushes, wooden spoons, pointers, batons, chair rungs, yard brushes, hoes, hay forks, pikes and pieces of wood with leather tongs attached) as the following examples illustrate:

> They used the leather for the least excuse. It was heavy, stitched and with waxed ends. It was very painful, you would scream in pain. As convent boys we didn't have a chance. The other boys, the city kids who were tough, and the Brothers, all picked on us. We stuck together which wasn't a good idea.

> Some of the Brothers had different leathers, I know because I made them when I was 14, in the boot room, some of them had little tiny leads in them, some had coins, some were straight. They weren't soft, they were hard. I'll never forget the cat-o'-nine-tails, 10 tongs … [thongs] … it used to have knots across the bottom. Observing other boys stripped and the blood running down as they were being flogged across the body, it was terrible. There must have been a new rule by the Government at some stage because it happened no more. (Ryan Report, 2009, Volume 3: paras 7.20 and 7.22)

Females were also subjected to severe physical abuse in the industrial school system, in which they traditionally constituted by far the larger gender group. The survivors reported high levels of violence by staff, with 166 female witnesses testifying to being beaten with various objects including wooden sticks, blackthorn sticks, rulers, pointers, window poles, wooden spoons, chair legs, wooden crutches, Hurley sticks, cricket bats, coat hangers, towel rollers and sally rods. In addition, seventy-seven witnesses reported being beaten with bamboo canes and ninety-nine with leather straps (Ryan Report, 2009, Volume 3: para. 9.14).

Apart from the infliction of severe beatings, female survivor witness statements record other serious forms of physical abuse including being hit, slapped, beaten, kicked, pushed, pinched, burned, bitten, shaken violently, physically restrained and force fed. This physical abuse ranged from being slapped on the hand to being beaten naked in public. The female witnesses also reported having their heads knocked against walls, desks and window ledges, being beaten on the soles of their feet, the backs of their hands, around their hands and ears, having their hair pulled, being swung off the ground by their hair, and made to perform tasks that they believed put them at risk of harm or danger (Ryan Report, 2009, Volume 3: para. 911). The following testimony from a female witness is illustrative:

> I remember once I got a big yellow blister on my hand, it was really painful … Normally when you got a beating from someone you had to hold your hand out for a slap like that … [demonstrated outstretched palm] not always of course, some of them would hit you anywhere on the legs or anywhere … She … [Sr X] … said Why are you holding your hand out like that? Give me the other hand …

You have to have 10 on that hand and 10 on the other. I couldn't part with this hand, it was yellow and throbbing it was, and she forced it open and slapped it. The blister burst, I'll never forget the pain. (*ibid.*)

Water punishments and burnings form another disturbing aspect of the ritualistic physical abuse of children in reformatory and industrial schools, highlighting the scale of human rights violations perpetrated against these children. Amongst the male survivors who gave evidence to the Confidential Committee of the Ryan Commission, thirty-four describe being forced into scalding or freezing showers or baths as deliberate punishments, including a number who reported being hosed with cold water before or after a severe beating (Ryan Report, 2009, Volume 3: para. 7.24). In addition, two male witnesses reported having their heads forcibly held under water (*ibid.*). Furthermore, twenty-two male survivors reported in their testimony being burned or scalded, which included the use of matches, cigarettes, electric sockets, leading to such severe disfigurement that they had to be hidden during inspectional visits (Ryan Report, 2009, Volume 3: para. 7.25). These assaults on children by staff appear to have been an everyday aspect of life in reformatory and industrial schools, underlining the tyrannical style of discipline and endemic scale of child abuse. Similarly, female witnesses reported a series of assaults involving water or burnings:

- Nineteen (19) witnesses reported being put into cold or scalding baths [or] showers.
- Twelve (12) witnesses reported having water thrown over them, five of whom were scalded with hot tea or water.
- Eight (8) witnesses reported having their heads held under water, including two whose heads were held under a cold running tap.
- Five (5) witnesses reported being burned with hot pokers or by having their hands held to a fire or on a hot stove.
- Two (2) witnesses reported having their fingers held to electric sockets. (Ryan Report, 2009, Volume 3, para. 9.18)

The scale of the alleged assaults perpetuated against children in Irish institutional care facilities was clearly on a mass scale. Inevitably, the children suffered many injuries. Survivors in their testimony to the Ryan Commission give us an idea of the scale and intensity of this physical abuse by cataloguing the number of injuries that were inflicted upon them.

Amongst the male witnesses to the Ryan Commission, 224 reported physical injuries arising from abuse, including breaks to ribs, noses, wrists, arms, legs, injuries to head, genitalia, back, mouth, eye, ear, hand, jaw, face and kidney. The physical consequences of some of these injuries were so severe that sixty-four witnesses reported being unable to walk, sit, stand or lie down (Ryan Report, 2009, Volume 3: para. 78.2).

- There were 136 reports of physical injury in the testimony of female survivors to the Ryan Commission that were attributed to abuse. These reports included: broken bones; head injuries; damage to eyes and ears, lacerations that required stitching as well as injuries to backs, legs and arms. Hospital treatment was required in 33 cases, eight witnesses reported no questions were asked.

What can we conclude from this survivor evidence relating to the physical abuse of children in care in Ireland over most of the twentieth century? First, institutionalisation was totally unsuitable for these children's needs. Second, the policy of dehumanisation practiced by the clergy administering these institutions constituted, as the Ryan Commission concluded, endemic violence. Third, the absence of human rights in the form of adequate child care legislation in line with modern child care practice left these children open to abuse on a mass scale. Fourth, 'the charity myth' perpetuated by the Irish state and supported by large and powerful elements within Irish civil society allowed this human rights tragedy to occur (see Raftery and O' Sullivan, 1999). While we have so far been discussing physical abuse it was compounded by and cannot be disaggregated from emotional abuse and sexual abuse. The evidence offered so far from survivor testimony clearly indicates that physical abuse was linked by an overall strategy of dehumanisation to other forms of abuse. The alleged assaults on children's bodily integrity demonstrate a serious neglect of their physical well-being. The culture of fear supported by ritualistic beatings and other forms of physical punishment calibrated to instill maximum fear and anxiety, demonstrate an atmosphere of emotional abuse that would be difficult to surpass. Finally, the survivors' testimony regarding the administration of corporal punishment strongly suggests that it was carried out in a highly sexualised way. The use of corporal punishment in Ireland's industrial and reformatory school system was beyond doubt a form of sexual abuse coupled with sadistic physical abuse and informed by policy of dehumanisation. This constitutes a profound indictment of Irish youth policy.

Neglect

The Ryan Report (2009, Volume 3: para. 7.156) defined neglect as 'failure to care for the child which results, or could reasonably be expected to result, in serious impairment of the physical and mental health or development of the child or serious adverse effects on his or her behavior or welfare'. Some 367 male witnesses (89%) made 408 reports regarding their care and welfare in twenty-two schools. Similarly, 367 female witnesses (97%) made 374 reports of neglect. Neglect was frequently reported in combination with other forms of child abuse. In the case of male witnesses, 41% reported neglect in combination with physical, emotional and sexual abuse. Reports from female witnesses reveal 60% reported neglect in combination with physical and emotional abuse, with a further 33% reporting neglect in combination with physical, emotional and sexual abuse (see Tables 10.3 and 10.4). Only one witness from both gender groups reported neglect as the only form of abuse that they had experienced.

Table 10.3 Neglect combined with other abuse types: male industrial and reformatory schools

Abuse type	Number of reports	%
Neglect, emotional, physical and sexual	166	41
Neglect, emotional and physical	120	29
Neglect and physical	66	16
Neglect, physical and sexual	49	12
Neglect and emotional	3	1
Neglect, emotional and sexual	2	>1
Neglect and sexual	1	>1
Neglect	1	>1
Total reports	408	100

Source: Report of Commission to Inquire into Child Abuse, 2009 (Ryan Report) Volume 3: 92

Table 10.4 Neglect combined with other abuse types: female industrial and reformatory schools

Abuse type	Number of reports	%
Neglect, emotional and physical	226	60
Neglect, emotional, physical and sexual	123	33
Neglect and physical	20	5
Neglect and emotional	3	1
Neglect, emotional and sexual	1	>1
Neglect, and sexual	1	>1
Total reports	374	100

Source: Report of Commission to Inquire into Child Abuse, 2009 (Ryan Report), Volume 3: 162

While all of the children were neglected within the industrial and reformatory schools system, some children were allegedly picked out for particularly severe neglect. These children were known as 'orphans' because of their association with the 'workhouse', or county home as it was officially referred to after the inception of the new independent state in 1922, or their membership of an ethnic minority such as Travellers or Afro-Irish. The following example highlights the discriminatory treatment of orphans, which subjected them to particularly intense forms of dehumanisation:

> The girls from the workhouse ... [orphans] ... they were treated worse, they suffered worse ... When we were out for a walk we would bring them back bits of chewing gum and haws that we found on the hedges and on the ground, we were all so hungry and they didn't get out ... [Orphans'] ... clothes were different, big patched knickers, boots with no soles in them. (Ryan Report, 2009, Volume 3: para. 9.126)

There were 379 reports from male witnesses of inadequate food in twenty-one schools and 168 female witnesses (46%) complained of being constantly hungry or 'starving' (Ryan Report, 2009, Volume 3: paras 7.163 and 9.126). The following examples illustrate the inadequacy of diet. Male witnesses reported having to survive on a diet of 'unsweetened sludge' made up of bread dipped in dripping and shell cocoa:

> In the morning you got 2 cuts of bread and dripping, the dripping was put on the night before. The food was terrible there, you were hungry, it was rationed even though the place was self-sufficient. They had their own tomatoes and orchard too, but we never got them.

> Hunger was extreme, we stole cattle nuts and mangels and the hosts from the altar because we were so hungry.

> You were hungry all the time, all the bloody time. We got bread and dripping, it would be rock hard by the time you got it ... I was always hungry, there was never enough ... I worked in the kitchen and you stole for your friends, if you were caught, you were terrified. (Ryan Report, 2009, Volume 3: para. 7.163)

Female witnesses told a similar story of hunger: 'if you saw anybody eating anything you just went up and grabbed it, we were always hungry' (Ryan Report, 2009, Volume 3: para. 9.127). Amongst the female witnesses, twenty-two reported eating grass leaves and berries and twenty-six remembered lack of drinking water. The following practice of drinking toilet water was reported from ten schools up to the 1970s:

You'd be more thirsty than anything else, we'd drink water out of the toilets, there would be little worms in the water, the older girls would show us how to spit them out like that … demonstrated … . But you weren't afeared … It was the nuns you feared. (Ryan Report, 2009, Volume 3: para. 9.132).

Ironically, many of the industrial and reformatory schools had farms attached to them, where the children worked as essentially forced labour. There was a plentiful supply of food. The clergy were apparently well-fed as the following witnesses reported:

I was hungry all the time. I was caught robbin' bread and they were all told not to talk to me … I was working in the kitchen and you'd see the carved roast for the convent but you never got it. You might get the leftovers if you worked in the kitchen. (Ryan Report, 2009, Volume 3: para. 9.129)

Hygiene standards were also extremely low. The Confidential Committee heard complaints from 277 female witnesses regarding the provision and maintenance of personal hygiene across thirty-five schools and 217 male witnesses in sixteen schools. Many of the female witnesses objected to the communal shared baths and unsanitary toilets:

You got in to the bath with the chemise and there were 2 nuns holding a big sheet so you got out and went into the toilet to dress, still in the chemise.

The toilets were always overflowing, it was terrible, we kept … [cleaned] … them, the girls, you had to keep the toilets the same as the floors, we unblocked them. The stench was terrible.

I had charge of the toilets downstairs and they were … filthy, you had to clean them. There was no toilet paper or anything, oh God, they were awful. (Ryan Report, 2009, Volume 3: paras 1.35 and 1.38)

Similarly, male witnesses reported a disturbing lack of hygiene in the reformatory and industrial school system:

We were on straw mattresses on the floor, the rats would go for you if you had any food … They were as hungry as we were. I got bitten on the ear, another fellow got bitten on the mouth … There were dry toilets, the boys cleaned them out. I never did myself, I avoided it … The clothes were very, very rarely washed. You'd have to go for a swim to wash.

The toilet situation was abominable, there were old toilets with no doors and you could not sit down on them, nobody cleaned them. You would prefer to go out to the field if you got a chance.

> There was a big trough, you got into that with togs on you to wash, that was
> the bath. You took off the togs then and gave it to the next guy, the water was
> never changed for the whole lot of the lads. (Ryan Report, 2009, Volume 3: paras
> 7.179–7.180)

Male witnesses discharged before 1970 made 156 reports of unsatisfactory bedding in sixteen schools. They reported that the bedclothes and mattresses were
neglected, 'filthy' and constantly smelt of urine (Ryan Report, 2009, Volume 3:
paras. 7.190–7.191). Similarly, forty-eight female witnesses from twelve schools
reported infestations and infections with some or all of the following conditions:
headlice/nits/scabies, thrush, ringworm, impetigo and fleas, which was frequently associated with unclean bedding, as the following example demonstrates.

> There was about 26 beds in each room. The beds were full of fleas, they used to
> put DDT on the bed. Sometimes it was entertaining, we'd watch it jump and say
> 'look at this one, look at this one'. (Ryan Report, 2009, Volume 3: para. 9.140)

The Ryan Report (2009, Volume 3: paras 7.170 and 9.141) recorded complaints
from 275 male witnesses and 272 female witnesses concerning inadequate clothing and footware. Testimony from male witnesses is illustrative:

> Misfits clothes, like hand me down clothes, and the boots clattering, they were
> too big, we would be like the German army.

> We had no underwear that changed in the 70s. You were in … pants and … shirt,
> they were all made in the School too, shoes, boots the lot, they were all made
> there. Anyone who had a hole in their sock at the inspections got a beating for
> that too; the boots were too big or too small. (Ryan Report, 2009, Volume 3: para.
> 7.170)

Favouritism in the allocation of clothing was an issue for female witnesses, with
nineteen reporting that the best clothing was reserved for the 'pets' of staff members (Ryan Report, 2009, Volume 3: para. 9.147). Generally speaking, female
witnesses reported their clothes being removed on admission and replaced by
inferior garments that were often ill-fitting and pre-worn. In some cases clothing
was made from sacking. The impact on children's identity and self-image was
serious, stigmatising them as the 'industrials' or 'orphans'.

Sixty-six male witnesses complained of inadequate health care. Similar
complaints were made by 138 females. Sometimes the need for health care was
the result of excessive punishment. As a result of this lack of attention to child
health within the reformatory and industrial school system several fatalities

were reported by survivors in their testimony to the Confidential Committee, which will be discussed here.

Neglect reports also focused on the lack of adequate heating in many industrial and reformatory schools, with 265 male witnesses from eleven schools and 241 female witnesses from thirty-five schools making complaints. In both male and female schools, prior to 1970, heating appliances were described as primitive. Dormitories were often unheated, with children suffering from chilblains during the winter season. Because children in industrial and reformatory school frequently lacked warm clothing and bedding their experience of the cold conditions within these primitive institutions was exacerbated (Ryan Report, 2009, Volume 3: paras 7.177–178 and 9.148–9.149).

One hundred and fifty seven male survivors reported being physically assaulted in the classroom (Ryan Report, 2009, Volume 3: para. 7.46). Education was neglected but also where it existed it was often associated with physical abuse. When at the age of sixteen the survivors of these institutions were discharged into the community, they had little preparation or support. Amongst male witnesses, 197 (48%) reported that no adequate arrangements were made for their discharge and aftercare. The areas of neglect most frequently identified by male witnesses were:

- Lack of acknowledgement regarding separation and loss
- Lack of preparation and training in basic life skills
- Lack of assessment, supervision and follow-up of placements
- Lack of opportunity to develop social and relationship skills. (Ryan Report, 2009, Volume 3: para. 7.205)

The systematic policy of discouraging links with their families and breaking up siblings in care between institutions left children very isolated on release. This compounded the problem of lack of aftercare. Manifestly, children placed in the industrial and reformatory school system were seriously neglected. That neglect was multi-dimensional. Children were hungry, cold, poorly dressed and frequently lacked basic hygiene. Health care was often neglected. So was the children's educational development. It appears many had basic literacy problems, which further constrained their life opportunities. There was little preparation for discharge into an uncertain and unsupported future.

Emotional abuse

The Ryan Report defines emotional abuse as 'any other act or omission towards the child which results, or could reasonably result, in serious impairment of the physical or mental health or development of the child or serious adverse effects on his or her behaviour or welfare' (Ryan Report, 2009, Volume 3, paras 7.213 and 9.190).

It recorded survivors' testimony of emotional abuse with regards to deprivation of family contact; personal identity; secure relationships; affection; approval and a lack of protection. The Ryan Report (2009, Volume 3: para. 7.221) observes:

> Witnesses reported a daily existence in the Schools that was dominated by fear, humiliation, loneliness, and the absence of affection. Fear was strongly associated with the daily threat of being physically and otherwise abused and seeing co-residents being abused. Constant apprehension about the next abuse to which they would be subjected was also a feature.

The Confidential Committee heard 327 reports of emotional abuse from 293 male witnesses (71%) and 354 from female witnesses (94%) (Ryan Report, 2009, Volume 3: paras 7.215 and 9.192). Amongst the male survivors, 194 described a lack of verbal and physical affection, which is illustrated by the example below:

> I remember the loneliness. You'd be in bed at night and you would be wondering, why didn't mam come or why didn't dad come? There was no one to hug you. I was not physically harmed there. It was emotional, nobody would come to you, it was just emptiness, nothing to latch onto. I don't understand how they didn't see it. You're lonely, unloved, unwanted. (Ryan Report, 2009, Volume 3: para. 7.222)

Other male survivors (thirty) reported on the lack of anybody to confide in or offer support: 'the worst thing was having no one to talk to, no one said a nice word to you' (Ryan Report, 2009, Volume 3: para. 7.224). Orphans and children from ethnic minorities (e.g. Travellers, Afro-Irish) were particularly vulnerable to this deprivation of affection, as the following male witness reports:

> It was a very tough place for me, one nun locked me in a closet, beat the hell out of me with a leather strap. She didn't like blacks, she called me Baluba,[2] every time the Irish soldiers were attacked in the Congo she attacked me. (Ryan Report, 2009, Volume 3: para. 7.236)

Other male witnesses (67) complained of being deprived of family contact with their parents, brothers and sisters, while they were institutionalised:

> We were all split up and we still are, 5 of us were in 4 different Schools. One brother, I did not know of his existence until I was 13 …

> I found out after 50 plus years that I had a brother, my brother was looking for me for 20 years and he couldn't find me. He was fostered out, he had a better life. He knew he had a brother. I was never sure but he was younger than me. It made an awful difference to me to meet him, it is brilliant like, it's a great thing. Why, why

did they break us all up? Why didn't they leave the 2 of us together? They didn't
have to break us up. They should have told us about each other. (Ryan Report,
2009, Volume 3: para. 7.237)

Frequently, the severance of family links was accompanied by designation of
parents as 'sinners', 'slags', 'old whores', 'scum', 'tramps' and 'from the gutter'
(Ryan Report, 2009, Volume 3: para. 7.236).

Female witnesses similarly described a pervasive atmosphere of emotional
abuse, including humiliation and ridicule; deprivation of contact with siblings
and family; rejection; loss of identity; lack of affection, threat of harm and deliberate exposure to frightening situations. They also complained of a variety of other
forms of emotional abuse based upon the systemic policy of mortification.

It involved a punitive emphasis on religion; public humiliation and personal ridicule, denigration of family of origin, isolation, criticism and verbal abuse,
and unreasonable imposition of responsibility (e.g. adolescent girls caring for in-
fants). A very large number of female witnesses (147) described being ridiculed
and humiliated in public through name-calling; humiliation regarding public
hygiene, constant criticism and various public humiliations, such as begging
for forgiveness, being placed at the 'penance table', being forced to stand naked
in public (Ryan Report, 2009, Volume 3: paras 9.198–9.199). Name-calling, according to female survivors, was prevalent including the following epithets:

> 'devil's handmaid', 'tar babies', 'shawlies', 'Baluba', 'pauper', 'tinker', 'trash', 'dirty
> stinking trollop', 'illegitimate', 'slut', 'sinners', 'bastards', 'idiot', 'dunce', 'thick', 'liar',
> 'bandy legs', 'wet the bed', 'Dublin nobodies', and 'street kids'. (Ryan Report, 2009,
> Volume 3: paras 9.197–9.203)

Fear dominated the experience of female witnesses, with 143 survivors describing it as a regular and at times constant feature of their young lives, as the
following survivor testimony illustrates:

> Always screaming, wailing, you would be hearing it as you would be going
> through the corridor, you would hear the screaming, and you would say 'Jesus
> Christ who is getting beaten today?'

> You lived in appalling fear, the most appalling fear, you would be terrified. You
> did not know at what time you would get a beating. I couldn't explain to you the
> fear, it was terrible. There was this nun … she was a very, very wicked woman
> … She beat you whenever she felt like it. (Ryan Report, 2009, Volume 3: para.
> 9.211)

The Ryan Report (Volume 3, 2009: para. 9.215) also records that fear of being sent
to a Magdalen Laundry struck terror into the female children in institutions:

The particular fear associated with these threats of being sent away was the belief that those who were transferred to other institutions were then never released. 'We suffered the fear of being sent to … laundry … that was the fear that hung over you … I saw many a girl go there, I can name them … named co-residents … We never saw them again.' One witness reported that a co-resident was accused of stealing a small amount of money from a local member of the clergy, as a result of which she was subsequently sent to a psychiatric hospital.

There was a room, it was my nightmare that room, I was never sent there. She … [Sr X] … would send them there, some girls, the ones who fought back, and you would hear them screaming, the screams! And you would never see them again, they would be sent away. I was terrified my sister would be sent to a laundry because some of them girls were.

Other female witnesses, particularly 'orphans' were fearful that their detention within the industrial and reformatory school system would be for life. (Ryan Report, 2009, Volume 3: para. 9.126)

Sexual abuse

The Ryan Report (2009, Volume 3: para. 7.109) defines child sexual abuse as 'the use by a person for sexual arousal or sexual gratification of that person or another person'. The testimony it received from survivors included sexual abuse ranging from contact sexual abuse including rape and associated physical violence to non-contact abuse such as enforced nakedness or voyeurism. Survivors understandably found it difficult to talk about their experiences of sexual abuse. One survivor described his reticence in talking about the experience of sexual abuse:

A priest sexually abused me … It's not very easy to talk about it … There is things there but I don't know how to get them out. I'd love to be able to come out with them, but I just can't … There's no easy way of saying things like that. (ibid.)

Some 253 reports of sexual abuse were made by 242 male witnesses (59%) in twenty schools. There were 128 reports of sexual abuse from 127 female witnesses (34%) (Ryan Report, 2009, Volume 3: paras 7.110 and 9.70). Sexual abuse almost invariably occurred in tandem with other forms of child abuse.

There were eighty-eight witness reports of sexual abuse and associated physical violence, fifteen of these reports related to one school. Many of the reports heard were of witnesses being beaten while their abusers masturbated, or of the witnesses being beaten on their bare buttocks while they were held against the abusers' genitals.

The Ryan Report (2009, Volume 3: para. 7.126) further notes that child sexual abuse was also accompanied by serious threats:

> Sexual abuse associated with violence was also reported to be accompanied at times by serious threats of physical harm, including risk to life, for the perceived purpose of instilling fear and enforcing compliance. For example, witnesses reported being threatened that if they ever told anyone what happened to them they would be '*drowned in the slurry pit*', '*sent to a worse place*', '*killed*' or in one instance, '*cut up and buried in a bag in the bog*'. This latter threat was issued by a lay ancillary worker who the witness reported challenged him with a knife.

Similarly, female survivors 'consistently reported that sexual abuse occurred in an environment of fear and secrecy (Ryan Report, 2009, Volume 3: para. 9.84). One female witness, who was raped by a lay ancillary worker on a number of occasions was intimated into silence by threats:

> He ... [X] got us back to his house, said he had a sandwich for us. After that he used to follow me around the place, the nuns would have to be blind not to see this. He threatened to burn down the School and threatened to kill my sisters, so you went to bed at night petrified, thinking he was going to break in and burn down the School. You were just petrified, so if I didn't go to his house, this is what he would do, burn down the School and kill my sisters. He ... [witness described anal rape] ... several time over years ... [crying] ... It stays with you, it sticks in my mind, and the threat to burn down the School. (Ryan Report, 2009, Volume 3: para. 9.86)

The most vulnerable children reported being particularly exploited by the perpetrators of child sexual abuse, including those labelled 'orphans' and the youngest, as survivor testimony vividly describes:

> The orphan children, they had it bad. I knew ... [who they were] ... by the size of them, I'd ask them and they'd say they come from ... [named institution] ... . They were there from an early age. You'd hear the screams from the room where [Br. X] ... would be abusing them.

> There was one night, I wasn't long there and I seen one of the Brothers on the bed with one of the young boys ... and I heard the young lad screaming crying and [Br. X] said to me 'if you don't mind your own business you'll get the same' ... I heard kids screaming and you know they are getting abused and that's a nightmare in anybody's mind. You are going to try and break out ... So there was no way I was going to let that happen to me ... I remember one boy and he was bleeding from the back passage and I made up my mind, there was no way it ... [anal rape] ... was going to happen to me. ... That used to play on my mind. (Ryan Report, 2009, Volume 3: para. 7.232)

Disclosure of abuse

Some 35% of males and 30% of females reported that they told adults that they were physically and sexually abused (Ryan Report, 2009, Volume 3: paras 7.262 and 9.258). The responses they recorded included being ignored, punished and not believed as the following male survivor testimony illustrates:

> Two fellas went to Confession and told the priests what was happening about the beating. The next day we were all brought up and they were beaten, severely beaten and we were told 'whatever happens in here stays here'.

> We ran away, made it to ... [named town] ... . The police car stopped us and asked us where we were going, and where we had come from ... and he said 'why are you running away?' My brother told him about the beatings ... we didn't want to say anything about the sexual .... He ... [garda] ... brought us back to ... [named School] ... and told the nun what we were saying. They really tortured us after that. There was a man ... [named lay care staff] ... and there was another woman and there was [Sr. X] .... They beat us with whatever come to hand. That time you couldn't say anything against nuns or priests or anything like that ...

> Afterwards I met [Br. X] ... going down the stairs, he beat the crap out of me. 'You know to keep your mouth shut' he'd say 'you know what you'll get if you don't keep your mouth shut' ... . It was complete fear, I couldn't tell anyone, the fear you know. (Ryan Report, 2009, Volume 3: para. 7.267)

While female survivors reported a similar reaction to their male counterparts in response to disclosure, a minority were believed and positive action was taken.

However, most of the survivors of abuse in institutional care who disclosed their experience, had a negative experience. This resulted in the endemic problem of child abuse being unchecked for so long.

Death, disappearance and suicide

Raftery and O'Sullivan (1999: 233) note that 'there are a number of accounts from survivors of deaths of children under suspicious or unexplained circumstances'. One of these reports was that of Barney O'Connell, a boy incarcerated in Artane Industrial School during the 1950s, who fell 40 feet down a stairwell to his death. There was concern among several of the witnesses that he had fallen because he was being chased and punished by a staff member. However, the Ryan Report (2009, Volume 3, para. 7.147) after a thorough investigation concluded that the Christian Brothers (who managed Artane) were not at fault for Barney O'Connell's death. But the Ryan Report (2009, Volume 3: para. 7.197) records:

Three (3) witnesses reported the death of boys who they described were ignored or neglected when they complained of being sick. One witness reported his belief that a co-resident died as a result of eating poisonous berries. Two (2) witnesses reported being hospitalised following suicide attempts in the context of abuse episodes. They were transferred back to the institution without psychological assessment or treatment.

Five male witnesses reported to the Confidential Committee that co-residents who disappeared following a severe beating may have died. Three were from the same school. The following case was reported to the Confidential Committee by a survivor:

> There were some Brothers there who were A1 ... Then there was ... [crying] ... [Br. X], nasty bastard. The man doesn't deserve to be called Brother. I was only 5 feet away the day it happened ... [crying] .... He had a habit, every day ... he'd walk up and down the refectory, that was his ritual. If he walked in everyone was on edge .... I'm not sure why but this evening he [Br. X] ... walked straight down the passage way and he dragged ... [named co-resident] ... out of his chair ... [crying] ... and he gave him an unmerciful beating, an unmerciful beating. I'm telling ye he did not stop with that leather strap. Now all the Brothers used to carry the leather strap, but I'm telling ye, you wouldn't beat an animal the way he beat ... [named co-resident] .... To this day it haunts me, the whole place was full and he was left lying. [Br. X] ... cleared the place out, you all had to get out of the refectory, I was even told to get out of the kitchen. That was the last time, the very last time, I seen ... [named co-resident] ... I think it was 3 days afterwards I heard he was dead ... It has haunted me. After that [Br. X] ... quietened down for awhile. I think he knew anyway ... (Ryan Report, 2009, Volume 3: para. 7.229)

Female survivors, as noted above, referred in their testimony to death threats to themselves or their siblings as a result of disclosing child abuse (Ryan Report, 2009, Volume 3: para. 9.212). Other female witnesses linked isolation in locked space (rooms and cupboards) with fears about their personal safety (*ibid.*). Male witnesses also expressed concerns about suicide as a result of beatings as the following example illustrates:

> We were marched up to a room ... we were put sitting around the gymnastic table, we called it ... the horse, we were put sitting around, from the youngest to the oldest boy. We watched 4 Brothers walk in with 3 boys ... [named co-residents] ... I know one of them, within a year of leaving he had hung himself ... they were stripped naked while the Brothers held their hands and their legs and this [Br. X] ... removing his soutane and his collar dramatically began to flog these guys within an inch of their life. Observing excrement coming out of the boys' behind and blood flowing down their legs, I literally trembled and I know kids all around us trembled in silence, some were crying for the poor boys. Their

screams for mercy were seared into your very brain. (Ryan Report, 2009, Volume 3: para. 7.250)

This harrowing testimony from the survivors can leave no doubt that the Industrial and Reformatory school regime was cruel and inhuman. The scale of deaths is difficult to assess. From the anecdotal evidence apparently some children died as a result of abuse. The paucity of records makes it difficult to assemble accurate figures. There clearly needs to be in-depth study of local cemetery records and death certificates before we will know the full scale of deaths in institutional care.

Conclusion

Irish industrial and reformatory schools were based upon a philosophy of violence that subjected the bodies and minds of their inmates to regimes of medieval-style terror, involving cruelty and in many instances torture. The Ryan Report (2009) is not simply a narrative of child abuse. Its revelations of human rights violations against children in institutional care belong to the same realm of violence and oppression as Soviet Gulags and Nazi concentration camps. In some respects the issues are even more morally challenging. These human rights crimes were not committed by a totalitarian state but by Church organisations in a society that purported to be democratic. All of the victims were children. Most of the alleged perpetrators were clergy. How do we make sense of these events? How do we deal with the moral issues? We have discussed the Catholic Church's difficulties with engaging in a process of truth-telling. The value of the Ryan Report (2009) is that it is an exercise in truth-telling, even if it is flawed by the anonymity of the accused. This was the compromise the Commission to Inquire into Child Abuse were prepared to make in order to provide the survivors with a forum to tell their truths and Irish society with the opportunity to bear witness to that truth. Accordingly, the challenge for Irish society is to engage with the moral and social legacy of the Ryan Report. The legacy of the Ryan Report (2009) is to confront Irish civil society with a deeply unpalatable truth about youth policy during the period after Ireland became independent. Life got harsher for the vulnerable poor. The promise of the revolution, despite rhetorical commitments in the Proclamation of 1916 and the Democratic Programme of 1919, was never realised. Instead a Kafkaesque world of violence perpetuated by clergy and unregulated by the Irish state was allowed to develop. Irish civil society was also complicit in this policy. While there is much that was positive in Irish youth policy during this period, the survivors' evidence is so damning of the Industrial and Reformatory School system that it is hard to reach any other conclusion that between 1922 and 1970 Irish youth from socially disadvantaged backgrounds were subject to cruelty and dehumanisation on a mass scale. Indeed there is evidence that some of these practices continued up to 1989. The dawn of the twentieth century has brought at least a partial acknowledgement of the truth about the underlying direction of Irish youth policy during the twentieth century. The challenge is to construct an entirely different policy approach based upon human rights and social justice.

Notes

1   The reader will notice a some slight statistical divergence in these figures, which the Ryan Report (2009: paras 7.11 and 9.07) explains as being due to rounding up and down.
2   Baluba was the name of a Congolese tribe where Irish peace-keeping troops were stationed during the 1960s.

References

Archives

Boys' Brigade (Dublin)
Boy Scouts Archive (Dublin and London)
Cork City and County Archives
Dublin Diocesan Archives
National Archive (Dublin)
National Archive (London)
National Library of Ireland
Representative Church Body Library (Dublin)
University College Dublin Archives

Parliamentary papers and government publications (pre-twentieth century)

Journal of the Irish House of Commons 1758, 1791, 1792, 1788.
Report of the Inter-departmental Committee on Child Care (Mundella Report), 1896 Local Government Board, London.
Report of the Reformatory and Industrial Schools Commissioners, H.C. 1884, c3876 XLV. 1.
Third Report of the Commissioners of Irish Education Enquiry, 1826–27.
Thirty-fourth Report of the Inspector of Reformatory and Industrial Schools of Ireland, 1896, C8204, XLV.

Official publications: Irish State since 1922

Bowden, M. and Higgins, L. (2000). *The Impact and Effectiveness of the Garda Special Projects: Final Report to the Department of Justice, Equality & Law Reform.* Dublin: Stationery Office.
Bunreacht na h-Eireann – Constitution of Ireland, 1937.
Central Statistics Office (CSO) (2006) *Census 2006. Volume 3: Household Composition, Family Units and Fertility.* Dublin: Stationery Office.

Central Statistics Office (CSO) (2009) *Community Involvement and Social Networks*. Dublin: Stationery Office.

Dail Eireann (2008) *Dail Debates*, 10 July, Volume 660.

Dail Eireann (2000) *Dail Debates*, Volume 525, 9 November, http://historical-debates.oireachtas.ie/D/0525/D.0525.200011090016.html, accessed 4 October 2010.

Dail Eireann (1977) *Dail Debates*, 25 May, Volume 299, http://historical-debates.oireachtas.ie/D/0299/D.0299.197705250016.html, accessed 1 September 2010.

Department of Community, Rural and Gaeltacht Affairs (2009) *National Drugs Strategy (interim) 2009–2016*, www.drugsandalcohol.ie/12388/1/DCRGA_Strategy_2009-2016.pdf, accessed 23 March 2010.

Department of Education and Science (2003) *National Youth Work Development Plan 2003–2007*. Dublin: Stationery Office.

Department of Justice, Equality and Law Reform (2006) *Report on the Youth Justice Review*. Dublin: The Stationery Office.

Department of Justice, Equality and Law Reform (2003) *Garda Youth Diversion Project Guidelines*, www.justice.ie/en/JELR/Garda%20Youth%20Diversion%20Project%20Guidelines.pdf/Files/Garda%20Youth%20Diversion%20Project%20Guidelines.pdf, accessed 14 April 2010.

Department of Justice, Equality and Law Reform (2002) *Guidelines Garda Youth Diversion Projects*. Dublin: Stationery Office.

Department of Local Government and Public Health (1932) *Annual Report, 1931–32*.

Department of Social, Community and Family Affairs (2000) *White Paper on a Framework for Supporting Voluntary Activity and for Developing the Relationship between the State and the Community and Voluntary Sector*. Dublin: Stationery Office.

Development of Youth Work Services in Ireland: A Report of the Committee Appointed by the Minister of State at the Department of Education (The O'Sullivan Report) (1980). Dublin: Stationery Office.

The Ferns Report: Presented to the Minister for Health and Children (2005). Dublin: Stationery Office.

Government Select Committee on Crime (1992) *Juvenile Crime: Its Causes and Its Remedies*. Dublin: Stationery Office.

Hanafin, M. (2005) *Dail Debates*, 3 November, Volume 609, http://historical-debates.oireachtas.ie/D/0609/D.0609.200511030200.html, accessed 29 September 2010.

Interdepartmental Group on Urban Crime and Disorder (1992) *Urban Crime and Disorder: Report of the Interdepartmental Group*. Dublin: Stationery Office.

Irish Youth Justice Service (2009a) *Designing Effective Local Responses to Youth Crime*. Dublin: Stationery Office.

Irish Youth Justice Service (2009b) *Mission Statement*, www.iyjs.ie/en/IYJS/Pages/Home, accessed 26 August 2009.

Irish Youth Justice Service (2008) *National Youth Justice Strategy 2008–2010*. Dublin: Stationery Office.

National Crime Council (2003) *A Crime Prevention Strategy for Ireland: Tackling the Concerns of Local Communities*. Dublin: Stationery Office.

National Crime Council (2002) *Tackling the Underlying Causes of Crime- A Partnership Approach*. Dublin: Stationery Office.

OECD (1966) *Investment in Education: Report of the Survey Team Appointed by the Minister of Education in October 1962*. Dublin: Stationery Office.

Office of the Minister for Children (2007) *Teenspace, National Recreation Policy for Young People*. Dublin: Stationery Office.

Office of the Minister for Children and Youth Affairs (OMYCA) (2010a) *Youth Cafés in Ireland: A Best Practice Guide*. Dublin: Stationery Office.

Office of the Minister for Children and Youth Affairs (OMYCA) (2010b) *Youth Café Toolkit: How to Set Up and Run a Youth Café in Ireland*. Dublin: Stationery Office.

Office of the Minister for Children and Youth Affairs (OMYCA) (2009a) *Funding Programmes and Initiatives*, www.omc.gov.ie/viewdoc.asp?fn=%2Fdocuments%2Fy outhaffairs%2Ffunding.htm&mn=yous, accessed 15 April 2010.

Office of the Minister for Children and Youth Affairs (OMYCA) (2009b) *The Young People's Facilities & Services Fund*, www.omc.gov.ie/viewdoc.asp?fn=%2Fdocumen ts%2Fpolicy%2Fyp_facilites.htm, accessed 15 April 2010.

A Policy for Youth and Sport (The Bruton Report) (1977). Dublin: Stationery Office.

Public Dance Halls Act, 1935, www.irishstatutebook.ie/1935/en/act/pub/0002/print. html, accessed 16 September 2010.

Reformatory and Industrial Schools Systems Report (The Kennedy Report) (1970). Dublin: Stationery Office.

Report into the Catholic Archdiocese of Dublin (Murphy Report) (2009), www.inis.gov. ie/en/JELR/Cover%20Part%201.pdf/Files/Cover%20Part%201.pdf, accessed 1 October 2010.

Report of the Commission on the Relief of the Sick and Destitute Poor, Including the Insane Poor (1927). Dublin: Stationery Office.

Report of the Commission on Youth Unemployment (1951). Dublin: Stationery Office.

Report of the Commission to Inquire into Child Abuse (The Ryan Report) (2009), www. childabusecommission.com/rpt/pdfs, accessed 1 September 2010.

Report of the Committee on the Criminal Law Amendment Acts (1880–85) and Juvenile Prostitution (Carrigan Report) (1931). Dublin: Stationery Office.

Report of Inter-Departmental Committee of Inquiry Regarding Venereal Disease (1926). Dublin: Stationery Office.

Report of the Inter-Departmental Committee on the Prevention of Crime and Treatment of Offenders (1963). Unpublished report.

Report of the Commission of Inquiry into the Reformatory and Industrial School System (Cussen Report) (1936). Dublin: Stationery Office,

Task Force on Active Citizenship (2007) *Statistical Evidence on Active Citizenship in Ireland*. Dublin: Task Force on Active Citizenship, www.activecitizenship.ie/ UPLOADEDFILES/Mar07/Statistical%20Report%20(Mar%2007).pdf, accessed 1 October 2010.

Task Force on Child Care Services (1980) *Final Report to the Minister of Health*. Dublin: Stationery Office.

Third Interim Report of the Commission to Inquire into Child Abuse (2003). Dublin: Stationery Office.

Voluntary and political organisations: annual reports, handbooks and other materials (pre-1940).

Boys' Brigade Dublin Battalion *Annual Reports* for the years 1908–09; 1911–12; 1921–22 and 1934–35. Boys' Brigade (BB) Dublin.

The Boys' Brigade 1st Dublin Company (St. Matthias): Souvenir [booklet] 1911. (BB)

Boy Scouts Association *Annual Reports*, 1911, 1912, 1913, 1915, 1917, 1919, 1920, 1921, 1922, 1924, 1925, 1926. Scouting Association Archive (SAA) London.

Dublin Boy Scouts' *Annual Handbook* (1919). Scouting Ireland Archive (SIA).

Dublin Boy Scouts (1917)[booklet]. (SIA)

Report of Inspection Tour by the Chief Scout in Ireland, August 1915. (SAA)

Report to Imperial Headquarters by the Chief Scout, 28 August 1928. (SAA)

Inghinidhe na hEireann, *First Annual Report 1900–1901*. National Library of Ireland (NLI).

Girls' Friendly Society (GFS) Annual Reports: 1880, 1883, 1884, 1885, 1887, 1888, 1889, 1890, 1891, 1901, 1902, 1903, 1905. Representative Church Body (RCB) Library.

Young Women's Christian Association (YWCA) Report for Ireland, 1887. (RCB)

Anon (c.1910) *Proposal Concerning the YWCA in Ireland*. (RCB)

Catholic Girls' Club and Hostel Annual Report 1919–1920. Dublin Diocesan Archives (DDA).

Report of the work of the Catholic Girls' Club produced by Eveleen Moore, Hon. Secretary, 1922. (DDA)

Girls' Brigade Minutes of Meeting 2 October 1908.

Fianna Eireann Central Council (1914) *Fianna Handbook*. Individually authored chapters within this publication include: Countess Markievicz, 'Introduction'; P.H. Pearse, 'The Fianna of Fionn'; and R. Casement, 'Chivalry'. (NLI)

O' Duffy, E. (1934) *An Outline of the Political, Social and Economic Policy of Fine Gael (United Ireland). Opening address delivered at first annual Ard-Fheis of Fine Gael in the Mansion House, Dublin, February 8, 1934*.

Blythe Papers P/24/657a. Draft speech of General Eoin O' Duffy on being elected leader of the Army Comrades Association. July 1933. University College Dublin Archive (UCDA).

Blythe Papers P/24/649a 'ACA Policy. Rough Draft for discussion'. (UCDA)

Blythe Papers P/24/658 'Constitution of the National Guard' 1933. (UCDA)

NI JUS 93/3/17. 'Statement by Commandant Cronin at ACA meeting, Mansion House, Tuesday, 6 December 1932'. (National Archive, Dublin).

Other reports

Police Reports CO 904/119 and CO 904/14. National Archive, London.

Books (pre-1940)

Association of Charities (1902) *Dublin Charities*. Dublin: Association of Charities.

Baden-Powell, R. (1908) *Scouting for Boys*. London: Arthur Pearson.

Carpenter, M. (1851) *Reformatory Schools for the Children of the Perishing and Dangerous Classes and for Juvenile Offenders*. London.

MacGull, P. (1914) *Children of the Dead End: The Autobiography of a Navvy*. London: Jenkins.

Malthus, T.R. (1878) *Essay on the Principle of Population*, London.

Correspondence

From the Scouting Archive, London:

Letter from Lord Meath to Lord Hampton, 27 January 1927;

Powerscourt to Meath, 27 October 1922;

Meath to Green, 18 November 1922;

Powerscourt to Meath, 16 October 1923;

Powerscourt to Meath, 27 October 1923;

Meath to Powerscourt, 29 October 1923.

Undated letter written by S.R. Barcroft to Miss McCarthy, giving the reasons for the Irish YWCA's decision to separate in 1916.

Newspapers and periodicals

The Blueshirt

Eire

Fianna

Headquarters Gazette (Boy Scouts)

The Irish Independent

The Irish Monthly

The Irish Scouts Gazette

The Irish Times

The Nation

Our Boys

United Ireland

The Weekly Irish Times

Books, articles and other references (post-1940)

Alexander, K. (2009) 'The Girl Guide Movement and Imperial Internationalism During the 1920s and 1930s', *Journal of the History of Childhood and Youth*, 2(1): 37–63.

Anderson, B. (1991 [1983]) *Imagined Communities: Reflections on the Origin and Spread of Nationalism*. London: Verso.

Aries, P. (1996 [1962]) *Centuries of Childhood*. London: Pimlico.

Arnold, B. (2009) *The Irish Gulag*. Dublin: Gill and Macmillan.

Barker (2008) *Cultural Studies: Theory & Practice* (3rd edn). London: Sage.

Barnes, J. (1989) *Irish Industrial Schools 1868–1908: Origins and Development*. Dublin: Irish Academic Press.

Beck, U. (1992) *Risk Society: Towards a New Modernity*. London: Sage.

Benton, S. (1995) 'Women Disarmed: The Militarization of Politics in Ireland 1913–23', *Feminist Review*, 50: 148–172.

Blanshard, P. (1954) *The Irish and Catholic Power*. Boston, MA: Beacon Press.

Blom, P. (2008) *The Vertigo Years: Change and Culture in the West 1900–1914*. London: Weidenfeld and Nicholson.

Bohn, I. (2007) *Report on the Socio-Economic Status of Young People in Europe*. Frankfurt: Insitut für Socialarbeit und Sozialpädagogik. Unpublished report.

Boys' Brigade (2010) *Mission of the Boys' Brigade*, www.boysbrigade.ie/about.htm, accessed 23 March 2010.

Brady, B. and Dolan, P. (2007) 'Youth Mentoring in Ireland: Weighing up the Benefits and Challenges', *Youth Studies Ireland*, 2(1): 3–16.

Brady, B., Dolan, P., O'Brien, M. and Canavan, J. (2005) *Big Brothers Big Sisters Ireland Youth Mentoring Programme, Galway, Mayo & Roscommon: Evaluation Report*. Report by HSE/NUI, Galway Child & Family Research & Policy Unit, www.nuigalway.ie/childandfamilyresearch/documents/big_brothers_big_sisters_pdf.pd, accessed 13 November 2009.

Brady, S. (2003) *Day of Prayer for Temperance*. Homily given by Archbishop Seán Brady, St Joseph's Church, Dundalk, 2 March 2003, www.catholiccommunications.ie/news/ArchbishopSeanBrady-TemperanceSunday2003.html, accessed 1 September 2010.

Brophy, C. (2009) *In the Spirit of Adventure: A History of the Catholic Guides of Ireland*. Dublin: Veritas.

Burke, H. (1999) 'Foundation Stones of Irish Social Policy 1831–1951', Kiely, G., O' Donnell, A., Kennedy, P. and Quin, S. (eds), *Irish Social Policy in Context*. Dublin: University College Dublin Press.

Burke, H. (1987) *The People and the Poor Law in Nineteenth Century Ireland*. Sussex: The Women's Education Bureaux.

Burleigh, M. (2000) *The Third Reich: A New History*. London: Pan Books.

Burnett, R. and Appleton, C. (2004) 'Joined-Up Services to Tackle Youth Crime: A Case Study in England', *The British Journal of Criminology*, 44(1): 34–54.

Bush, J. (2000) *Edwardian Ladies and Imperial Power*. London: Leicester University Press.

Bush, J. (1993) 'Moving On: And Looking Back', *History Workshop*, 36 (1): 183–194.

CARE (1974) *CARE Newsletter*, 1(2) November 1974.

CARE (1972) *Children Deprived: The Care Memorandum on Deprived Children and Children's Services in Ireland*. Dublin: CARE.

Carroll, J. and Meehan, E. (2007), *The Children Court: A National Study*. Dublin: Association for Criminal Justice Research and Development.

Coakley, J. (2004) 'Mobilizing the Past: Nationalist Images of History', *Nationalism & Ethnic Politics*, 10(4): 531–560.

Cohen, S. (1985) *Visions of Social Control: Crime, Punishment and Classification*. Oxford: Polity Press.

Cohen, S. (1979) 'The Punitive City: Notes on the Dispersal of Social Control', *Crime, Law and Social Change*, 3(4): 339–363.

Comhairle le Leas Óige (CLLO) (1944) *Souvenir and Programme of Youth Week (11th–18th June)*. Dublin: CLLO.

Condon, J. (2000) 'The Patriotic Children's Treat: Irish Nationalism and Children's Culture at the Twilight of Empire', *Irish Studies Review*, 8(2): 167–178.

Connell, J. (undated): *History of B-P Scouts in Southern Ireland: 1908–1958*. Unpublished report.

Considine, M. and Dukelow, F. (2009) *Irish Social Policy: A Critical Introduction*. Dublin: Gill and Macmillan.

Coolahan, J. (1981) *Irish Education: History and Structure*. Dublin: Institute of Public Administration.

Cooney, J. (1999) *John Charles McQuaid: Ruler of Catholic Ireland*. Dublin: O'Brien Press.

Coussee, F. (2009) 'The Relevance of Youth Work's History', in Verschelden, G., Coussee, F., Van de Walle, T. and Williamson, H. (eds), *The History of Youth Work in Europe and its Relevance for Youth Policy Today*. Strasbourg: Council of Europe Publishing.

Cronin, M. (1997) *The Blueshirts and Irish Politics*. Dublin: Four Courts Press.

Cronin, M. (1995) 'The Blueshirt Movement, 1932–5: Ireland's Fascists?', *Journal of Contemporary History*, 30(2): 311–332.

Crook, S., Pakulski, J. and Waters, M. (1992) *Postmodernization: Change in Advanced Society*. London and New Delhi: Sage.

Cunningham, H. (1990) 'Leisure and Culture', in Thompson, F.M.L. (ed.), *The Cambridge Social History of Britain 1750–1950. Volume 2. People and Their Environment*. Cambridge: Cambridge University Press.

Curtis, J.R. (1996) 'Ireland in 1914', in Vaughan, W.E. (ed.), *A New History of Ireland. Volume VI: Ireland Under the Union, II: 1870–1921*. Oxford: Clarendon Press.

Cusack, J. (2009) 'Bishops Gave Editor Sack Over Articles on Sex Abuse', *Sunday Independent*, 7 June.

Cusack, T. (2001) 'A "Countryside Bright with Cosy Homesteads": Irish Nationalism and the Cottage Landscape', *National Identities*, 3(3): 221–238.

Davies, B. (2005) 'Youth Work: A Manifesto for our Times', *Youth & Policy*, 88: 7–27.

Davies, B. and Merton, B. (2009) 'Squaring the Circle? The State of Youth Work in Some Children and Young People's Services', *Youth & Policy*, 103: 5–24.

Denman, T. (1994) '"The Red Livery of Shame": The Campaign Against Army Recruitment in Ireland, 1899–1914', *Irish Historical Studies*, 29(114): 208–233.

Devlin, M. (2008) 'Youth Work and Youth Policy in the Republic of Ireland 1983–2008: "Still Haven't Found What We're Looking For ...?"', *Youth & Policy*, 100: 41–54.

Devlin, M. (1989) 'Official Youth Work Discourse: Aims, Orientations and Ideology in Irish Youth Work Policy'. Unpublished M.Soc.Sc. thesis, University College Dublin.

Devlin, M. and Gunning, A. (2009) *The Purpose and Outcomes of Youth Work: Report to the Youth Services Interagency Group*. Dublin: Irish Youth Work Press.

Dolan (2006) *Foróige Neighbourhood Youth Projects: Enhancing Support for Young People*. Summary research report commissioned by Foróige and the Health Service Executive, www.nuigalway.ie/childandfamilyresearch/downloads/NYP_PDF_copy. pdf, accessed 14 April 2010.

Dolan, P. and Kane, S. (2005) *Neighbourhood Youth Projects in the Health Services Executive Western Area, Counties Galway, Mayo and Roscommon. Review Report 1992–2004: Strengthening Existing Practice, Building Future Capacity*, www. nuigalway.ie/childandfamilyresearch/documents/nyp_review_1992_2004_final. pdf, accessed 14 April 2010.

Dorr, D. (2009) 'Who was Responsible?', in Flannery, T. (ed.), *Responding to the Ryan Report*. Blackrock: Columba Press.

Duncan, P. (2009) 'Charity Shops Welcome a Downturn Donation: People', *The Irish Times*, 23 July.

Elias, Norbert (1994 [1939]) *The Civilizing Process: Sociogenetic and Psychogenetic Investigations*. Oxford: Blackwell.

Engels, F. (1999 [1887]) *The Condition of the Working Class in England*. Oxford: Oxford University Press.

Fanning, B. (2008) *The Quest for Modern Ireland: The Battle of Ideas 1912–1986*. Dublin: Irish Academic Press.

Ferguson, H. (2007) 'Abused and Looked After Children as "Moral Dirt"', *Journal of Social Policy*, 36(1): 123–139.

Ferriter, D. (2010) 'A Scholar with a Passion on his Mind' (interview with Fintan O' Toole), *Irish Times*, 28 May.

Ferriter, D. (2009) *Occasions of Sin: Sex and Society in Modern Ireland*. London: Profile Books.

Ferriter, D. (2005) *The Transformation of Ireland 1900–2000*. London: Profile Books.

Finnegan, F. (2001) *Do Penance or Perish: A Study of Magdalen Asylums in Ireland*. Piltown: Congrave Press.

Fionda, J. (2005) *Devils and Angels: Youth Policy and Crime*. Oxford: Hart Publishing.

Fitzpatrick, D. (1984) *Irish Emigration 1801–1921*. Dublin: Economic and Social History Society of Ireland.

Flannery, T. (2009) *Responding to the Ryan Report*. Dublin: Columba Press.

Forde, W. (1995) *Growing up in Ireland: The Development of Irish Youth Services*. Gorey: Kara Publications.

Furlong, A. and Cartmel, F. (2007) *Young People and Social Change: New Perspectives*. London: Open University Press.

Garda Siochana (2008) *Annual Report of An Garda Síochána 2007*. Dublin: Garda Siochana.

Garda Síochana (2005) *Annual Report of an Garda Siochana 2004*. Dublin: Garda Síochana.

Garda Síochana (2000) *Annual Report of an Garda Siochana 1999*. Dublin: Garda Síochana.

Garland, D. (2001) *The Culture of Social Control: Crime and Social Order in Contemporary Society*. Oxford: Oxford University Press.

Gaughan, A. (2006) *Scouting in Ireland*. Blackrock: Currach Press.

Giddens, A. (1991) *Modernity and Self-Identity: Self and Society in the Late Modern Age*. Cambridge: Polity Press.

Gilchrist, R., Jeffs, T. and Spence, J. (eds) (2003) *Architects of Change: Studies in the History of Community and Youth Work*. Leicester: The National Youth Agency.

Gilligan, R. (1991) *Irish Child Care Services: Policy, Practice and Provisions*. Dublin: Institute of Public Administration.

Gilroy, P. (2010) *Darker than Blue*. Cambridge, MA: Belknap Press.

Girls' Brigade (1983) *The Growth and Development of the Girls' Brigade: Ireland 1893–1983*. Belfast: Girls' Brigade.

Girls' Friendly Society (2010) *Constitution*, www.girlsfriendlysociety.ie/index.php/members/constitution, accessed 15 April 2010.

Goffman, E. (1961) *Asylums*. New York: Doubleday.

Gothard, J. (1992) 'A Compromise with Conscience: The Reception of Female Immigrant Domestic Servants in Eastern Australia', *Labour History*, 62: 38–51.

Graham, E. (2004) *For Such a Time as This: Background and Highlights of the Irish YWCA 1860–2003*. Dublin: YWCA.

Griffin, C. (1993) *Representations of Youth: The Study of Youth and Adolescence in Britain and America*. Cambridge: Polity Press.

Guinnane, T. (1990) 'Coming of Age in Rural Ireland at the Turn of the Twentieth Century', *Continuity and Change*, 5 (3): 443–472.

Hamilton, C. and Seymour, M. (2006) 'ASBOs and Behaviour Orders: Institutionalised Intolerance of Youth?', *Youth Studies Ireland* (1)1: 61–76.

Hanley, B. and Millar, S. (2009) *The Lost Revolution*. Dublin: Penguin Ireland.

Harrison, B. (1973) 'For Church, Queen and Family: The Girls' Friendly Society 1874–1920', *Past and Present*, 61: 107–138.

Hay, M. (2008) 'The Foundation and Development of Na Fianna Eireann, 1909–16', *Irish Historical Studies*, 36(141): 53–71.

Hegarty, K. (1995) 'Foreword', in Moore, C., *Betrayal of Trust: The Father Brendan Smyth Affair and the Catholic Church*. Dublin: Marino Books.

Heywood, J. (1978) *Children in Care: The Development of the Service for the Deprived Child*. London: Routledge and Kegan Paul.

Hobsbawm, E. (1983) 'Introduction: Inventing Traditions', in Hobsbawn, E. and Ranger T. (eds), *The Invention of Tradition*. Cambridge: Cambridge University Press.

Hobson, B. (1968) *Ireland Yesterday and Tomorrow*. Tralee: Anvil Books.

Hooper, J. and Siddique, H. (2010) 'Catholics Angry as Church puts Female Ordination on Par with Sex Abuse', *The Guardian*, 17 July.

Hunt, M. (1990) 'The De-Eroticization of Women's Liberation: Social Purity Movements and the Revolutionary Feminism of Sheila Jeffreys', *Feminist Review*, 34: 23–46.

Hurley, L. (2002) 'Youth Work and Young People', ADM Community Based Youth Initiatives Discussion Papers. Dublin: Area Development Management (ADM).

Hurley, L. (1992) *The Historical Development of Irish Youth Work*. Dublin: Youth Work Research Centre.

Hurley, L. and Treacy, D. (1993) *Models of Youth Work: A Sociological Framework*. Dublin: Irish Youth Work Press.

Hynes, S. (1968) *The Edwardian Turn of Mind*. London: Oxford University Press.

Inglis, T. (1987) *Moral Monopoly: The Catholic Church in Modern Irish Society*. Dublin: Gill and Macmillan.

Instituto di Ricerca (IARD) (2001) *Study on the State of Young People and Youth Policy in Europe: Final Reports*. Milan: IARD. http://ec.europa.eu/youth/archive/doc/studies/iard/summaries_en.pdf, accessed 1 September 2010.

Irish Council for Civil Liberties (ICCL) (1977) *Children's Rights Under the Constitution*. Dublin: ICCL.

Irish Times (2010) 'Tracey Fay's Legacy', *Irish Times*, 5 March.

Irish Times (2009) 'The Savage Reality of Our Darkest Days', *Irish Times*, 21 May.

Jackson, A. (1990) 'Unionist Politics and Protestant Society in Edwardian Ireland', *The Historical Journal*, 33 (4): 839–866.

Jeal (2001) *Baden-Powell: Founder of the Boy Scouts*. London: Yale University Press.

Jeffs, T. and Smith, M. (2008) 'Valuing Youth Work', *Youth & Policy*, 100: 277–302.

Jeffs, T. and Smith, M. (2002) 'Individualisation and Youth Work', *Youth and Policy*, 76: 39–65.

Jenkinson, H. (2000) 'Youth Work in Ireland: The Struggle for Identity', *Irish Journal of Applied Social Studies*, 2(2): 106–124.

Jenkinson, H. (1996) 'History of Youth Work', in Burgess, P. (ed.), *Youth and Community Work: A Course Reader*. Centre for Adult and Continuing Education, University College Cork.

Johnson, N. (1997) 'Making Space: Gaeltacht Policy and the Politics of Identity', in Graham, B. (ed.), *In Search of Ireland: A Cultural Geography*. London: Routledge.

Jones, G. (2009) *Youth*. Cambridge: Polity Press.

Jordan, T.E. (1998) *Ireland's Children: Quality of Life, Stress and Child Development in the Famine Era*. Westport: Greenwood Press.

Kadushin, A. (1980) *Child Welfare Services*. New York: Macmillan.

Keane, J. (2009) *The Life and Death of Democracy*. London: Simon and Schuster.

Keohane, K. and Kuhling, C. (2004) *Collision Culture: Transformations in Everyday Life in Ireland*. Dublin: Liffey Press.

Kerrins, L. (2008) 'Coming of Age in the 21st Century: The New and Longer Road to Adulthood', *Youth Studies Ireland* (3)1: 45–51.

Kiely, E. (2009) 'Irish Youth Work Values: A Critical Appraisal', in Forde, C., Kiely, E. and Meade, R. (eds), *Youth and Community Work in Ireland: Critical Perspectives*. Blackrock: Blackwell Publishing.

Kiely, E. and Kennedy, P. (2005) 'Youth Policy', in Quin, S., Kennedy, P., Matthews, A. and Kiely, G. (eds), *Contemporary Irish Social Policy*. Dublin: University College Dublin Press.

Kilkelly, U. (2008) *Children's Rights in Ireland: Law, Policy and Practice*. West Sussex: Tottel Publishing.

Kilkelly, U. (2006) *Youth Justice in Ireland: Tough Lives, Rough Justice*. Dublin: Irish Academic Press.

Kirby, P. (2008) *Explaining Ireland's Development: Economic Growth with Weakening Welfare* (UNRISD Social Policy and Development Programme Paper no. 37). Geneva: United Nations Research Institute for Social Development (UNRISD).

Kornitzer, M. (1952) *Child Adoption in the Modern World*. London: Putnam.

Kornprobst, M. (2005) 'Episteme, Nation-builders and National Identity: The Reconstruction of Irishness', *Nations and Nationalism*, 11 (3): 403–421.

Lalor, K., de Roiste, A. and Devlin, M. (2007) *Young People in Contemporary Ireland*. Dublin: Gill Macmillan.

Lesko, N. (2001) *Act Your Age: A Cultural Construction of Adolescence*. London: Routledge.

Levene, M. (2005) *The Rise of the West and the Coming of Genocide*. London and New York: I.B. Taurus.

Luddy, M. (1997) "Abandoned Women and Bad Characters': Prostitution in Nineteenth-century Ireland', *Women's History Review*, 6(4): 485–504.

Luddy, M. (1995a) *Women and Philanthropy in Nineteenth-Century Ireland*. Cambridge: Cambridge University Press.

Luddy M. (1995b) *Women in Ireland, 1800–1918: A Documentary History*. Cork: Cork University Press.

Lyons, F.S.L. (1973) *Ireland Since the Famine*. London: Fontana.

MacCurtain, M., O' Dowd, M. and Luddy, M. (1992) 'An Agenda for Women's History in Ireland, 1500–1900', *Irish Historical Studies*, 28 (109): 1–37.

MacGill, P. (1914) *Children of the Dead End*. London: H. Jenkins.

MacKeogh, C. (2002) *Participant Observation: A Team Study of Young People and Television* (Irish Sociological Research Monographs). Maynooth: National University of Ireland.

Maffesoli, M. (1996) *The Times of Tribes: The Decline of Individualism in Mass Society*. London: Sage.

Maguire, M. (2009) *Precarious Childhood in Post-Independence Ireland*. Manchester: Manchester University Press.

Mann, M. (2005) *The Dark Side of Democracy*. Cambridge: Cambridge University Press.

Manning, M. (1970) *The Blueshirts*. Dublin: Gill and Macmillan.

McDonagh, P. (2010) 'More Vaccine Trials Were Kept Secret by the State', *Irish Independent*, 27 August.

McDowell, R.B. (1979) *Ireland in the Age of Imperialism and Revolution, 1760–1801*. Oxford: Clarendon.

McGarry, F. (2005) *Eoin O'Duffy: A Self-made Hero*. Oxford: Oxford University Press.

McGrath, B. (2006) "Everything is Different Here …': Mobilizing Capabilities Through Inclusive Education Practices and Relationships', *International Journal of Inclusive Education*, 10(6): 595–614.

McLoughlin, D. (2001) 'From Women and Sexuality in Nineteenth-century Ireland', in Hayes, A. and Urquhart D. (eds), *The Irish Women's History Reader*. London: Routledge.

McRobbie, A. (1991) *Feminism and Youth Culture*. London: Macmillan.

Miles, S., Cliff, D. and Burr, V. (1998) 'Fitting in and Sticking Out: Consumption, Consumer Meanings and the Construction of Young People's Identities', *Journal of Youth Studies*, 1(1): 81–96.

Millerson, G. (1964) *The Qualifying Association*. London: Routledge and Kegan.

Mokyr, J. (1983) *Why Ireland Starved: A Quantitative and Analytical History of the Irish Economy 1800–1850*. London: Allen and Unwin.

Mollan, C. (1979) *Children First*. Dublin: Arlen House, The Women's Press.

Mooney, G. (1998) "Remoralising' the Poor: Gender, Class and Philanthropy in Victorian England', in Lewis, G. (ed.), *Forming Nation, Framing Welfare*. London: Routledge.

Moore, C. (1995) *Betrayal of Trust: The Father Brendan Smyth Affair and the Catholic Church*. Dublin: Marino Books.

Morgan, M. and Kitching K. (2009) *Report on Quality Standards Framework (QSF) Evaluation*, www.omc.gov.ie/documents/youthaffairs/Report_on_Quality_Standards_Framework_(QSF)_Evaluation.doc, accessed 20 April 2010.

Morris, A., Giller, H., Szwed, E. and Geach, H. (1980) *Justice for Children*. London: Macmillan.

Morris, R.J. (1990) 'Clubs, Societies and Associations', in Thompson, F.M.L. (ed.), *The Cambridge Social History of Britain 1750–1950. Volume 3: Social Agencies and Institutions*. Cambridge: Cambridge University Press.

Morton, R.S. (1972) *Venereal Disease* (second edition). Harmondsworth: Penguin.

Mosse, G.L. (1997) *Nationalism and Sexuality: Respectability and Abnormal Sexuality in*

Modern Europe. New York: Howard Fertig.

Mulcahy, A. (2007) 'Crime, Policing and Social Control in Ireland', in O'Sullivan, S. (ed.), *Contemporary Ireland: A Sociological Map*. Dublin: University College Dublin Press.

Muncie, J. (2004*) Youth & Crime*. London: Sage.

National Economic and Social Council (2005) *The Developmental Welfare State*. Dublin: NESC.

National Federation of Youth Clubs (1983) *Youth Services 2000*. Dublin: National Federation of Youth Clubs.

National Youth Council of Ireland (NYCI)(2009) *Briefing March 2009*, www.youth.ie/ advocacy/youth_work_funding/briefing_march_2009, accessed 13 April 2010.

National Youth Policy Committee (1984) *National Youth Policy Committee Final Report* (Costello Report). Dublin: Stationery Office.

Obelkevich, J. (1990) 'Religion', in Thompson, F.M.L. (ed.), *The Cambridge Social History of Britain 1750–1950. Volume 3: Social Agencies and Institutions*. Cambridge: Cambridge University Press.

O'Brien, C. (2010a) 'Child Deaths While in Care or Contact With Services Now at 188', *Irish Times*, 5 June.

O'Brien, C. (2010b) 'HSE accused of Potential Dereliction of Duty over Foster Care', *Irish Times*, 13 July.

O'Brien, C. (2009) 'Government to Review Effectiveness of Asbos', *Irish Times*, 29 June.

O'Broin, D. and Kirby, P. (2009) *Power, Dissent and Democracy: Civil Society and the State in Ireland*. Dublin: A. & A. Farmar.

O' Connell, L. (1974) 'Travelers' Aid for Polish Immigrant Women', *American Studies*, 31(1): 15–19.

O' Connell, P.J., Clancy, D. and McCoy, S. (2006) *Who Went to College in 2004: A National Survey of New Entrants to Higher Education*. Dublin: Higher Education Authority.

O'Connor, B. (2003) 'Ruin and Romance: Heterosexual Discourses on Irish Popular Dance, 1920–1960', *Irish Journal Of Sociology* (12)2: 50–67.

O'Connor, P. (2008) *Irish Children and Teenagers in a Changing World: The National Write Now Project*. Manchester: Manchester University Press.

O'Day, R. (1994) *The Family and Family Relationships 1500–1900: England, France and the United States of America*. Basingstoke: Macmillan.

O'Donoghue, T.A. (1999) *The Catholic Church and the Secondary School Curriculum in Ireland, 1922–1962*. New York: Peter Lang.

O'Dwyer, K. (2002) 'Juvenile Crime and Justice in Ireland', in Bala, N., Hornick, J. and Snyder, H. (eds), *Juvenile Justice Systems: An International Comparison of Problems and Solutions*. Toronto: Thompson Educational.

O'Gorman, C. (2009) *Beyond Belief*. London: Hodder and Stoughton.

O'hAdllmhnran, G. (2005) 'Dancing on the Hobs of Hell: Rural Communities in Clare and the Dance Halls Act of 1935', *New Hibernia Review* (9)4: 9–18.

O'hAodain, M. (2010) 'The Contemporary Relevance of Historical Trends on Youth Work in Ireland', in Burgess, P. and Hermann, P. (eds), *Highways, Crossroads and cul de sacs: Journeys into Irish Youth & Community Work*. Bremen: Europaischer Hochschuverlag.

O'Reilly, E. (1992) *Masterminds of the Right*. Dublin: Attic Press.

O'Sullivan, D. (1992) 'Cultural Strangers and Educational Change: The OECD Report. Investment in Education and Irish Educational Policy', *Journal of Education Policy* (7)5: 445–469.

O'Sullivan, E. (1998) 'Juvenile Justice and the Regulation of the Poor: Restored to Virtue, to Society and to God', in Bacik, I. and O'Connell, M. (eds), *Crime and Poverty in Ireland*. Dublin: Round Hall Sweet & Maxwell.

O'Sullivan, E. (1997) 'Restored to Virtue, to Society and to God: Juvenile Justice and the Regulation of the Poor', *Irish Criminal Law Journal*, 7(2): 171–194.

O'Sullivan, E. and O'Donnell, I. (2007) 'Coercive Confinement in the Republic of Ireland: The Waning of a Culture of Control', *Punishment and Society*, 9(1): 27–48.

O'Toole, F. (2009) 'Law of Anarchy, Cruelty in Care', *Irish Times*, 23 May.

Ozkirimli, U. (2000) *Theories of Nationalism: A Critical Introduction*. Basingstoke: Palgrave.

Papal Encyclical *Quadragesimo Anno* (1936 [1931]), London.

Papal Encyclical *Rerum Novarum* (1983 [1891]), London.

Parsons, T. (1963) 'Youth in the Context of American Society', *Daedalus*, 91(1): 97–123.

Parsons, T. (1942) 'Age and Sex in the Social Structure of the United States', *American Sociological Review*, 7(5): 604–616.

Paxton, R. O. (2005) *The Anatomy of Fascism*. New York: Vintage Books.

Pedersen, J. Senders (1981) 'Victorian Headmistresses: A Conservative Tradition of Social Reform', *Victorian Studies*, 24(4): 463–488.

Piven, F. and Cloward, R. (1971) *Regulating the Poor: The Functions of Public Welfare*. London: Tavistock.

Pollock, L. (1983) *Forgotten Children: Parent-child Relations from 1500–1900*. Cambridge: Cambridge University Press.

Powell, F. (2007) *The Politics of Civil Society*. Bristol: Policy Press.

Powell, F. (1992) *The Politics of Irish Social Policy 1600–1992*. New York: Edwin Mellen Press.

Powell, F. and Geoghegan, M. (2004) *The Politics of Community Development*. Dublin: A.& A. Farmar.

Powell, F., Geoghegan, M., Scanlon, M. and Swirak, K. (2010) *Working with Young People: A National Study of Youth Work Provision and Policy in Contemporary Ireland*. Cork: Institute for Social Sciences in the 21st Century.

Powell, F. and Guerin, D. (1997) *Civil Society and Social Policy*. Dublin: A.A. Farmar.

Power, V. (2000) *Send 'Em Home Sweatin': The Showband Story*. Cork: Mercier Press.

Preston, M.H. (2004) *Charitable Words: Women, Philanthropy, and the Language of Charity in Nineteenth-Century Dublin*. Westport, CT: Praeger.

Prochaska, F.K. (1990) 'Philanthropy', in Thompson, F.M.L. (ed.), *The Cambridge Social History of Britain 1750–1950. Volume 3: Social Agencies and Institutions*. Cambridge: Cambridge University Press.

Proctor, T.M. (2002) *On my Honour: Guides and Scouts in Interwar Britain*. Philadelphia: American Philosophical Society.

Prunty, J. (1995) *Dublin Slums 1800–1925: A Study in Urban Geography*. Dublin: Irish Academic Press.

Pryke, S. (1998) 'The Popularity of Nationalism in the Early British Boy Scout Movement', *Social History*, 23(3): 309–324.

Putnam, R. (2000) *Bowling Alone: The Collapse and Revival of American Community*. London and New York: Simon and Schuster.

Quinn, M. (2002) 'Youth Crime Prevention', in Mahony, P. (ed.), *Criminal Justice in Ireland*. Dublin: Institute of Public Administration.

Raftery, M. (2009a) 'Report a Monument of a Society's Shame', *Irish Times*, 21 May.

Raftery, M. (2009b) 'Bishops Lied and Covered-Up', *Irish Times*, 27 November.

Raftery, M. and O' Sullivan, E. (1999) *Suffer the Little Children: The Inside Story of Ireland's Industrial Schools*. Dublin: New Island Books.

Richardson, V. (1999) 'Children and Social Policy', in Quinn, S. Kennedy, P., O'Donnell, A. and Kiely, G. (eds), *Contemporary Irish Social Policy*. Dublin: University College Dublin Press.

Richmond, V. (2007) "It is not a Society for Human Beings but for Virgins': The Girls' Friendly Society Membership Eligibility Dispute 1875–1936', *Journal of Historical Sociology*, 20(3): 304–327.

Robins, J. (1980) *The Lost Children: A Study of Charity Children in Ireland 1700–1900*. Dublin: Institute of Public Administration.

Rose, N. (1996) *Governing the Soul: The Shaping of the Private Self*. London: Routledge.

Rosenthal, M. (1986) *The Character Factory: Baden-Powell and the Origins of the Boy Scout Movement*. London: Collins.

Rosenthal, M. (1980) 'Knights and Retainers: The Earliest Version of Baden-Powell's Boy Scout Scheme', *Journal of Contemporary History*, 15(4): 603–617.

Ruddle, H. and Donoghue, F. (1995) *The Organisation of Volunteering: A Study of Irish Voluntary Organisations in the Social Welfare Area*. Dublin: Policy Research Centre, National College of Industrial Relations.

Ruddle, H. and Mulvihill, R. (1999) *Reaching Out: Charitable Giving and Volunteering in the Republic of Ireland: The 1997/98 Survey*. Dublin: Policy Research Centre, National College of Industrial Relations.

Ruddle, H. and Mulvihill, R. (1994) *Reaching Out: Charitable Giving and Volunteering in the Republic of Ireland*. Dublin: Policy Research Centre, National College of Industrial Relations.

Ryan, F. (2009) "A Lingering Shame", in Flannery, T. (ed.), *Responding to the Ryan Report*. Blackrock: Columba Press.

Seymour, M. (2006) 'Transition and Reform: Juvenile Justice in the Republic of Ireland', in Junger-Tas, J. and Decker, S. (eds), *International Handbook of Juvenile Justice*. Dordrecht, the Netherlands: Springer Academic Publications.

Share, P., Tovey, H., and Corcoran, Mary P. (2007) *A Sociology of Ireland*. Dublin: Gill & Macmillan.

Sheard, J. (1992) 'Volunteering and Society 1960 – 1990', in Hedley, R. and Davis-Smith, J. (eds), *Volunteering and Society: Principles and Practice*. London: Bedford Square Press.

Sisson, E. (2004) *Pearse's Patriots: St Enda's and the Cult of Boyhood*. Cork: Cork University Press.

Skidmore, P. and Craig, J. (2005) *Start with People: How Community Organisations Put Citizens in the Driving Seat*. London: Demos.

Smart, C. (1999) 'A History of Ambivalence and Conflict in the Discursive Construction of the 'Child Victim' of Sexual Abuse', *Social and Legal Studies*, 8(3): 391–409.

Smith, A. (1997) 'The "Golden Age" and National Renewal', in Hosking, G. and Schopflin,

G. (eds), *Myths and Nationhood*. New York: Routledge.

Smith, J. (2007) *Ireland's Magdalen Laundries and the Nation's Architecture of Containment*. Notre Dame, IN: University of Notre Dame Press.

Smith, R. (2007) *Youth Justice: Ideas, Policy, Practice*. Cullompton: Willan Publishing.

Smyth, J. (2010) 'Children's Rights Poll Unlikely Before 2011', *The Irish Times*, 28 July.

Smyth, J. (1993) 'Depravity and all that Jazz: The Public Dance Halls Act of 1935', *History Ireland*, 1(2): 51–54.

Springhall, J. (1987) 'Baden-Powell and the Scout Movement before 1920: Citizen Training or Soldiers of the Future?', *The English Historical Review*, 102 (405): 934–942.

Springhall, J. (1977) *Youth, Empire and Society: British Youth Movements, 1883–1940*. London: Croom Helm.

Springhall, J.O. (1970) 'Lord Meath, Youth and Empire', *Journal of Contemporary History*, 5(4): 97–111.

Springhall, J., Fraser, B. and Hoare, M. (1983) *Sure and Steadfast: A History of the Boys' Brigade 1883 to 1983*. London and Glasgow: Collins.

Summers, A. (1976) 'Militarism in Britain before the Great War', *History Workshop*, 2: 104–123.

Swanwick, G. (1997) 'Suicide in Ireland 1945–1992: Social Correlates', *Irish Medical Journal*, 90(3): 106–108.

Sweeney, J. and Dunne, J. (2003) *Youth in a Changing Ireland*. Dublin: Foróige.

Tobin, F. (1984) *The Best of Decades: Ireland in the Nineteen Sixties*. Dublin: Gill and Macmillan.

Treacy, D. (2009) 'Irish Youth Work: Exploring the Potential for Social Change', in Forde, C., Kiely, E. and Meade, R. (eds), *Youth and Community Work in Ireland: Critical Perspectives*. Blackrock: Blackwell Publishing.

Tuairim (1966) *Some of our Children: A Report on Residential Care of the Deprived Child in Ireland*. London: Tuairim.

Turner, B. (1995) *Medical Power and Social Knowledge*. London: Sage.

Tyrrell, P. (2006) *Founded on Fear*. Dublin: Irish Academic Press.

Viney, M. (1966) 'The Young Offenders' (Series of 8 Articles), *Irish Times*, 27, 28, 29 April and 2, 3, 4, 5, 6 May.

Wallace, C. and Kovatecheva, S. (1998) *Youth in Society: The Construction and Deconstruction of Youth in East and West Europe*. Basingstoke: Macmillan.

Walsh, D. (2005) *Juvenile Justice*. Dublin: Thomson Round Hall.

Ward, M. (1983) *Unmanageable Revolutionaries: Women and Irish Nationalism*. Dingle: Brandon Book Publishers.

Warren, A. (1986) 'Sir Robert Baden-Powell, the Scout Movement and Citizen Training in Great Britain, 1900–1920', *The English Historical Review*, 101(399): 376–398.

Wayman, S. (1980) '£20,000 Campaign for Youth Work', *Irish Times*, 21 October.

Whyte, J. (1980) *Church and State in Modern Ireland 1923–1979*. Dublin: Gill and MacMillan.

Whyte, J. (1979) 'Church, State and Society 1950–70', in J. Lee (ed.), *Ireland: 1945–70*. Dublin: Gill and Macmillan.

Wilkinson, P. (1969) 'English Youth Movements, 1908–30', *Journal of Contemporary History*, 4(2): 3–23.

Williams, M. (1983) 'Ancient Mythology and Revolutionary Ideology in Ireland, 1878–1916', *The Historical Journal*, 26(2): 307–328.

Willis, P. (1977) *Learning to Labour: How Working Class Kids Get Working Class Jobs.* Farnborough: Saxon House.

Woodroofe, K. (1960) 'Social Group Work and Community Organization in Nineteenth-century England', *The Social Service Review*, 34(3): 309–322.

Index

Books named in the text are indexed under their authors. Matter in notes and tables is indicated by the letters 'n' and 't'

EU authorised representative for GPSR:
Easy Access System Europe, Mustamäe tee 50,
10621 Tallinn, Estonia
gpsr.requests@easproject.com